Exploring Hindu Philosophy

Global Philosophy

Series Editor—Mohammed Rustom, Carleton University

Given the tremendous amount of interest in non-Western philosophy today, teachers, students, and the general public are beginning to come away with a clearer picture of what "philosophy" means in various civilizations and to large sectors of humanity beyond the Anglo-American and European worlds. This series in global philosophy seeks to further this interest by highlighting the epistemic diversity and profound insights of Islamic, Jewish, Hindu, Jain, Buddhist, Confucian, Taoist, Africana, Mesoamerican, Native American, and Latin American philosophy. To accomplish its goals, the series focuses on publishing accessible and lively books on these philosophical traditions and scholarly translations of their key works.

Exploring Hindu Philosophy

ANKUR BARUA

equinox

SHEFFIELD UK BRISTOL CT

Published by Equinox Publishing Ltd.

UK: Office 415, The Workstation, 15 Paternoster Row, Sheffield, South Yorkshire S1 2BX

USA: ISD, 70 Enterprise Drive, Bristol, CT 06010

www.equinoxpub.com

First published 2023

British Library Cataloguing-in-Publication Data

A catalogue record for this book is available from the British Library.

ISBN-13 978 1 80050 269 7 (hardback)
978 1 80050 270 3 (paperback)
978 1 80050 271 0 (ePDF)
978 1 80050 316 8 (ePub)

Library of Congress Cataloging-in-Publication Data

Names: Barua, Ankur, 1977- author.
Title: Exploring Hindu philosophy / Ankur Barua.
Description: Bristol : Equinox Publishing Ltd, 2023. | Series: Global philosophy | Includes bibliographical references and index. | Summary: "This introductory text points to some of the diverse tapestries of Hindu worldviews where scriptural revelation, logical argumentation, embodied affectivity, moral reasoning, and aesthetic cultivation constitute densely interwoven conceptual threads"--Provided by publisher.
Identifiers: LCCN 2022038356 (print) | LCCN 2022038357 (ebook) | ISBN 9781800502697 (hardback) | ISBN 9781800502703 (paperback) | ISBN 9781800502710 (pdf) | ISBN 9781800503168 (epub)
Subjects: LCSH: Hindu philosophy.
Classification: LCC B131 .B329 2023 (print) | LCC B131 (ebook) | DDC 181/.4--dc23/eng/20221107
LC record available at https://lccn.loc.gov/2022038356
LC ebook record available at https://lccn.loc.gov/2022038357

Typeset by Scribe Inc.

To all my students
at the Faculty of Divinity, University of Cambridge
for thinking through my thinking

Contents

Preface ix

Series Foreword xi
Mohammed Rustom

Introduction: Conceptual Constellations 1

1 Unity and Its Concrete Multitudes 21

2 Knowing the Roots of Reality 47

3 Therapies for Liberation 73

4 Finding a Home in the World 99

5 Multiple Modes of Morality 125

Conclusion: Reorienting the Mind's Compass 151

Glossary 165

Notes 167

Bibliography 173

Further Reading 179

Index 181

Preface

I set out to write *Exploring Hindu Philosophy* with first-year undergraduate students as my intended audience. I would write it without using any technical terminology at all—this was my plan of action. However, midway through writing, I realized that some of the discussion here can be a bit too involved for students who have not taken a Philosophy 101 course. So in my revised estimate, this book is meant for advanced undergraduate and postgraduate students.

In this book, I have sought to convey one key point to you: while the patterns of arguments and counterarguments in Hindu styles of reasoning occasionally become quite rarefied, such patterns do "touch base" with some of our basic experiences, ideas, and thoughts. You have probably not encountered Sanskrit words such as *ātman*, ***vyāpti***, and *sāmānya*—in this book, you will see how they constitute the conceptual glue of some formidable structures of thought. They are formidable in the sense that you may need several years of patient and systematic study before you begin to inhabit them. However, even if you do not set out on such an undertaking, their key questions may resonate with some of your own inquiries based on everyday occurrences: Is the book that you are holding in your hand as unqualifiedly real as your dream last night? How important is it to remain rational at all times? Can you step outside yourself for three seconds and get to know how other people see you? Does the red flower in the green vase remain red when the lights are switched off in the room? Can we find any meaning in this world that is suffused with suffering on multiple fronts? Do you become less free or more free if you move to some place that is far from the madding crowd?

If you have taken a Philosophy 101 course and you wish to explore whether, and to what extent, the themes that are standardly covered in such courses in Anglophone settings can be resituated or recalibrated in Hindu contexts of reasoned-based argumentation, the chapters in this book will point you toward some important texts, teachers, and traditions.

In an overview of this type, precisely which themes are introduced and in what fashion they are discussed relate to interpretive choices that depend on who the overviewer is. My understanding of what "philosophy" is has been shaped by two different sets of institutional affiliation over the last fifteen years. I have taught undergraduate and postgraduate students both in a department of philosophy and in a faculty of divinity. In my former self, I taught symbolic logic, British empiricism, and the philosophy of science, and in my current avatar, I teach Hindu metaphysics and theology from philosophy of religion perspectives. Depending on one's intellectual proclivities and background training, the content in this book may be judged as being overly philosophical or overly theological.

As shall become clear from this book, whether one should draw a line between "philosophy" and "theology" is itself a topic of philosophical debate. That some Hindu traditions work with spirit-centered idioms is not sufficient reason to deny them a seat at the philosophical roundtable. These kinds of traditions' projected destinations may be some transcendental states or entities, but even they cannot bypass the arduous task of making sense of their earthly pilgrimage by collecting evidence from the world, arranging it into coherent tapestries of meaning, assessing it critically, and defending it against rival viewpoints. For some other Hindu traditions, in contrast, spiritual questions do not constitute the central focus of inquiries into the meaning of life and our place in the world. All these distinctively Hindu styles of philosophical reasoning will be explored in the following chapters that make up this book.

Series Foreword

Given the tremendous amount of interest in non-Western philosophy today, teachers, students, and the general public are beginning to come away with a clearer picture of what "philosophy" means in various civilizations and to large sectors of humanity beyond the Anglo-American and European worlds. This series in Global Philosophy seeks to further this interest by highlighting the epistemic diversity and profound insights of Islamic, Jewish, Hindu, Jain, Buddhist, Confucian, Taoist, Africana, Mesoamerican, Native American, and Latin American philosophy. To accomplish its goals, the series focuses on publishing accessible and lively books on these philosophical traditions, as well as scholarly translations of their key works.

Mohammed Rustom
Series Editor, *Global Philosophy*

Introduction

Conceptual Constellations

Over the last three millennia, the landmass of South Asia has been host to several kinds of cosmological visions, reasoned discourses, moral evaluations, social analyses, and spiritual quests. The aim of this introductory book is to highlight the conceptual motifs that have structured or inflected the forms of life that are today classified as "Hindu." Given the densities of these intellectual worlds, which often developed through dialectical negotiations with one another, it is wise to first take account of the methodological lenses with which we will explore their fine-grained textures. As it turns out, the two questions "What is *Hindu* about Hindu philosophy?" and "What is *philosophical* about Hindu philosophy?" do not have straightforward answers and are shaped by multiple presuppositions that may be variously defended, contested, or rejected.

If the term "Hindu," following its Perso-Arabic etymology rooted in the river Indus, is applied in an ethnolinguistic sense to all inhabitants of the subcontinent (*al-Hind*), this survey would have to include the Buddhist deconstructions of Nāgārjuna (c. 200 CE), the Jaina compositions of Umāsvāti (c. 200 CE), the Sufi meditations of Dārā Shukhōh (1615–59), the Christian reflections of Brahmabandhab Upadhyay (1861–1907), and so on. Avoiding the cognitive hubris of trying to write an encyclopedia under the pretense of presenting an introduction, I will follow the pathway of reception history and include only those intellectual tapestries that have come to be categorized as "Hindu." Thus, I will explore the mythic narratives, logical disputations, moral visions, and spiritual practices relating to the texts, themes, thinkers, and traditions that would be accepted, more or less readily, as vital markers of present-day "Hindu" self-understandings. Having said that, I will occasionally discuss how Hindu philosophical standpoints were forged in active disputation with Buddhist notions such as not-self, impermanence, and so on.

The other question that I approach with trepidation presents an equally daunting challenge. If I were writing in an Indian vernacular such as Bengali or Hindi, and with speakers of these languages as my intended audience, I could straightforwardly invoke the Sanskrit term ***darśana***, which has become established in some of these sociolinguistic milieus as a correlate of the English term "philosophy." However, to write in English on the theme of "Hindu philosophy" is to simultaneously generate a metaphilosophical query as to how the cognitive boundaries of "philosophy" are to be demarcated in the first place. A hallowed European tradition, starting roughly from 1850 and enduring into the present in some Anglo-American institutional contexts, would deny forthrightly that there is anything specifically philosophical in Hindu worldviews.[1] On the basis of the descriptive premise that the English word "philosophy" is derived from the Greek word *philosophia*, the normative diktat is sometimes issued that intellectual systems that are not infused with Greco-Roman modes of inquiry should not be granted the honorific status of philosophical sophistication. Thus, Hindu matrices of belief and practice are often characterized as a tropical jungle bristling with exotic forms of otherworldly mysticism whose heart of darkness can be exorcised only with the liberating light of European reason. These matrices are said to be suffused with unrestrained flights of fantasy, in contrast to the rigorously theoretical exercises of *philosophia*, in which representations of the world are systematically worked out by following rationally transparent and, therefore "objective," methods.

Schematically stated, here is the argument.

Premise 1: *Philosophia* is a quest of purely objective inquiry independent of scripture, religion, other-worldly phenomena, and so on.
Premise 2: Hindu worldviews are shackled to scriptural testimony (*śabda*) and are practically orientated toward liberation (*mokṣa*) from worldly finitude.
Conclusion: Hindu worldviews are devoid of *philosophia*.

The leitmotif running through the next six chapters is that Hindu ways of being-in-the-world often enshrine complex interplays of reason, revelation, experience, and tradition, and the persisting summarization of these existential textures as antirational is largely a result of insufficient attention paid to these dynamic interconnections.[2] The occasional invocation of scriptural revelation did not prevent, and indeed was concurrent with, the development of rich traditions of reasoned investigation into the structure of reality, the purpose of human existence, the moral fiber of social life, the sources of knowledge, and so on. Conversely, some Anglophone philosophical contexts are marked by a much greater disciplinary plurality than was acceptable around a century ago, when adherence to certain norms of methodological purity was par for the course in institutional domains. In recent decades, a few influential philosophical styles have critiqued the quest for "pure" reason whose invariant structures are said to be universally replicable by an impartial observer and instead highlighted the interconnections between cognitive competence, embodied experience, and cultural location. Rejecting the model of a solitary individual who dispassionately sketches a world-picture on a clean slate, these styles present social epistemologies according to which knowledge acquisition takes place within specific traditions of critical inquiry. Thus, a recent introduction to epistemology argues that many testimony-based beliefs are justified beliefs and such beliefs play an important role in the generation of our stock of knowledge.[3] While I do not directly engage with contemporary debates in Anglophone frameworks, some of their paradigms, problems, and perplexities—relating to metaphysics, philosophy of mind, philosophy of science, ethics, and philosophy of language—have resonating counterparts across Hindu intellectual worlds. Because these Hindu counterparts are often shaped by presuppositions that are not neatly transferable into European registers, an exploration of their conceptual contours reveals the insight that the project of human reasoning is deeply inflected by distinctive regional settings. In this way, what may initially seem to be a parochial inquiry into *Hindu* philosophy is repositioned as a critical contribution to contemporary conversations about the concept of *philosophy* across European and Indian intellectual landscapes.

Consider a related argument involving the equally contested term "religion," commonly derived from the Latin *religio.*

Premise 3: *Religio* is structured by the commitments of the European enlightenment relating to the centrality of doctrinal belief and the separation of private life from public sphere.
Premise 4: Hindu worlds are complete ways of living that integrate the sacred and the secular and are not exclusively focused on systems of belief.
Conclusion: Hindu worlds are devoid of *religio*.

To those who are uninitiated into scholarly debates in the critical study of religion, this conclusion may seem to suggest the absence of religion in Hindu universes, and it may also seem highly counterintuitive to them—if anything, various individuals, European as well as Indian, have claimed that there is too much of religiosity in Hindu social spaces. Without assessing these premises, I present the argument only to highlight the point that concepts such as philosophy and religion are not natural kinds such as water, oxygen, and gold. Therefore, with respect to any such concept *x*, the question "Do we find *x* here?" should be asked concurrently with the question "How do we delineate the boundaries of *x*?" If we define *x* in a certain way, *x* becomes ubiquitous, while after a certain redefinition of *x*, we will not find a trace of *x* even after relentlessly scanning the intellectual horizon. For another instance of this deep interrelation between fundamental presupposition and result of inquiry, consider the opposition of many Hindu intellectuals, over the last hundred years or so, to the application of the term "theology" to Hindu spiritual visions on the grounds that the *theologia* of the Abrahamic religions is rooted in blind faith, sociopolitical intolerance, and subservience to ecclesiastical authorities. Once again, the question "Is there theology in a Hindu tradition?" may generate, at best, an entertaining parlor game and, at worst, a dialogue of the deaf, unless there is some measure of agreement on whether *theologia* indeed has these distinctive markers.

Therefore, to return to philosophy, the process of defining the term "philosophy" is itself a philosophical inquiry, and the question of whether Hindu visions are philosophical cannot be settled through definitional fiat. Rather, the question demands a careful exploration of their thematic content. In the narratives of European intellectual history, "philosophy" has been applied to somewhat different cognitive paradigms inhabited by the ancient Greeks, the medieval Christian scholastics, and trained specialists in Anglo-American settings in our own times. It is precisely in these settings that professional philosophy has developed a disciplinary identity partly through an alliance with the tools of "science," on the one hand, and an opposition to the idioms of "religion" and "theology," which are associated with irrationalism, on the other hand. One aspect of this identity is a piecemeal approach to problems that are meticulously analyzed with the apparatus of formal logic and mathematics so that academic philosophers who operate within these paradigms shaped by an insistence on clarity and rigor tend to be opposed to an overarching "philosophy of life." Thus, the soteriological goal of overcoming worldly finitude that shapes some Hindu traditions is often stated as the grounds for refusing them the status of the "philosophical."

However, the conception of inquiry as a therapy for the ailments of the human self has several parallels across Western traditions. Epicurus highlights an important aspect of Hellenistic worldviews when he says, "Empty are the words of the philosopher who offers therapy for no human suffering. For just as there is no use in medical expertise if it does not give therapy for bodily diseases, so too there is no use in philosophy if it does not expel the suffering of the soul."[4] This therapeutic impulse, as Pierre Hadot emphasized, was central to many forms of *philosophia* in Greek antiquity, where discourse was enfolded in exercises through which a student, as auditor or interlocutor, could undergo a spiritual transformation.[5] Thus, if a "History of Western Philosophy" were written with individual chapters on Plato, Aristotle, Plotinus, Augustine, Aquinas, Kant, Carnap, Wittgenstein, Kripke, and Davidson, one academic may be willing to accord the title of "philosopher" only to the first five and another academic only to the last five—and neither of them might agree with the inclusion of Heidegger, or Derrida, or Rorty, and so on. As Bertrand Russell once pointed out, "If someone asks the question what is mathematics, we can give him a dictionary definition, let us say the science of number, for the sake of argument. . . . But philosophy cannot be so defined. Any definition is controversial and already embodies a philosophic attitude."[6]

Be that as it may, since I have undertaken the task of writing about Hindu "philosophy," I bear the conceptual burden of providing some pointers to how this term will be employed in this book. Echoing the semantic timbre of ***darśana***—derived from the Sanskrit root *dṛś* ("to see")—the Hindu intellectual formations that I will discuss are "philosophical" in the sense that they offer *structured visions* of the world. In this sense, ***darśana*** is not so much a static schema of propositional statements as a synthetic tapestry that holds together multiple threads that we may classify as ontological, ethical, epistemological, and so on. Somewhat akin to its counterparts among the ancient Greeks, the medieval Christians, and the Muslims in premodern Persianate contexts, ***darśana*** is a conceptually capacious horizon on which questions such as "How should I live my life?" "What is really out there?" "How may I know the structures of the world?" "How do I develop a logically valid argument?" "What is the significance of beauty?" and so on form densely interrelated pathways of inquiry. In this sense, ***darśana*** is an exploratory map with a dynamic set of orientations and not a firm territory with established landmarks.

At the same time, however, ***darśana*** should not be construed as a cognitively spineless set of speculations about who or what there is, for the visionary sketches clustered under this rubric are often animated by systematic patterns of reasoning, rules of dialogical engagement, classifications of categories, and citations of experiential evidence. Reflecting the German concept of *Weltanschauung* ("worldview"), certain styles of ***darśana*** can be classified as life-philosophy with the caveat that they should not be presented as leading to an erasure of the intellect. Moreover, we encounter patterns of critical inquiry in ancient India that are not directly oriented to soteriological ends. For instance, the *Artha-śāstra* ("the science of wealth"), a treatise on statecraft and military strategy attributed to Kauṭilya (c. 300 CE), mentions a cognitive discipline called *ānvīkṣikī*. The text rejects the view that it is only a special branch of the scriptures (***Vedas***) and presents it as an independent science (*vidyā*) (1.2.1–12). The author cites a traditional couplet that states that *ānvīkṣikī* is the source of light for all branches of knowledge, a means for all activities, and a support for social and religious duties.[7] A significant amount of intellectual labor was expended in the milieus of Hindu ***darśana*** in developing meticulous analyses of linguistic forms and practices. The *Aṣṭādhyāyī* ("Eight Chapters") of Pāṇini (c. 400 BCE) is a treatise on Sanskrit grammar that sets out general rules that apply to words and also specific rules that override the former. Keeping in the mind the significant developments made in ancient India in the fields of arithmetic, astronomy, metallurgy, medicine, and the like, it would be as misleading to view these domains of intellectual productivity and material culture exclusively through a "spiritualist" lens as it would be to construct a narrative about European civilization solely on the basis of the contemplative reflections of Christian monks in premodern France.

Having laid out a pathway through various semantic minefields, I will now sketch, with broad brushstrokes, some intellectual trajectories of Hindu philosophy.[8] At the root of various cosmological forms of inquiry in ancient India stands the Vedic corpus, of which the earliest strata are the hymns of the *Ṛg Veda* (c. 1200 BCE) and the early ***Upaniṣads*** (c. 800 BCE), which begin to rework certain dimensions of Vedic visions. These compositions—with diverse textures woven with mythic narratives, aphoristic expressions, and cosmogonic speculations—embody the "mapping" dimensions of ***darśana*** (the more scholastic enterprise of distilling conceptual categories from these textures has not emerged at this stage). Regarding the fundamental themes that would soon become the staple of some substantial platters of food for thought, the ***Upaniṣads*** seemingly speak with different and even discordant voices. On themes such as the status of the human individual in the cosmos, the structure of reality, the relation between the finite and the nonfinite, and the shape of living that is properly aligned with truth, we encounter different modes of inquiry. For instance, the *Praśna Upaniṣad* is structured in the form of six questions relating to the origin of finite beings, the syllable Oṃ, the nature of the human person, and so on, and the answers given by a sage are couched in symbolic terms. The ***Bhagavad-gītā*** ("The Song of the Lord"; c. 200 CE), a text of great significance in these spiritual milieus, is often presented as a synthetic fabric that seeks to bring together diverse strands relating to ritual activity, self-knowledge, devotion to a supremely personal divine reality, and meditative concentration. The ***Upaniṣads*** are *śruti* ("that which is heard") or *śabda* (verbal testimony), which is infallible revelation in contrast to various *smṛti* ("that which is remembered") compositions, which are attributed to specific human authors. The ***Bhagavad-gītā*** is presented as a dialogue between Lord Kṛṣṇa and his disciple Arjuna; as the word of the divine reality, it is sometimes accorded the status of *śruti*. Although Hindu scripture was written down at some point, the Sanskrit words *śruti* and *śabda* remind us that, somewhat akin to the connotations of recitation in the Arabic word *qur'ān*, a revelatory message is primarily an utterance that resonates and becomes etched in human memory. This motif of the world-generating dynamism of the sacred word would prove to be a significant one for various forms of Hindu philosophy of language.

It is with the multiple strands of exegetical discourse called **Vedānta** that we arrive at some "territorial" cartographies of ***darśana***. Several preceptors such as Śaṃkara (c. 800 CE), Rāmānuja (1017–1137), Madhva (1238–1317), and Vallabha (1479–1531) developed highly influential systematizations of scriptural texts such as the ***Upaniṣads*** and the ***Bhagavad-gītā*** in the process of spinning threads of rational inquiry that would, from contemporary Anglo-American perspectives, be recognized as metaphysical, epistemological, ethical, and aesthetic. While the multiple configurations of Vedāntic discourse lay down structured pathways toward liberation from the cycles of reincarnation (***saṃsāra***), they do not mindlessly cast reason to the wind. In fact, a central Vedāntic question is the precise relation between rational discourse (*tarka*) and revelatory horizon (*śabda*). So we find Vedāntic thinkers asking whether ***darśana*** is animated by reason within the bounds of revelation or by revelation within the bounds of reason. These Vedāntic distillations of the essence of scriptural wisdom constitute living streams that vitally shape many contemporary iterations of ***darśana***. An entire galaxy of Hindu thinkers, poets, contemplatives, and social activists—such as Rabindranath Tagore (1861–1941), Swami Vivekananda (1863–1902), Mahatma Gandhi (1869–1948), Sri Aurobindo (1872–1950), Rama Tirtha (1873–1906), Ramana Maharshi (1879–1950), Sarvepalli Radhakrishnan (1888–1975), Paramhansa Yogananda (1893–1952), Jiddu Krishnamurti (1895–1986), and Swami Prabhupada (1896–1977)—creatively reenvisioned the cartographical projections of premodern Vedāntic systems.

Over the last two hundred years, these Vedāntic compositions have featured prominently in many discoveries of "Oriental religion" so that in the process of assessing or retrieving their philosophical content, one has to walk down a hall in which multiple mirrors—some Indian and some European—reflect one another.[9] Therefore, it is important to keep in mind that the question "Is there such a thing as Hindu philosophy?" is enmeshed in transactional processes characterized by intersections and oppositions between Indic idioms of ***darśana*** and European self-understandings of *philosophia*. The semantic range that has developed in modern Indian languages to translate "philosophy" encompasses Sanskrit terms such as *tattva-darśana* and *tattva-jñāna*, but—to repeat—whether or not the latter are adequate equivalents will depend significantly on one's assessment of the meanings associated with the former.

A key moment in these intellectual trajectories was the translation into English of scriptural texts such as the ***Bhagavad-gītā*** (1785) and the *Ṛg Veda* (1869) that reinforced the projection of India as an antique land saturated with an undiluted mysticism. These romanticized images were reworked by some Hindu gurus, from within the crucible of colonial modernity in British India, to project a civilizational contrast between westerners as essentially materialistic and Hindus as essentially spiritual. In such crisscrossing Indo-British and Indo-European currents, the specifically reason-shaped dimensions of ***darśana***—which I have characterized as structured vision—have often been ignored or insufficiently highlighted, generating the contemporary perceptions of Hindu worlds as logically bankrupt. And as numerous waves of yoga, meditation, holistic health, and mindfulness wash onto Western shores with increasing intensity, it is important to highlight the fact that they are not yet more iterations of an Oriental mysticism that is cognitively vacuous. Rather, they are rooted in systematic classifications, produced between 200 BCE and 500 CE, of cognitive-experiential worldviews through *sūtras*, which are strings of aphorisms. These pithy expressions became the urtexts upon which detailed commentaries (*bhāṣya*), subcommentaries (*vārttika*), and glosses were written for the exposition and the defense of one's own ***darśana*** and the refutation of rival viewpoints.

These discursive processes operated partly by generating fine-tuned definitions of key concepts such as perception, error, causation, and reality that would avoid the errors of underextension (for instance, "the cow is an animal with a reddish skin," which leaves out many cows) and overextension (for instance, "the cow is an animal with four feet," which includes horses, dogs, and cats). To be sure, a certain style of **Vedānta** makes the startling claim that our everyday world populated by laptops, chairs, and cars is not ultimately real but has a dream-like quality; however, this statement is not pulled out abruptly like a rabbit from a magician's hat but defended partly by developing a carefully chiseled definition of "error" and critiquing competing definitions. Indeed, in these contexts of reasoning, it is common for a thinker to lay out a spectrum of definitions, D_1, D_2, D_3, . . . D_N; methodically work out the implications of D_1, D_2, D_3, . . . ; and put forward D_N (one's own definition) as the most plausible and logically defensible. Moreover, these definitional maneuvers are often enmeshed in forms of analogical reasoning that are centered on everyday objects. For instance, to highlight the capacity of human consciousness to "illuminate" objects, the metaphor of a lamp is often employed: I light a lamp in a dark room and I instantly see a table with a laptop and books on it. What philosophical lesson I should draw from this everyday occurrence is, however, deeply disputed. Some Hindu thinkers claim that this analogy reflects, and properly reinforces, our common-sense belief that objects such as tables, laptops, and books exist independently of human perception. Some others would argue that the proper way to read this analogy is to say that consciousness lights up the world in the active sense of bringing it into existence: it is because of light that there are objects to be illuminated in the first place.

Here is a conversation between two friends, William (W) and Iris (I), that reflects the dialectical skein of such Hindu philosophical debates:

W: Let me begin by defining "perception" as any process of knowledge acquisition that involves conscious thinking.

I: That definition applies to the drawing out of inferential chains of reasoning ($2 + 2 = 4$, $4 > 3$, $2 + 2 > 3$), but it does not cover our immediate encounters with everyday objects such as chairs and tables. So let's say that "perception" has sensory awareness as a fundamental constituent.

W: According to your definition, prelinguistic babies are capable of perception. Do you mean to say that a baby can think in this way: "Now I see my mother bringing me a wonderful meal"?

I: No, not quite. Perhaps the baby is not capable of higher-order reflective thinking.

W: So there is a difference between *perceiving* something and *thinking about* it? If yes, which mode is prior—do we perceive the world in an experiential rawness and then apply concepts to the world, or is the world packaged with concepts all the way down, and then these concepts structure our experience of the world?

I: Let's step away for a moment from this question of priority. The current definition of perception implies a contact between a sense organ and the world. I think this definition underextends.

As a Christian, I believe that God perceives me at all times but God has no sensory bases.

W: Perhaps we can define "perception" as a way of knowing that is not dependent on another way of knowing? Let's return to this topic tomorrow.

I: Before you go, let me remind you about your other claim that there is a spiritually refined mode of perception—the mode that you call "intuition"—which reveals everything to be ultimately unreal. Is it not the case that your statement, "everything is ultimately unreal," is itself ultimately unreal?

W: Yes, it is. And yet, it penultimately points to the truth, which is the ultimate unreality of every finite thing—including itself.

I: Tomorrow, you must tell me what definition of "reality" you are working with here.

The forging of such definitional pathways is carried out, often in painstaking detail, across vast tomes of commentarial literature. This industrious production of reasoned discourse developed through active engagements not only with Buddhist milieus of teaching and spiritual practice but also with various other standpoints that are today labelled as "Hindu." Partly to highlight the dialectical shape of these engagements, I do not adopt the "six ***darśana***" typology that is sometimes employed in introductory textbooks on Hindu philosophy. According to this classification, there are six *āstika* schools—**Sāṃkhya**, **Yoga**, **Nyāya**, **Vaiśeṣika**, **Mīmāṃsā**, and **Vedānta**—in contrast to the *nāstika* schools of Buddhists, Jains, and others. The *āstika* schools accept Vedic scriptural authority, which is denied by the *nāstika* schools. This overly schematic structure obscures two vital currents of rational inquiry running across the argumentative spaces that were developing from around the turn of the first millennium.

First, some forms of Hindu philosophy acquired their distinctive contours through spirited counterresponses to the *nāstika* Buddhists who were formulating critiques of concepts relating to supraempirical essence, diachronic identity, and the like. In opposition to the key Buddhist teaching that the "I" is not an enduring entity but is a causally connected dynamic stream of momentary events, various Hindu philosophers claimed that it does not adequately capture the subjectivity of recognitive statements such as "The *I* who am writing this essay today is the *I* who was listening to Nusrat Fateh Ali Khan last week." This fundamental debate across Hindu-Buddhist borderlines over personal identity—Is the substantial self (*ātman*) a presupposition of embodied agency?—would take participants into diverse fields, such as ontology, moral philosophy, philosophy of language, and philosophy of mind. On these intellectual landscapes where scholastic identities were dialectically negotiated, thinkers could differ on the number of "schools"—Bhāviveka, a sixth-century Buddhist, mentions **Sāṃkhya**, **Vaiśeṣika**, **Vedānta**, and **Mīmāṃsā**, in addition to two Buddhist systems; in a compendium of Haribhadra, an eighth-century Jain philosopher, the Buddhists, the Jains, and the followers of **Nyāya**, **Vaiśeṣika**, **Sāṃkhya**, and **Mīmāṃsā** are presented as the six ***darśanas***; and in the fifteenth century, Vidyāraṇya discusses, from a Vedāntic Hindu perspective, as many as fifteen ***darśanas***.

Second, even though the *āstika* systems were indeed shaped by different degrees of fidelity to Vedic revelation (*śabda*), this scriptural affiliation did not arrive fully formed with a uniform set of ontological commitments or substantive conclusions. While **Nyāya** logicians worked with rational inference (*anumāna*) to demonstrate the existence of a personal divine reality (*īśvara*), Vedāntic exegetes generally rejected the claim that such inferential processes can lead us from the finite world to the nonfinite being. Several **Mīmāṃsā** and **Sāṃkhya** standpoints even concurred with the Buddhist project of using reasoning to argue for the nonexistence of a cosmic deity. In the naturalistic outlook of **Vaiśeṣika**, all physical entities are composed of atoms (*aṇu*), and these are set in motion through the divine will. Somewhere on this fine-grained continuum are the spiritual technologies of **Yoga**—they envision the divine reality as a cosmic person who is untouched by any imperfections and is a teacher of world-afflicted humanity but does not possess any cosmos-generating power. Skeptical standpoints are also foregrounded in the *lokāyata* milieus, paradigmatically *nāstika*, which affirm a robust form of ontological naturalism—consciousness is emergent from material entities, and there is no means of knowledge to demonstrate the existence of supraspatiotemporal entities. Highlighting these strands in ancient Indian cultures, Amartya Sen points out that "Indian traditions are often taken to be intimately associated with religion, and indeed in many ways they are, and yet Sanskrit and Pali have larger literatures on systematic atheism and agnosticism than perhaps in any other classical language–Greek, Roman, Hebrew, or Arabic."[10]

I have drawn out this sliver of intellectual discourse to highlight one type of the trans-***darśana*** disputations that structured Hindu philosophical engagements.[11] In contrast to the homogenizing image of Hindus as "God-crazy"—which, as alluded to already, has often been deployed to project the spiritual superiority of a timeless India over a materialistically degraded Europe—the lines of inquiry of the *āstika* schools often sharply diverged on the crucial question of the existence and the nature of the divine foundation of the world. These two labels—*āstika* and *nāstika*—are, to some extent, abstractions that can mask the innovations made by a thinker who belonged to a traditional lineage or may have ranged across multiple discourses. For instance, Vācaspati Miśra (c. 1000 CE), often regarded as a proponent of a style of **Vedānta**, worked with themes from **Nyāya**, **Mīmāṃsā**, and **Sāṃkhya**, and Vijñāna-bhikṣu (c. 1600 CE) composed treatises on **Sāṃkhya**, **Yoga**, and **Vedānta**. Again, while **Nyāya** is indeed a "school" with a root text and several commentaries, its account of knowledge sources (***pramāṇa***) and objects of knowledge (*prameya*), pseudoreasons (*hetvābhāsa*), and formal procedures for engaging in rational dispute (*tarka*) were highly influential and integrated into many other intellectual systems.

In contexts of public, truth-directed disputation (*vāda*), the defender of a particular viewpoint would begin with an outline of a rival viewpoint (*pūrvapakṣa*) and carefully assess it on its own terms before seeking to refute it—only then a conclusive statement (*siddhānta*) would be presented. For instance, the proponent of a form of **Vedānta** who is disputing a Buddhist standpoint should be able to offer an immanent critique of this standpoint with respect to the form of reasoning employed in it, even though both groups would have differing epistemic resources. Given this immersive familiarity with the presuppositions of competing systems of thought, it is not surprising that these traditions of inquiry sometimes borrowed one another's argumentative strategies. For a sophisticated instance of this trans-***darśana*** intellectual traffic, consider the argumentative style of Bhaṭṭa Rāmakaṇṭha (c. 1000 CE) who assimilated certain features of Buddhism, thereby strengthening his own conceptual repertoire, and then used these tools to critique those features of Buddhism that conflicted with his own tradition.[12]

With the caveat that **Sāṃkhya, Yoga, Nyāya, Vaiśeṣika, Mīmāṃsā,** and **Vedānta** should be viewed as clusters of presuppositions, disciplines, and practices that were developing in contiguous spaces, I highlight some key markers of these systems with respect to their accounts of what truly exists ("ontology") and the means of knowing what there is in the world ("epistemology").

1. In the **Sāṃkhya** vision outlined in the *Sāṃkhya-kārikā* of Īśvarakṛṣṇa (c. 400 CE), the world has evolved from the conjunction (*saṃyoga*) of two independent principles: *puruṣa*, which is contentless consciousness, and *prakṛti*, which is primordial matter. The *puruṣa*, which is nonagential witness (*sākṣin*), forgets that it is ontologically distinct from the mind-body complex, which is a product of dynamic *prakṛti*, and this misidentification leads to reincarnations in a world that is steeped in suffering (*duḥkha*). Including *puruṣa* and *prakṛti*, **Sāṃkhya**'s enumerative cartography of reality delineates twenty-five fundamental principles (*tattva*). Crucially, it accepts a plurality of *puruṣa*—each human person is a distinct *puruṣa* embodied as a psychophysical *prakṛti*-shaped complex.
2. In the context of the styles of ***darśana*** noted here, readers in Western locations would perhaps be most familiar with the term "yoga." However, while in these milieus it is often associated with the cultivation of certain postures, in many premodern Hindu worlds the term "yoga" encompasses a diverse range of spiritual disciplines, psychosomatic subjectivities, and soteriological goals, such as the cultivation of meditative stability, the yoking of the human individual to the divine reality, and the development of superhuman powers. Some of these motifs and practices are first systematized in the *Yoga-sūtras* of Patañjali (c. 300 CE), where the supreme end is the realization of one's spiritual identity as pure witness and as distinct from the transient modifications of the mind. The *Yoga-sūtras* are divided into four chapters. The first defines yoga as the termination of the activities of the mind, which is a state of pure awareness not directed toward any object; the second lays down certain moral observances that lead toward the supreme

goal; the third outlines certain supranormal powers that an individual can attain through meditative states; and the fourth discusses liberation from all worldly afflictions. An important commentary on the *Yoga-sūtras* is attributed to Vyāsa, with a gloss on it penned by Vācaspati Miśra. The **Yoga** traditions adopt **Sāṃkhya** cosmology and develop various accounts of the nature of the self, consciousness, and agency to promote the liberation (*kaivalya*) of the immutable *puruṣa* from the impermanent domains of *prakṛti*.

3. As we have seen, one central motif of **Nyāya** is a reflective inquiry into the nature and the operation of reason, and especially the rules that govern inferential reasoning. The **Nyāya** tradition holds that the overcoming of erroneous beliefs is geared toward final liberation. Its foundational text, the *Nyāya-sūtras*, attributed to Akṣapāda Gautama (c. 200 BCE), states that this highest good is to be attained through the knowledge of sixteen categories, five of which are the knowledge sources or means of right knowledge (***pramāṇa***), the objects of right knowledge (*prameya*), doubt (*saṃśaya*), ascertainment (*nirṇaya*), and truth-directed debate (*vāda*). More specifically, *vāda* has characteristics such as these: the debate is generated by the ascription of incompatible attributes to the same subject, the proof of a thesis or a refutation is based on evidence and argument (*tarka*), and the reasoning does not involve contradictions with accepted doctrine. In other words, an individual seeks to establish a viewpoint and refute opposing viewpoints, while all parties in the debate draw on a background of common knowledge and use established methods for gathering and assessing evidence. Four important commentators on the *Nyāya-sūtras* are Vātsyāyana (c. 400 CE), Uddyotakara (c. 550 CE), Vācaspati Miśra (c. 900 CE), and Udayana (c. 1000 CE). Around the time of Gaṅgeśa Upādhyāya (c. 1300 CE), the tradition enters into the phase of "new reason" (*navya-nyāya*), vigorously discussing motifs such as double negation, failure of reference, and definition.
4. The worldview of **Vaiśeṣika** is rooted in Kaṇāda's *Vaiśeṣika-sūtras* (c. 100 BCE) and develops a form of atomism in which

the substances of earth, water, air, and fire are composed of atoms (*aṇu*) that are indivisible and indestructible. The **Nyāya** traditions generally accept the developed ontological scheme of the **Vaiśeṣika**, in which the world is constituted of seven fundamental categories (*padārtha*): substance, quality, action, universal, particularity, inherence, and absence. The term *padārtha* is sometimes glossed as the *artha* (meaning) of a *pada* (word), so in the **Vaiśeṣika** worldview, there is a fundamental equivalence between language and world. It seeks to provide a detailed inventory of what there is in the world, and it possibly receives the name "**Vaiśeṣika**" from one of these categories—*viśeṣa* (particularity). Praśastapāda (c. 600 CE) wrote an important treatise, *Padārtha-dharma-saṅgraha* ("A Compendium of the Characteristics of Categories"), which is based on the *Vaiśeṣika-sūtra*.

5. The central concern of **Mīmāṃsā** is an investigation of *dharma*, a term with multiple meanings that resists straightforward translation into English—its conceptual range includes such things as cosmic order, natural regularity, social stability, and moral structure. The root text is the *Mīmāṃsā-sūtras* of Jaimini (c. 200 BCE), which consists of 2,745 *sūtras* and is accompanied by two distinctive commentarial traditions associated with Kumārila Bhaṭṭa (c. 700 CE) and his contemporary Prabhākara. This tradition is nontheistic in the sense that while different deities are indeed accepted as the recipients of Vedic sacrifices, there is no creator or divine reality who has produced and sustains the world. The ***Vedas*** are authorless in the sense that no agent—human or divine—has generated them: the Vedic utterances, in the sacred script of Sanskrit, are self-validating. These texts are to be read not as attempts to delineate the nature of reality but in terms of certain injunctions toward action. According to a traditional distinction, while this system, presented as "prior" **Mīmāṃsā**, focuses on the proper performance of ritual action (*karma*), "later" **Mīmāṃsā** or **Vedānta** explores the significance of liberating knowledge (*jñāna*).
6. The term "**Vedānta**" ("end of the **Vedas**") encompasses multiple traditions, such as the Advaita of Śaṃkara (c. 700 CE), the

> Viśiṣṭādvaita of Rāmānuja (1017–1137), the Dvaita of Madhva (1238–1317), and the Śuddhādvaita of Vallabha (1479–1531). These worldviews often diverge on ontological and epistemological themes, but they agree that Vedic statements are truly revelatory of the nature of reality—especially that of the human self (*cit*, *jīva*, *ātman*) and the divine source of all things (*brahman*). They accept the ***Upaniṣads***, the ***Brahma-sūtras***, and the ***Bhagavad-gītā*** as the triple scriptural foundations (*prasthāna-trayī*) of the worldviews that they sketch through exegetical reasoning. The ***Brahma-sūtras*** are a collection of aphorisms that seek to refute the **Sāṃkhya** duality of *puruṣa* and *prakṛti*, and they proclaim *brahman* as the unitary basis of all worldly phenomena. If the *Mīmāṃsā-sūtras* begin with an inquiry into *dharma*, the ***Brahma-sūtras*** begin with an inquiry into *brahman*.

As this overview indicates, different styles of Hindu ***darśana*** are characterized by varying intersections between rational analysis, spiritual discipline, naturalist inquiry, and cosmological vision. In each chapter, I will highlight a set of key motifs and indicate how some of these styles have engaged with them. That is, instead of devoting six chapters to **Sāṃkhya**, **Yoga**, **Nyāya**, **Vaiśeṣika**, **Mīmāṃsā**, and **Vedānta** respectively, I will foreground specific motifs relating to themes like perception, reality, action, language, beauty, and consciousness, discussing how these styles of Hindu ***darśana*** grappled with them. These forms of argumentation developed certain standardized formulations of their own viewpoints and also critiques of rival viewpoints. Thus, **Nyāya** philosophers such as Gaṅgeśa responded to the Advaita vision of Śrīharṣa (1125–80) and also critiqued the viewpoints of **Mīmāṃsā**; defending an Advaita perspective, Madhusūdana Sarasvatī (c. 1600) attempted a refutation of the worldview of Madhva; and Utpaladeva (c. 950 CE), a Śaiva philosopher, borrowed specific aspects of the viewpoints of Kumārila and the Vijñānavāda strands of Buddhism.

We begin chapter 1 with a fundamental question that will stay with us throughout the book's subsequent chapters: "How many *kinds* of things are there?" Sitting in a garden beside the University of Cambridge's Faculty of Divinity, I look around and ask myself what it is that I see. In response to this question, I do not craft a long sentence that reads something like this: "A human being walking by, another human being walking by, another human being walking by . . . a tree, another tree, another tree . . . a bench, another bench, another bench . . . a blade of grass, another blade of grass, another blade of grass . . ." Instead, I say, "Human beings walking past, trees, benches, and grass." The latter report is more economical because I am able to conceptually aggregate things into particular kinds—human beings, trees, benches, and grass. You and I may be satisfied with this report, but someone else, who is watching us, may demand, "But what is ultimately there? Like really, really, really, there?" In other words, this questioner is asking, "What is the fundamental stuff of it all—that is, the cement that holds the different things that populate our everyday world together?" Perhaps there is no such cement out there, but we human beings, who cannot bear too much chaos, project order into the blooming, buzzing confusion of our existence. Or perhaps there really is such cement and our epistemic tools help us uncover it from within the scaffolding of the everyday objects and processes that we encounter in our daily lives. Our questioner, in effect, is demanding a comprehensive catalog of these tools, which is the focus of chapter 2. If I place a stick in a beaker that is half filled with water, the stick is not really bent but only *appears* to be bent—or at least that is what I say. Our questioner might disagree; she might claim that such is the wonderful power of water: it can bend sticks. And she might add that such is the wonderful power of sticks: they regain their original shape when they are taken out of water. So we need a careful discussion of how we build up our webs of belief, and a lot of intellectual labor in Hindu ***darśana*** is devoted to this enterprise.

In some styles of Hindu ***darśana***, such accounts of what there is in the world and how we get to know the constituents of the world are oriented toward the goal of overcoming suffering. In one straightforward sense, human well-being is deeply correlated with the formation of correct beliefs about the structure of the world—if we ingest poison, we may die, whereas if we regularly consume sufficient amounts of protein, we remain healthy. Likewise, if there is nothing that is everlasting, the attempt to hold on to things with a mistaken belief in their endurance will lead, sooner or later, to great misery. Conversely, if everything is ultimately rooted in the eternal source of being, truth, and goodness ("God"), then a constitutive aspect of our flourishing lies in cultivating a proper alignment with this spiritual foundation. Such matters of life and death—and everything that lies between them and beyond them—are the foci of the discussions in chapters 3, 4, and 5.

Given the distinctive origins and lineages of Hindu ***darśana*** and Euro-American *philosophia*, the topics that Anglophone philosophers debate may not have precise equivalents in Hindu settings. For instance, the analytic truth versus synthetic truth distinction, the ontological argument, and the Kantian a priori cannot readily be translated into them. On the other hand, some aspects of the Fregean view that a word has meaning in the context of a sentence is paralleled in the theory of "expression through what has been connected" (*anvitābhidhāna-vāda*), which states that isolated words are not meaningful and only a sentence expresses a complete meaning. This sentential holism was opposed by the theory of "the connection of what has been expressed" (*abhihitānvaya-vāda*), which states that the meaning of a sentence is composed of the meanings of individual words.[13] Hindu thinkers raised other questions that correspond in certain respects to European philosophical disputes relating to whether consciousness is a substance, property, or event; whether logic is based on formal validity or material truth; whether being is a real predicate or a linguistic construct; and so on. Thus, Gaṅgeśa assiduously worked his way through as many as twenty-nine formulations of the definition of "pervasion" (***vyāpti***), which is a crucial term in the *navya-nyāya* style of logical discourse. Referring to this system, a scholar begins his book with the following anecdote:

> A Western philosopher with whom I used to argue once expressed a prejudice in . . . the following terms: "The Indians," he said, "were never really interested in philosophy. They were interested in religion. Their philosophy always leads to a religious or mystical goal, which is all very fine, I dare say, but it is not what I call philosophy; it is not at all the sort of thing that I am interested in." He admitted that his knowledge of the subject was limited to translations of religious texts and to selections from Buddhist and Vedānta idealism, and he agreed to read any two books I should give him before reasserting his judgment. I gave him two translations of Navya-nyāya texts. Actually, they were the only translations of Navya-nyāya available at that time. My philosopher . . . persevered, until one day he

said, "I admit I was hasty. Your Navya-nyāya is talking about problems of philosophy all right, problems that interest me greatly. My only trouble now is that I find their talk so difficult to understand."[14]

What is vital in such explorations as the one presented in this book is not whether we are able to locate exact correlates of European *philosophia* in Hindu ***darśana*** or vice versa. Some Anglo-American academic settings are increasingly characterized by a diversity of philosophical perspectives so that *philosophia* is not strictly associated with a specific set of methods, doctrines, or debates but with ongoing exercises in rational inquiry. In this vein, Tyler Burge argues that philosophy "lies in the detailed posing of questions, the clarification of meaning, the development and criticism of argument, the working out of ideas and points of view."[15] This type of generic rationality—reason at work in illuminating meanings, relating concepts, and offering explanations—can be readily located in Hindu philosophy, as we will see in the following five chapters. Many Hindu forms of reasoning pay meticulous attention to the formulation of arguments based on examples drawn from everyday settings, although the philosophical disputants will often draw different conclusions from these examples.

1

Unity and Its Concrete Multitudes

Some strands of Vedic literature (c. 1200 BCE) raise the momentous question of the origin of all things, and by the time we arrive at Vedāntic systematizations (c. 1000 CE), some intricately layered worldviews have emerged that engage with it from multiple perspectives. According to their visions of reality, the multiplicity that we encounter in our quotidian lives is rooted in, pivoted on, and supported by a spiritual unity that is immutable and indivisible. The crucial terms are *sat* ("existence") and *asat* ("nonexistence")—*brahman*, the divine ground of finite being, is at times characterized as unqualified existence, and at times as transcending the duality of *sat* and *asat*, which are said to apply only to worldly entities. These Vedāntic ontological frames had to compete with those of **Sāṃkhya** and **Yoga**, which speak of a duality between the principles of pure consciousness (*puruṣa*) and physical reality (*prakṛti*), and those of **Nyāya** and **Vaiśeṣika**, which outline seven categories. The inquiries that unfolded across these systems of ***darśana*** over several millennia can be characterized as "ontological"—that is, an exploration into the conditions that make possible and give recognizable shape to empirical experience. More precisely, one fundamental question that they sought to address is this: What is a thing?

WHAT IS A THING?

Consider the following three statements:

1. A laptop is an instrument on which essays can be typed.
2. A dog is an animate being who sometimes lives with humans.
3. A thing is . . .

In the case of words such as "laptop" and "dog," which refer to empirical entities that populate our everyday world, we can define them quite readily and also find ways of arriving at a consensus on whether a certain entity is indeed encompassed by that definition. For instance, someone who has defined a dog as "an animate being who can bark" may be happy, on being presented with a basenji, to sketch a redefinition so that the extension of "dog" includes the nonbarking basenji. However, with respect to the word "thing," our intuitions, presuppositions, or convictions may take us in different directions—some of us may have an austere ontology and regard only that which is directly perceptible to us as a "thing"; others may have a slightly more abundant ontology and refer to genes, positrons, viruses, and quarks as "things"; and others may have an even more luxuriant ontology in which a nonspatiotemporal entity such as the soul is put forward as a "thing." Even those who belong to the first group may disagree about specific details—someone drinking a cup of tea while a storm is gathering in the sky may apply the term "thing" only to the fairly stable cup and not to the dynamically evolving cloud formation in the sky. Moreover, even if two people agree that a certain *x* is indeed a "thing," they may yet disagree over whether a collection of *x* should be characterized as an independent "thing." For instance, a scientist may claim that the table in her office is not truly a "thing," reserving this label only for the subatomic entities or processes that constitute the table, but her colleague may happily apply the term "thing" to both macroscopic and microscopic entities.

WORKING WITH WORDS TO UNDERSTAND THE WORLD

We begin our ontological explorations with the **Nyāya** and the **Vaiśeṣika** systems. According to them, not only cups and typhoons, and their atomic constituents, but also the absence (*abhāva*) of a dog in my house is a kind of "thing." We shall work our way toward Advaita **Vedānta**, as systematized by Śaṃkara (c. 700 CE), according to whom empirical distinctions are, in the ultimate analysis, misconceptions associated with our state of worldly ignorance. Here, *brahman*—the unitary source, foundation, and telos of everything in the world—is not *this* thing or *that* thing but, if such an idiom can be applied at all, the indivisible super-Thing that is beyond even the concept of thing. In contrast, **Vaiśeṣika** has a down-to-earth feel: the world with its manifold differences—such as that between a basenji and a collie, and between the head of that basenji and its tail, and so on—is robustly real. Moreover, it is meaningful to say that the medium-sized objects in our environment have mind-independent existence in the sense in which we may say that an apple continues to exist inside a refrigerator after we have shut its door. Call this viewpoint "ontological realism" or simply "realism": the world has a fine-grained texture such that even though it is human perceivers with specific linguistic skills and conceptual repertoires who make classificatory statements (such as "this basenji is more friendly than that collie"), there is something out there that these statements represent. Therefore, while it is true that a world devoid of human observers would also be a world in which a description such as "this grass in the garden is green" is not uttered, *that* to which this description applies is not itself fabricated or constructed by this utterance. Thus, consider a scientist of a realist persuasion who declares, "When I write out a differential equation for a positron, there is something out there that is behaving in the ways that are depicted by this equation."

Perhaps most people whose minds have not been illuminated—or contaminated—by philosophical thinking are proponents of realism. We do not usually spend a sleepless night pondering whether the milk and the porridge in the kitchen will be waiting for us in the morning after we fall asleep; we assume, or even claim to know, that these entities are really out there. Our concepts of milk and porridge help us to navigate breakfast, and the reason why we are successful is because of an appropriate "fit" between our capacities of cognition and action on the one hand and the world that contains objects that answer to the descriptions of milk and porridge on the other hand. Even if such a tough-minded realism is presupposed by many (or perhaps all) of us in our quotidian lives, things get complicated pretty quickly when we start analyzing the *that* that is said to be the basis of our realism-infused utterances. While **Vaiśeṣika**, **Sāṃkhya**, and many strands across **Vedānta** articulate different styles of realism, they disagree significantly over the nature of the *that* in question, and this disagreement relates partly to the issue of how many categories we need in order to make sense of the world we inhabit and with which we engage.

Suppose John, who has 858 books in his office, is asked, "What things do you have in your office?" He would not usually start a long sentence of this type: "I have a book written by Martineau, another book by Green, another book by Bradley . . ." On this occasion, it may be more economical to use the category "book" and reply, "I have many books." Suppose, however, the much more magnificent question "What things do we have in our world?" were put to John. He could start in this way: "We have dogs, and here we have dog_1, dog_2. . . . We have cats, and here we have cat_1, cat_2. . . . We have laptops, and here we have $laptop_1$, $laptop_2$ . . ." However, instead of attempting this complex type of description, John could simply say, "We have living things and nonliving things." While this description is much more economical in its use of categories—only two—someone who is compiling a comprehensive inventory of what there is in the world may have to rework it. A microbiologist may struggle to situate viruses in this categorial scheme—as a thing, a virus seems to be neither living nor nonliving. A devout Roman Catholic may be puzzled about where to place God, the soul, and Saint Teresa of Avila—for instance, God is certainly not nonliving, but God is also so much more than just *a* living thing. Poets of a mystical temperament may claim that the absence of the beloved is a thing too—indeed, this hole in the fabric of being is the most tangible presence in their lives.

These thought exercises indicate that even if in the days of our prephilosophical innocence we tend to be realists, we may not quite agree on the *that* that we claim exists independent of our perceptual cognitions. Someone may need millions of categories to go over the terrain of reality with a fine-tooth comb, while someone else may be happy with just two categories. At this stage, introduce a philosopher who says that they will bite the bullet and give up our linguistic practices of presupposing or referring to *that* and view *that* simply as a construct of our interests and needs. Call this viewpoint "ontological idealism" or simply "idealism": the world does not arrive with a ready-made structure, and what there is in our surroundings is a function of what types of concepts we use and for which ends. Idealism is conceptually diffuse, encompassing as it does a range of philosophical perspectives. Consider this statement: "Julius Caesar suffered from clinical depression." Assuming that the neurophysiological constitution of the human organism has not changed significantly over the last two thousand years, it is reasonable to assume that some of the ancient Romans too suffered from what *we* categorize as "clinical depression," and yet it seems somewhat odd to impute such a set of psychosomatic experiences to a Roman general. For us, "clinical depression" exists within some present-day biomedical worldviews—that is, it is a meaningful term with which we negotiate certain features of our environment such as hospitals, doctors, and so on—and it did not exist within the existential milieus of the ancient Romans. This claim would be a weak iteration of idealism (WI): the question "Is there clinical depression?" cannot be detached from, and has to be answered concurrently with, the question "What types of concepts are we using and for what purposes?" However, once WI has been proposed, a stronger form of idealism (SI) is often not too far away. In the case of WI, clinical depression is said to be concept-dependent, but a hospital is assumed to have mind-independent existence. Now, SI demands that "hospital" too be properly recognized as a category shaped or informed by human interests and that this deconstructive process be carried out with respect to the "walls" that constitute the hospital, the "matter" that constitutes the walls, the "quarks" that constitute the matter, and so on. Given that Hindu philosophy is often associated with "idealism"—where this standpoint is understood as the proclamation "It's all in your mind" or the consolation "Life is but a dream"—it is important to note that SI is associated primarily with the lineages of Advaita **Vedānta**, and even they affirm some form of WI-shaped realism with respect to mundane objects such as chairs and cups.

MAPPING THE MULTITUDES IN THE WORLD

In the realist outlook of **Vaiśeṣika**, the world is said to be structured by (six and later) seven categories (*padārtha*) that encompass its nuanced features and details: substance (*dravya*), quality (*guṇa*), action (*karma*), universal (*sāmānya*), particularity (*viśeṣa*), inherence (*samavāya*), and nonexistence (*abhāva*).[1] Regarding the first six *padārtha*, Praśastapāda (c. 600 CE), an influential commentator, writes that they possess reality, cognizability, and nameability. Three important commentaries were written, in turn, on Praśastapāda's treatise by Vyomaśiva (c. 900 CE), Śrīdhara

(c. 1000 CE), and Udayana (c. 1000 CE)—by the time of Udayana, the **Nyāya** and **Vaiśeṣika** traditions had largely become integrated as one universe of discourse. This Nyāya-Vaiśeṣika categorial scheme is presented as a comprehensive outline of the kinds of things that can be known and linguistically expressed. The ontological account is pluralist in the sense that these kinds are not reducible to one another—thus, if we sought to subsume *guṇa* into *dravya*, dissolve *sāmānya*, and so on, the very scaffolding of the world would collapse.

To begin with, substance (*dravya*) is that in which qualities and actions exist, and it is ontologically distinct from the latter. Therefore, *dravya* is that which stands under qualities and actions as their substantial locus. There are nine types of *dravya*—namely, earth, water, fire, air, ether, time, space, self, and mind. The first five have a specific quality that is apprehended by a sense modality—smell for earth, taste for water, color for fire, touch for air, and sound for ether. The first four are of two kinds—the atoms (*aṇu*) of earth, water, fire, and air are indivisible and indestructible, while the specific combinations of these atoms are physical objects such as pots, which are subject to disintegration. Ether, which is singular, invisible, and all-pervading, is inferred as the medium of sound. This is because sound cannot be a quality of earth, water, fire, and air, since their distinctive qualities are not perceived by the ear. Space and time are each singular and omnipresent—they are the basis of our spatial distinctions, such as distance and nearness, and our temporal distinctions, such as past and future. The self (*ātman*) is the nonphysical subject of the various dimensions of our embodied life through time. It is all-pervading and indestructible and is inferred as the substratum of cognitions, feelings, volitions, and the like. Crucially, it is not intrinsically conscious, and consciousness is its contingent property when it is embodied in a psychophysical complex with a mind (*manas*). This understanding of the self—which is not shared by **Sāṃkhya**, **Yoga**, and the Vedāntic visions of Śaṃkara and Rāmānuja—plays a crucial role in the **Nyāya** opposition to styles of WI and SI.

While a substance exists in itself, a quality (*guṇa*) determines the character of a substance but does not constitute it. A quality is a nonmoving and nonrepeatable property, and it belongs to a substance and not to another quality. That is, one quality cannot itself be the substratum of another quality—thus, the blue color qualifies a sapphire and does not itself belong to another color. In a minute dissection of the fibers of reality, there are said to be twenty-four types of qualities, including color, taste, magnitude, conjunction, disjunction, cognition, pleasure, pain, desire, aversion, volition, character traits, and so on. Next, an action (*karma*) belongs to a substance and is distinct from both substance and quality. Unlike a quality, which is static, an action is a dynamic feature that is located in a substance and is also an independent cause of conjunction and disjunction. There are five types of action, and these are located only in the five corporeal substances (namely, earth, water, fire, air, and the mind)—there can be no action in ether, space, time, and the self, which are omnipresent and thus not subject to any change in position. These definitions, traversing the spaces of ontology and philosophy of psychology, are crafted with clear-cut precision: in the triad of *dravya*, *guṇa*, and *karma*, each item is distinct from the other two.

This understanding of *dravya* as the substratum of different aspects of an object resonates with some commonsense notions that shape our everyday lives. Thus, after listening for fifteen minutes to a friend we may say, "Now that's a substantial argument you have developed," or we may comment on her dinner: "Why, that's a substantial meal!" Such linguistic practices embody two notions of substance with which we work through our environments, even if unreflectively. When I turn toward a certain object in my visual field—say, the laptop on the table—I notice that it has a substantial presence: what I see is *one* "thing" with a fairly stable structure and not a mobile heap of colors, shapes, and sounds streaming back and forth or hovering above the table. It is because of this synchronic identity that at any given moment I can point to *it* and say, "That is a laptop and not a dog." Moreover, after looking at a payment receipt, I can report to customer service that the laptop that I am working on today is the very same laptop that I bought three years ago. Because of the diachronic identity that this rectangular and black-colored object *seems to* have, I state confidently, "I have had this laptop for three years now."

These notions of substance, with some distinctive variations, are shared across different styles of Hindu ***darśana***, in opposition to their formidable Buddhist interlocutors. In my reports from the frontlines of experience, I added the qualifier "seems to." Buddhist forms of teaching and spiritual practice are constant reminders that if all that glitters is not gold, we should exercise great caution in invoking everyday experience as a reliable guide into the hinterlands of reality. In this case, I may have concluded a bit too hastily, on the basis of my perception of a fairly unified configuration in front of me, that I can individuate *a* substance called a laptop persisting across temporal moments. According to a fundamental Buddhist tenet, whatever there is in the world is a momentary product of antecedent causes and conditions, and when these pass away, the product too ceases to be. Therefore, instead of speaking of a substantial laptop that exists over the course of three years, I should view it as a causally connected stream of events. From Buddhist perspectives, all talk of *dravya* is based on a fundamental misconception about the world, and such essences are to be disaggregated or "deconstructed" into interrelated processes of evanescent moments. If we were to rapidly whirl a stick that is lit at one end, a passerby would perceive an unbroken circle—likewise, the sense that the world is populated by multiple *dravya* is, in truth, the illusion of persistence.

We may happen to view this debate across Hindu and Buddhist conceptual borderlines over whether a laptop is a continuing substance or an aggregate of stages as a somewhat academic disputation. The stakes get raised significantly, however, when we realize that it applies not only to objects out there but also to the "I" itself. Across the landscapes of Hindu ***darśana***, an important presupposition is the spiritual center of gravity, which is the enduring locus of cognition, volition, and action. While the psychophysical complex is mutable and dissolves at death, this unchanging center—*ātman*, *jīva*, *cit*, or *puruṣa* in different contexts—is the basis of personal identity in one lifetime and across lifetimes within cycles of reincarnation. For Buddhists, generally speaking, the world is shaped by matrices of momentary events connected through causal relations, and there is no such enclave with ontological solidity. Therefore, if the question "Are you more like a tomato or more like a typhoon?" were raised, Nyāya-Vaiśeṣika would affirm the first view and Buddhism the second. Regarding a little boy whose name is Devadatta, the former would say that the different stages that he goes through—adolescence, middle age, and old age—are different temporally indexed properties that are rooted in a substantial self, just as the green color of the tomato when raw three days ago and the red color of the tomato when ripe this morning are located in the self-same tomato. The latter would claim that these stages are densely connected on a causal continuum such that a subsequent moment is related to an antecedent moment, but these moments themselves are not held together by a substantial self, just as distinct vortices of air are causally interrelated within the matrix of a typhoon, but the typhoon itself is not an abiding entity.

Such Hindu and Buddhist dialectical exchanges often involve debates over the criterion of reality—that is to say, the distinguishing mark with which we may demarcate between what is real and what is not real. These debates are much more intractable than disputes relating to boundaries in everyday social contexts. For instance, it may be possible to get thirty people to agree that one criterion for getting a particular job is that the candidate should have received a PhD in astrophysics within the last five years. In contrast, in a Hindu-Buddhist argumentative setting, if the criterion for what is real is stipulated as "*x* is real if *x* is a substance," it will not be acceptable to the Buddhist interlocutor. Conversely, Buddhist viewpoints, which deny the existence of an enduring self as the substratum of momentary events, are shaped by criterial statements such as "Whatever is real is momentary" or "Whatever is real has causal efficacy."

WHAT IS THE CRITERION OF REALITY?

Reflecting the **Nyāya** standpoint, Udayana, in his *Ātma-tattva-viveka* ("Determining the Truth of the Self"), sets out to critique the Buddhist equivalence between existence and momentariness and also defends the distinction between qualities and the substantial basis of those qualities.[2] One argument involves the claim that we are able to both see and touch the same object, and this cross modality points to an identical self in which these sensations are located. This line of argument is indicated in the aphorism *Nyāya-sūtra* 3.1.1, which cryptically says, "Because the same thing is apprehended by sight and by touch." The commentator Vātsyāyana (c. 400 CE) offers the following analysis: We may apprehend an object visually and then touch that object, saying "that thing that I saw earlier, I now touch." This statement indicates that the two cognitions apprehend the same object and also belong to the same subject. The "I" who both sees and touches the object must be distinct from sense organs, because one sense organ cannot perceive the object of another.

In short, there is something that recognizes itself as seeing and touching the same object, and this something is the spiritual self that is distinct from sensory processes.[3]

Another strategy that was developed in these argumentative contexts was to appeal to the subjective feel (or the "phenomenology") of one's recollection of the past and claim that this subjectivity can be more adequately elucidated by one's preferred ontological account. For Nyāya-Vaiśeṣika, there is a plurality of substantial selves and consciousness is a property of each substantial self, and it opposes the Buddhist understanding on the grounds that it cannot capture the phenomenology of this statement: "I who perceived *x* in the past am the I who remember it now." On a Buddhist account, the cognizer is not an enduring self but a causal stream of discrete cognitions that are momentary. Therefore, when Devadatta remembers in the afternoon that he had seen a cat sitting in the garden in the morning, this is how we should analyze the recognitive process—an antecedent temporal stage when a cat was observed is causally related to a subsequent temporal stage when a cat-impression is revived. Thus, a statement such as "It is *I* who remember the cat" should be reformulated through translation as "Cognition $_{\text{afternoon}}$ is causally connected with cognition $_{\text{morning}}$." In other words, a present cognition is in causal continuity with a past cognition, and we do not need to invoke a substantial self that "embeds" these momentary cognitions. The Nyāya-Vaiśeṣika responds that because these stages are transient, by the time the latter arrives, the former has vanished. However, what needs to be explained is Devadatta's sense that *he* remembers seeing the cat—and this is distinct from the sense *that* a cat is remembered. If the two stages do not belong to the self-same cognizer who is transcendent to them, the subsequent stage cannot know that its object (in this case, a cat) is the object cognized in the previous stage.

This argument from memory is often developed on the basis of *Nyāya-sūtra* 1.1.10, which states, "Desire, aversion, volition, pleasure, pain, and cognition are characteristics of the self." With respect to the first, Vātsyāyana argues in this way in his commentary: if an individual experiences pleasure through contact with a certain object, when a similar object is perceived in the future, there is desire for this object; however, such desire is possible because there is one unified self who both cognizes and re-cognizes the object.[4] In other words, there is an implicit "binder" that links past cognition with present cognition, and this singular subject of synthesis is the self. Across the tissues of cognitive existence, there is a subtle—and indeed imperceptible—glue that binds them, and this glue is the "I" that re-claims past cognitions as its own.

The substantial identity of the self across time

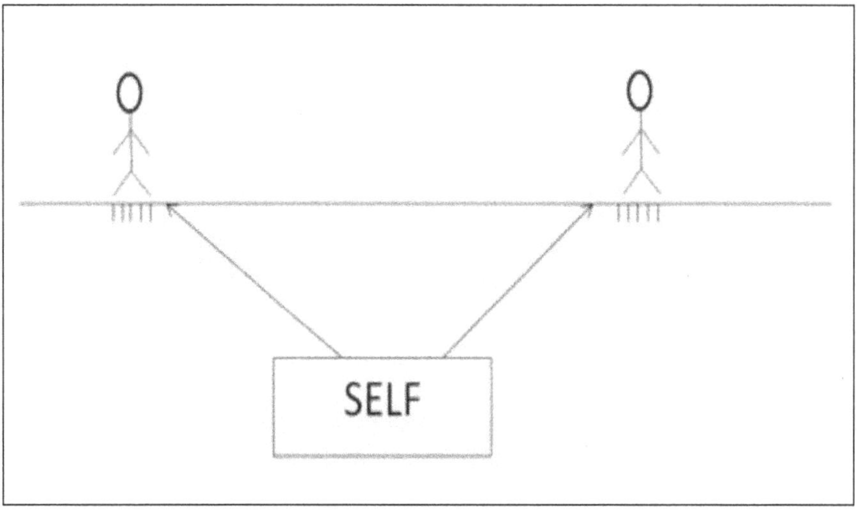

This analysis of psychic processes is related to the understanding of a substantial mind (*manas*) as the organizing unit with which a self is contingently associated—that is, when the self is embodied. As the inner sense, the mind receives information from the different senses about the environment, and since each sense operates within a specific sphere, it is the mind that coordinates these distinct sensory reports. If Mary is intently looking at a painting in a room where someone is playing a piece from Beethoven on the violin, the strains of music may fade away from Mary's perceptual space, and this is because her mind is directly attending to a visual object. She can subsequently turn to the music, and on the next day, she can remember that it was she who both observed a painting and listened to some Beethoven. Therefore, on the basis of certain theses about memory, such as "One can remember only what one has seen before," Nyāya-Vaiśeṣika tries to establish that the memory criterion of personal identity—according to which personal identity is based on an individual's memory of past experiences—presupposes the existence of a permanent self. This is because a certain cognition can be regarded as a genuine memory (say, of a picnic in the summer in Cornwall) only if the individual with this cognition is the same individual as the one who had the experience earlier. Therefore, notions of psychological continuity seem to presuppose personal identity in the attempt to explain it. It is not meaningful to say, "What Devadatta experienced once is what Yajñadatta currently remembers," and this is because remembering is a form of mental grasping in which I declare, "This thing I cognize now is something I cognized earlier." For Buddhists, however, this postulation of a spiritual self that holds together discrete cognitions is ontologically extravagant, and as noted earlier, they claim that the subjectivity of remembering episodes from the past is captured in the notion of a causally connected stream of cognitions. Just as a seed before sprouting and the seed at the moment of sprouting are two distinct things, and yet they are causally related in one stream, so too is the "I" a dynamically interconnected bundle of cognitions, volitions, affectivities and so on, and not a unitary substance.

The crux of the matter can be highlighted with this question: Is humanity characterized by a condition of "self-*obsession*" (this is the Buddhist charge, generally speaking) or by a condition of "self-*forgetfulness*" (this is the Hindu charge, generally speaking)? Someone could regard this dispute as yet another grand exercise in crafting hair-splitting distinctions: after all, whether we regard ourselves as a substance or as a stream, we are usually able to remember in the evening what we had eaten at lunch. However, for Hindu—as well as for Buddhist—philosophical systems, the question "To self or not to self?" is not simply an inquiry into what exists out there but is integrally linked with the question "What is the pathway toward liberation from worldly suffering?" If it turns out that the "I" is more like a typhoon than a tomato, then by holding on to the misconception that one is a unitary thing, one becomes even more enmeshed in structures of ignorance. Conversely, if the "I" is more akin to a tomato than to a typhoon, then in failing to discern a stable anchor, one sinks much deeper into the swirling waters of change and decay. Thus, as we will see in subsequent chapters, the question of self-identity is vitally connected to topics relating to how we may acquire knowledge of what there is in the world, and how we may use our embodied capacities of cognition, emotion, and volition to find a way through the vales of worldly misery.

The scaffolding outlined so far—with *dravya*, *guṇa*, and *karma* as its nuts and bolts—is further reinforced by universals (*sāmānya*) and inherence (*samavāya*). Looking at three animals on a grassy field we say, "That is a *cow*, that too is a *cow*, and that is also a *cow*." According to Nyāya-Vaiśeṣika, linguistic predicates such as "cow" are not psychological projections onto objects in the world—rather, they are aligned with mind-independent constituents called universals. There are certain objective identities across the individual cows on a field, and the description "cow" is a linguistic correlate of these identities. While a concrete particular such as a cow—which is on the field and not inside the house—has a specific spatiotemporal location, a universal such as cow-ness is multiply exemplifiable in the sense that the indivisible cow-ness is present in more than one cow at the same time. Likewise, when we describe Julius Caesar as courageous and General Eisenhower too as courageous, we are invoking the universal called "courage," which is exemplified by these two individuals from two distinct historical epochs. Such universals help us re-cognize an individual across time and exercise predictive power over objects in space-time; indeed, in a world devoid of them, there would be no meaningful inquiry and no intersubjective communication.[5]

This line of argument can be spelled out schematically in this way.

Premise 1: In our everyday experiences, we perceive qualitative similarities across distinct individuals. We never cognize a bare particular but always a particular under a certain description, such as "cow."

Premise 2: These descriptions are not linguistic artifacts—they successfully latch on to the deep structures of reality.

Premise 3: In the absence of this success in identifying stable features of the environment, our encounters with the world would be thrown into disarray.

Conclusion: The best explanation for our success is the existence of mind-independent universals.

Developing the second premise, the recurring features are said to be universals (*sāmānya*) or class-essences (*jāti*), which are unitary and which exist independently of specific instances, such as that cow in the field. They are eternal in the sense that they are not affected by transformations in their instantiations. They cut the natural world at its joints, and they are to be distinguished from arbitrary collections (*upādhi*) of individuals such as "a group of cooks." For instance, cow-ness is the common nature present in multiple cows, and because cow-ness is incorporated into the fabric of reality, our practices of classification relating to animals are not arbitrary.

In short, *dravya*, *guṇa*, *karma*, and *sāmānya* are distinct from one another. The ontological glue that binds them together into the real-world objects that we perceive and live with—cows, books, and laptops—is inherence (*samavāya*). More precisely, this is the relation that obtains between qualities and a substance, actions and a substance, a universal and its instantiations, and a relational whole and its parts. Crucially, inherence, which is an independent category of reality, is an eternal relation that is to be distinguished from contingent relations of conjunction. When Mary gets up from a chair after sitting on it for an hour, both Mary and the chair continue to exist beyond this temporary conjunction. However, as long as a particular exists, a universal is always *in* that particular, so that the two relata are inseparably linked. With these categories in place, we can make sense of Praśastapāda's careful definition of a universal as that which "brings about the idea of its own form in one, two or many things; and it is the cause or basis of the notion of inclusion, inhering as it does in all its substrates simultaneously."[6]

In delineating the constitution of the world in this way, Nyāya-Vaiśeṣika philosophers seem to be seeking a sort of reflective equilibrium between what is observed in the everyday world on the one hand and what needs to be postulated as the basic constituents of the world to make sense of these quotidian observations on the other. Quite remarkably, the developed Nyāya-Vaiśeṣika system adds to this inventory of what there is in the world the category of nonexistence or absence (*abhāva*). That is to say, the absence of an entity in a particular spatiotemporal location is as objective a feature of the world as the presence of that entity in that particular location. It is claimed that the awareness of something absent—such as the sun in the night sky—has a subjective feel that is distinct from that of the awareness of the sun as present in the sky in the daytime. Such absences are perceived and not inferred on the basis of something that is present—for instance, "A pot on this floor is not perceived; therefore, there is the absence of a pot on this floor." Rather, we perceive the floor and also the floor as qualified by the absence of a pot on it. There are four types of absence: prior nonexistence (*prāgabhāva*), such as the nonexistence of a house in bricks before it is built; posterior nonexistence (*dhvaṃsa*), such as the nonexistence of a jar in its pieces after it is destroyed; absolute absence (*atyantābhāva*), such as the constant nonexistence of heat in ice; and difference (*anyonyābhāva*), which is the nonidentity of one thing (say, a pot) with another (say, a book).

Stepping back from the detailed argumentation, it is clear that Nyāya-Vaiśeṣika and the Buddhists are battling over a fundamental question regarding the relation between language and the world: Can our commonsense reports about our psychic lives and our physical environments be taken as helpful guides to how "deep reality" is structured, or is it the case that "deep reality" has no stable structure and our commonsense reports need to be radically revised? According to Buddhist philosophers, we are misled by the surface grammar of everyday language—as articulated through statements such as "*I* am eating a *cake*"—into believing that it picks out translinguistic entities such as a spiritual self and enduring objects. Just as in the sentence "It is raining," the word "it" does not refer to anything out there but is only a logical subject that is required by syntactical rules, the sentence "I am reading a book with a brown cover" also does not describe the action of an ontologically unitary agent. From one Buddhist perspective, what there is in the world is dynamic streams of unique—that is, nonrepeating—particulars (*svalakṣaṇa*), and these particular streams are broken up through human language into specific objects such as books. Designations of this type are indeed useful for everyday purposes—such as writing or reading a book—but there is no enduring book-ness inhering in a book. A name, such as "cow," is applied to certain entities not because they all share an essence but because this name is a conventional tool that distinguishes these entities from others. In contrast, Nyāya-Vaiśeṣika claims that its ontological outline, with categories such as substance, (static) quality, (dynamic) action, universal, and inherence, is a comprehensive scheme that adequately maps out and explains our complex world.

COMPREHENDING THE FORM OF UNITY

Relative to Nyāya-Vaiśeṣika, therefore, Buddhists have an austere ontology—in addition to locating space-time points on an *xy* plane, Nyāya-Vaiśeṣika argues for a real *z* axis along which these points are organized in stable configurations. On these conceptual landscapes, Advaita **Vedānta**, as systematized by Śaṃkara (c. 700 CE), occupies an intermediate space—Advaita is vigorously opposed to the Buddhist rejection of the spiritual self (*ātman*), but at the same time, Advaita claims that Nyāya-Vaiśeṣika is, ontologically speaking, too extravagant.[7] The basic Advaita thesis can be expressed through a question: "Why demand as many as seven independent categories when *one* supercategory will do the job of making sense of the manifold entities we encounter in the world?" Trying to spell out the worldview of Advaita is a deeply paradoxical exercise, because the fundamental cement that holds together the world of finitude cannot be apprehended through human thought. Just as the "war to end all wars" would itself be another war and, at the same time, would somehow transcend the limitations of an earthly conflict, the "supercategory to sublate all categories" is itself a category insofar as we can point to *it* from within the space of reasoned discourse, all the while transcending the limitations of reasoned discourse.

WHAT IS THE MOST ECONOMICAL INVENTORY OF THE WORLD?

For Nyāya-Vaiśeṣika, the sevenfold categorization is an "objective" outline of the world—it is not that someone who happened to like the number seven a lot went on adding categories till they arrived at this wonderful figure. Therefore, it is crucial to establish that these categories are logically independent of one another. Since one does not perceive a universal (such as cow-ness) separately from a particular in which that universal is instantiated (such as a cow in the grassy field), a critic of Nyāya-Vaiśeṣika could charge that they have been presented with an inflated ontology and some of its categories should be popped by a conceptual pin. According to Nyāya-Vaiśeṣika, however, it is because of the intimate connection called inherence that although universals and their particulars are ontologically distinct, they are not found separately. The commentator Śrīdhara argues that while cow-ness is not perceived apart from individual cows and individual cows too are not perceived apart from their cow-ness, we should not conclude that universals have no independent existence over and above their particulars—rather, they are both perceived in the way that an iron ball is perceived to be red hot because of its contact with fire. That is, the iron ball and the fire are perceived together while they are the causes of two distinct cognitions. In this way, the *cow-ness*-exemplified-in-every-cow causes our cognition of identity across different cows, and the cow-ness-exemplified-in-every-*cow* causes our cognition of a particular cow.

But for Śaṃkara (c. 700 CE), to count cow-ness as a distinct category is already to add one thing too many to one's inventory of the world. Śaṃkara is an exegetical thinker who seeks to weave together a harmonious tapestry with scriptural threads from the ***Upaniṣads***, the ***Brahma-sūtras***, and the ***Bhagavad-gītā***. One fundamental question that he seeks to answer, by drawing on the vocabulary of the human self (*ātman*) and the divine self (*brahman*), is the relation between the finite world and the nonfinite ground. Paradoxically, he concludes that the relation is, in fact, a nonrelation. While we may meaningfully say, "Mary is related to Jane as a niece of Jane," because Mary and Jane can indeed be enumerated as two distinct individuals, we cannot point to the finite world as one *this* and its nonfinite foundation as another *this*, and then raise the question of how *this* and *this* are related. One does not solve a question if it can be shown that it is not properly phrased in the first place; one seeks to *dis*solve it. Whether or not the question itself—"What is the relation between humanity and divinity?"—is coherent, therefore, became an intensely debated theme across the worldviews of Vedāntic philosophical discourse.

While Advaita has sometimes been presented as the epitome of "Oriental irrationalism," it is vital to highlight the point that its scriptural readings are animated partly by a quest for the criterion of reality and a systematic application of this criterion to the everyday world. In our busy lives, we do not usually need to formulate a precise criterion; we operate with rough and ready classifications that state that squared circles are not real at all, Santa Claus is only "real" for children, and the laptop on the table is "real" for everyone. However, we may need a standard rule for things or processes whose reality is disputed: telekinesis, ESP, reincarnation, the archangel Michael, and, of course, God. In such situations, we realize that it is not enough to say, "I *feel* that reincarnation is real," for we may receive the stern rejoinder, "I *feel* that reincarnation is not real." We have already encountered two criteria—the Buddhist criterion that *x* is real if it is an evanescent point-instant, streams of which we organize with labels such as "cow" and "laptop," and the Nyāya-Vaiśeṣika criterion that *x* is real if it conforms to the sevenfold categorial scheme.

In the case of Buddhism, the conceptual equivalence between reality and momentariness is put forward not simply as someone's subjective preference ("I don't like permanent entities—those ghastly beings!") but as the teaching of the Buddha, the enlightened individual who possesses the correct discernment of the way the world is. Advaita is shaped by the mirror-inverse conceptual equivalence—namely, between reality and eternality—and this too is not Śaṃkara's fanciful conjecture but drawn out by him from scriptural texts. Consider, for instance, this verse from the ***Bhagavad-gītā*** (2.16): "There is no being of the non-existent (*asat*) and there is no non-being of the existent (*sat*). The difference between the two is discerned by those who see the truth." For Śaṃkara, such verses indicate that only the immutable ground of mutable entities—the *sat*—is robustly real in the sense that it cannot undergo any transformation whatsoever, and the impermanent fabric woven together as the everyday world is not fully real. As noted in the introduction, the exegetical reasonings of Śaṃkara, Rāmānuja (1017–1137), Madhva (1238–1317), Vallabha (1479–1531), and others are classified under the rubric of **Vedānta**, which are multiple attempts to construct a coherent tapestry of meaning from the scriptural data. While Rāmānuja would dispute some of the conclusions that Śaṃkara draws from scripture, in his exegeses, too, the divine foundation—*sat* or *brahman*—is the ontological "stuff" that binds together the finite entities in the world. When I look around the room in which I am sitting, I do not see a blooming, buzzing confusion of thirty different things flying about but a relatively stable environment. Things do not fall apart, and *brahman* is the transcendental center of coherence in a world of constant change. When I look at the tree in my garden in December, I see that it has no leaves, and when I look at it in July, I see that it is full of green leaves—I do not doubt, at least in my unreflective moments, that *it* is the *same* tree, though with very different properties. To the question "Why do I seem to inhabit a universe in which things undergo change against a wider background of relative stability?" a Vedāntic answer would be, "Because *brahman* is the still point in our moving world and remains the unchanging foundation upon which all empirical processes are based."

One distinctive marker of Advaita in these Vedāntic streams is the claim that these processes are not robustly or unqualifiedly real. In his commentary on *Taittirīya Upaniṣad* 2.1.1, Śaṃkara argues that something is said to be substantially real (*satya*) when, once it has been ascertained to be in a certain condition, it does not undergo any change in that condition. On the basis of this conceptual equivalence between "reality" and "immutability," one Advaita argument can be presented in this schematic form:

Premise 1: If *x* is not absolutely immutable, then *x* is not real.
Premise 2: The world is not absolutely immutable.
Conclusion: The world is not real.
Premise 3: Whatever is not real is substantially nonexistent.
Conclusion: The world is substantially nonexistent.

This equivalence (premise 1) would be rejected by various other Hindu philosophers. In *Ślokavārttika* ("Exposition on the Verses"), Kumārila presents the objection that if at the time of performing action, and when pain and pleasure emerge, the self is transformed, its eternality (*nityatā*) disappears. Kumārila replies that he is willing to characterize the self as "noneternal" in the sense of its liability to modification; however, such a liability does not necessarily mean annihilation (*uccheda*). The self is modified in the sense that it assumes a different state, just as an individual goes from childhood to youth.[8] Again, the commentary of Vyāsa on *Yoga-sūtra* 4.33 states that permanence is of two types: one is the permanence of the immutable (*kūṭastha-nityatā*), which belongs to the spiritual principle (*puruṣa*), and the other is the permanence that belongs to the strands (*guṇas*) of worldly reality that are mutable (*pariṇāmi-nityatā*). Since that is said to be permanent in which the essence is not destroyed while it is changing, both the *puruṣa* and the *guṇas* are permanent because their essential nature is not destroyed.[9]

While Advaita operates with a stronger reading of *nityatā* and concludes that the world is nonexistent, we should not overlook the crucial qualifier in premise 3—"substantially." It is not the case that the world is as utterly nonexistent as a squared circle that cannot even be conceptualized, but the world does not have a self-generated ontological momentum, and it exists insofar as it is rooted in *brahman*. Therefore, the entities that populate the everyday world—cows, chairs, cups, books, laptops, and so on—indeed exist in the sense that when I type on a laptop or drink coffee with a cup, these entities are not hallucinatory wisps flitting in and out of my sensory vistas. We are not zombies who are sleepwalking our way through the world. From this perspective, Advaita leaves the world as it is—when a disciple in an Advaita lineage feels hungry, they eat food, and neither the food nor the experience of hunger is utterly nonexistent. However, because these entities and processes are mutable, they are not unequivocally real in the sense that only *brahman* is (premise 1). This conceptual distinction may seem arcane, but we often invoke it in negotiating optical illusions such as mirages. When we perceive a mirage, it seems very real to us, and yet we comment later that it was not "substantially" out there: the mirage *is* and yet the mirage is *not*. The Advaita claim is that the world of impermanence has a mirage-*like* feel to it: we mistakenly think that we are surrounded by objects of ontological solidity when, in truth, they do not contain such solidity in themselves but derive it entirely from *brahman*. The world is precariously poised at the edge of a precipice: without the continuing support of the immutable *brahman*, the world would fall into nothingness.

To use the more characteristic terminology found in Advaita commentarial texts, the world of mutability is "conventionally real" (*vyāvahārika*) but not "ultimately real" (*pāramārthika*). Consider a five-pound banknote from two standpoints: the conventional and the ultimate. From the first perspective, it is a highly useful piece of paper that can buy me bread because people around me agree to ascribe to it the value that it has. From the second perspective, however, it is a piece of paper with some beautiful inscriptions on it, but it does not have any intrinsic monetary value, as I realize if I try to use it in a small village in Mongolia or Japan. Money is, as it is said, a social construct—it is not real in itself but real only to the extent that some people collectively consent to participate in certain financial practices with respect to it. Likewise, the world with its multiple differences too does not possess any intrinsic reality, and it exists insofar as *brahman* undergirds and suffuses its existence at all times. This conclusion can be highlighted with the stock Advaita analogy of a snake and a rope. If I am walking down a road that is poorly illuminated, I may think that I am about to step on a snake and move away in fright. Shining a torch on the road, however, I realize that what lies ahead is only a rope. Just as the snake felt very real to me for a few fleeting seconds but later turned out to be nonexistent, the Advaita claim is that the whole world of plurality, which feels very real, is not ultimately real. Again, just as the "snake" has a certain locus (namely, the rope), so too is the world not an aggregate of disconnected entities; rather, it has some stable configurations because it is rooted in its transcendental ground (namely, *brahman*).

Therefore, if we seek to classify the objects we see in the world, we do not need to enumerate them independently of one another, since every object is *brahman*-structured. If there are ten different pots of clay with ten different colors, instead of enumerating them individually as pot_1, pot_2, pot_3, . . . pot_{10}, we can simply say, "These are ten different variations of the one substantial basis of clay." Even though each pot does have a distinctive name and form (*nāma-rūpa*), because it is subject to change, it is not ultimately real (premise 1). Again, after reading through a book with 158 pages, I do not usually say to a friend, "I have finished reading the book that you have written," and then add after ten minutes, with reference to the same book, "Oh, I forgot to mention that I have finished reading 158 pages." We do not need two independent categories—"this book" and "158 pages"—because the former encapsulates the latter. We can repeat this exercise with various other entities that we see around us: thus, a wave in an ocean is substantially water and necklaces of gold are substantially gold. Developing this analogy with respect to a golden necklace and *brahman*, we do not have to count twice in the logical space of categories: one ontological category called a golden necklace and another called *brahman*. Rather, the essence of the golden necklace is *brahman* through and through. Between a golden necklace and *brahman*, there is ontological nonduality or "not-two-ness," and this is what the term *a-dvaita* literally means. Just as a brown pot would continue to exist as a pot even if it were painted blue but would dissolve at once if the clay, with which it is *advaita*, were somehow eradicated, so too would the world vanish at once if its underlying support, with which it is *advaita*, were removed. Therefore, if the question were put to us, "What is out there?" we do not have to compile a massively long list with items such as cats, cows, cups, stars, Norwegians, cousins, laptops, bridges, and so on and then add *brahman* to it; rather, *brahman* is the ontological ground of all the items on that massively long list. In other words, unlike spatio-temporal beings, which can be individuated and placed in distinct conceptual boxes, the unchanging basis of reality is not *this* being or *that* being: it is the being-itself that makes possible the existence of individual beings.

One way to summarize the discussion so far is to say that Advaita simultaneously affirms and denies difference from two different perspectives. While Śaṃkara's Advaita is sometimes read as the declaration that "everything is just the same," this proclamation of spiritual identity does not negate mundane differences. Thus, the distinctive markers of Chinese porcelain from the Tang dynasty (618–907 CE) and Wedgwood pottery from 1850 are affirmed; again, it is affirmed that across the world, human beings have different nationalities, and therefore different sets of passports. What is denied, however, is that in such descriptions, we are speaking of distinct ontological categories such as *dravya*, *guṇa*, *karma*, and the like. The presupposition here is that if the existence of one thing (such as a blue-colored clay pot) can be explained in terms of the existence of another thing (clay), then the former is not ontologically real over and above the latter. The clay pot depends on the clay for its contingent existence, but the clay itself does not depend on an individual clay pot for its substantial existence. Therefore, the question "How is the clay pot related to the clay?" is not properly phrased, because it assumes that it is possible to distinguish between a clay pot and clay as two ontologically independent things. There is, strictly speaking, no *relation* per se between a clay pot and clay: the clay pot is nondual with clay. Analogously, since the world is not ultimately real, the question of an essential relation between the world and *brahman* does not arise: this paradoxical (non)relation is nonduality.

On the basis of this conceptual equivalence between "reality" and "causal independence," here is the outline of another Advaita argument:

Premise 4: If *x* is causally dependent, then *x* is not ultimately real.
Premise 5: The empirical world is causally dependent on *brahman*.
Conclusion: The empirical world is not ultimately real.

In his commentary on ***Brahma-sūtra*** 2.1.18, Śaṃkara invokes this motif against a **Vaiśeṣika** account of independent categories. Regarding the relation between a quality (such as brown) and its substance (such as a book), the **Vaiśeṣika** argues, on the one hand, that they are ontologically different and, on the other hand, that they are connected through inherence (*samavāya*). Śaṃkara argues, however, that this postulation of *samavāya* generates the following dilemma: On the one hand, we have to postulate a second-order *samavāya* to connect each of the two relata and the first-order *samavāya*, and in this way, we would trigger an infinite regress. On the other hand, if the *samavāya* is not connected in any manner to the two relata, the bond between the two relata would dissolve.[10] We should *dis*solve this dilemma by denying the ontological reality of *samavāya*. When we see a blue lotus, the proper way to analyze our cognition is to say not that the blue color and the lotus in which this quality inheres are *two* distinct categories but rather that the former is nondual with the latter. Because the blue has its basis in the lotus, it is not independently real, just as because the finite world is dependent on the nonfinite *brahman*, it is ultimately unreal (premise 4).

Inherence and the threat of an infinite regress

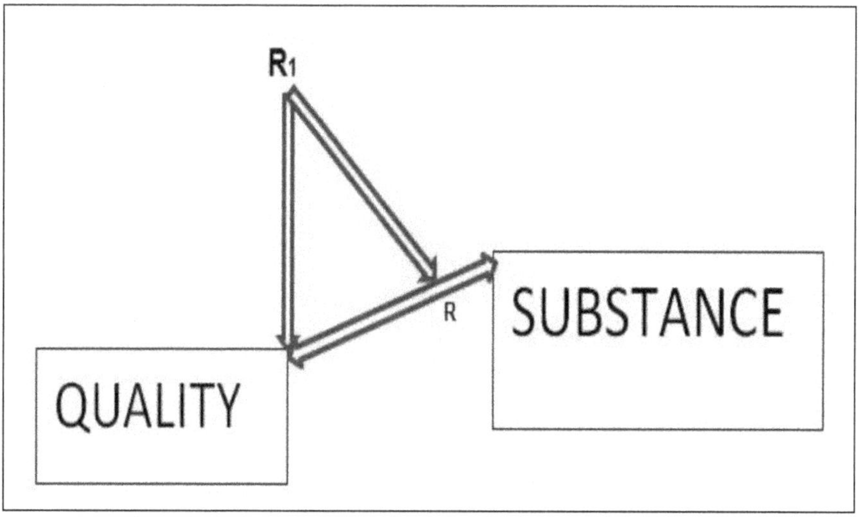

One Nyāya-Vaiśeṣika response to this problem is to claim that inherence is not externally related to the two relata, in which case a higher-order inherence would indeed have to be posited as an additional entity; rather, the very nature of inherence is to be self-linked to the relata (*svarūpa-sambandha*).[11] Just as when two sheets of paper are stuck together with glue, we do not need superglue, which would stick the glue itself to the two sheets, so too does inherence bind together the two relata and itself to them without generating an infinite regress. A similar line of reasoning is used to avoid a replication of the particularities or haecceities (*viśeṣa*) that individuate partless entities such as atoms, selves, minds, space, time, and ether. Such individuators are, conceptually speaking, the polar opposites of universals—if a universal gathers many entities under one description, an individuator distinguishes one individual from another in a particularized way. Two atoms of water that are qualitatively indistinguishable are yet individuated through their *viśeṣa*—thus, *this* atom of water is distinct from *that* atom of water. Crucially, these individuators are to be regarded as self-differentiating because, otherwise, we would have to postulate additional individuators to distinguish one individuator from another individuator, thus generating an infinite regress.

A somewhat different way to address the problem of an infinite regress can be found in the Vedāntic worldview of Madhva, where *brahman* is the sole independent support of the world that is ontologically real. Rejecting premise 1 and premise 4, its defenders argue that we cannot deny ontological reality to finite entities simply because they are not independent of *brahman*—rather, they continue to have real existence in time through their dependence on *brahman*. These entities have a *viśeṣa* through which we are able to distinguish between qualities and substances, particulars and universals, and so on. That is, a thing is constituted in such a manner that it is able to relate itself to, and also distinguish itself from, its modes, predicates, and properties without having to appeal to any higher-order entities.[12] In the *Ślokavārttika* of Kumārila, we find yet another style of engaging with this problem: Kumārila says that the universal (*sāmānya*, *jāti*) and the particular (*viśeṣa*) are different aspects of the same thing, and neither is intelligible in distinction from the other. The universal is distinct from the particulars and yet pervades each one of them, and their relation is natural (*svābhāvika*) and does not have to be established through any specific reasoning.[13]

Thus, Nyāya-Vaiśeṣika, the Vedāntic vision of Madhva, and the **Mīmāṃsā** of Kumārila, which do not accept premises 1 and 4, develop distinctive ways of relating general features and specific properties. In contrast, Advaita holds that the finite "I"—the agent who drinks coffee, reads books, and so on—is not ultimately real, since it is not immutable. In a statement such as "I am writing a book," the word "I" ultimately points not to the mutable ego but to the *ātman*, which is ineffably nondual with *brahman*. While the conscious subject is directed toward particular objects in the world, the *ātman* is the onlooker witnessing these transient states without becoming engaged in their unfolding. As a remote analogy, consider how worldly activities, shaped by the distinctions of cognizer and cognized, proceed in the light of the sun. While sunlight enables me to make judgments such as "Now I am eating a pizza," the sun's luminosity is devoid of such subject-object dichotomies—sunlight just *is*. As we will see in chapters 3 and 4, the nondual luminosity of reality seems to have become characterized as the finite "I" (*jīva*) because of spiritual ignorance (*avidyā*) or *māyā*—a term that is sometimes translated as "illusion." The center of spiritual gravity in the human person (*ātman*) is not one more ontological category over and above the transcendental ground of finitude (*brahman*); to think that it is so is an expression of *avidyā*. As the Advaita traditions developed after Śaṃkara, certain questions that were not explicitly discussed by him, especially relating to the site and the object of *avidyā*, became loci of active disputation.[14] The Vivaraṇa school is associated with the view that the world exists before it is perceived (*sṛṣṭi-dṛṣṭi-vāda*), and the Bhāmatī school with the view that the perception of the world is simultaneous with its production (*dṛṣṭi-sṛṣṭi-vāda*). According to the WI varieties of the former, the world has an existence independent of specific perceivers but not independent of *brahman*. According to the SI varieties of the latter, when an individual self enters into deep sleep, the world of diversity dissolves, and upon awakening, a new world of diversity is presented through the individual's vision (*dṛṣṭi*). Again, the Bhāmatī school holds that there are multiple instances of *avidyā* located in many *jīvas* and these *jīvas* are the limitations of *brahman*. The Vivaraṇa school argues that there is one *avidyā* that operates through many *jīvas* that are the reflections of *brahman*. In contrast, the more robustly theistic forms of **Vedānta** argue that the finite "I" is ontologically real as a distinct thing that is existentially dependent on *brahman* at all times. They vigorously claim that the postulation of the principle of *avidyā* or *māyā*—which is neither existent nor nonexistent—is not logically coherent.

In sum, Advaita **Vedānta** and Nyāya-Vaiśeṣika offer two different conceptual ways of identifying, cataloging, and organizing the things that we see in the world around us. The latter has a "thick" ontology packed with substances, qualities, and actions, while the former has a "thin" ontology in which the diversity of mundane milieus is regarded as ultimately unreal. Thus, if I see a brown dog on the street, according to Nyāya-Vaiśeṣika, the brown color is distinct from the dog, which is the substantial locus of the color, and *this* dog is distinct from *that* dog and from that *cat*. Advaita simultaneously affirms these distinctions as empirically valid and denies that they isolate distinct categories at the bedrock of reality. In the next chapter, we will move further into the epistemological and the logical landscapes of Nyāya-Vaiśeṣika and look at some aspects of the debate over whether reason is capable of leading human beings from the finite world toward the divine ground.

2

Knowing the Roots of Reality

In a famous soliloquy from Shakespeare, Macbeth asks, "Is this a dagger which I see before me, the handle toward my hand?"[1] Macbeth wants to know whether the object suspended in his visual field is reality-rooted or simply a fabrication of his feverish mind. To reiterate a key theme of chapter 1, a proponent of idealism would claim that both this dagger and the world at large are dependent—strongly or weakly—on a mental state or process. Consider an alternative play in which such a philosopher tries to convince Macbeth that the kingdom of Duncan is a mind-dependent construct and asks Macbeth to renounce any attachment to such a fragile entity. However, one does not perceive "mind-dependence" in the straightforward way in which one points to an apple on the table and says, "I see that it is red." Rather, arguments about whether the world has a mind-dependent existence have to be developed by carefully investigating the structure and content of everyday perceptual experience. Perhaps there is indeed an apple-shaped thing out there, and perception latches onto this configuration, or perhaps the apple-configuration is a fabrication of our minds. Either the apple is a reflection of what is already out there, or it is a projection by us toward what is not yet there.

WHAT IS THE CORRECT ANALYSIS OF COGNITIVE PROCESSES?

Sidestepping these philosophical debates for a moment, one pathway would be analogy. Macbeth could be asked to compare the kingdom to a dagger and understand that any human-made kingdom is dagger-*like* in the sense that it is subject to decay and decline and has no existential solidity. Macbeth may not be impressed by this move, however, for he could lay out various disanalogies between a dagger and a kingdom. For one, Macbeth can marshal a thousand people who readily affirm that he rules over a kingdom, but none of his trusted ministers endorse his claim that there is a dagger in front of them. At this stage, the philosopher, who has read some Advaita **Vedānta**, offers him this argument shaped by inference:

All that is different from *brahman* is ultimately unreal,
because it is different from *brahman.*
Whatever is different from *brahman* is ultimately unreal,
for instance, silver in a mother-of-pearl.

Variations on this argument appear in various commentarial texts of Advaita **Vedānta**, and it can be partly reworked in this form—if *p* then *q*; *p*; therefore, *q*.

Premise 1: If *x* is different from *brahman*, then *x* is ultimately unreal.
Premise 2: A finite spatiotemporal object is different from *brahman.*
Conclusion: A finite spatiotemporal object is ultimately unreal.

THE REALITY OF REASONING

Crucially, the real-world instance ("silver in a mother-of-pearl") in the Advaita argument does not appear in the proposed reformulation. The logical template for this argument was developed, and refined across several centuries, by **Nyāya** philosophers. In the very first aphorism of the root text *Nyāya-sūtras*, we read about sixteen categories (*padārtha*), one of which is precisely the instance (*dṛṣṭānta*) that exemplifies a general rule. Someone who argues that there is a fire on a distant hill where smoke is currently perceived, on the basis of the rule that "where there is smoke, there is fire," could point to a kitchen and a camping site where they have seen smoke generated by a fire. In this form of inferential reasoning (*anumāna*), one starts with what one directly perceives (smoke) and proceeds through an invariable association (between smoke and fire) to what one does not directly perceive (fire). The word *anumāna* means "after-cognition," so that here one begins with perceptual cognition and tries to establish a link between inferential reason and the inferential target. To invoke the idioms of Aristotelian logic, the hill is the minor term (*pakṣa*), the fire is the major term (*sādhya*), and the smoke is the middle term (*hetu*). That is, the hill is the inferential subject under consideration, the fire is the object that we seek to establish with respect to the hill, and the smoke is the sign or prover that connects the fire and the hill. We see that the sign (smoke) qualifies the inferential subject (the hill); we remember the concomitance between the sign and the probandum—namely, the thing that needs to be proved (fire)—and we reflect that the probandum is related to this inferential subject. However, unlike the Aristotelian categorical syllogism, which has three propositions, the full outline of the **Nyāya** inference has five members (*avayava*).[2]

To take another case, the inferential reasoning for the conclusion that Devadatta is mortal would proceed through the following steps:

1. Devadatta is mortal
2. because Devadatta is a human being (*hetu*).
3. All human beings are mortal; for instance, Śakuntalā, Devadatta, and Yajñadatta.
4. Devadatta too is a human being.
5. Therefore, Devadatta is mortal.

Here the inferential reasoning invokes a relationship between a property to be proved (mortality) and the inferential subject that bears that property (Devadatta). The keystone of this logical structure is point 3, which reflects the strong empirical orientation of **Nyāya** philosophers—inferences about the structure of reality have to proceed by providing concrete instances that are not disputed by the parties in the debate. Moreover, point 3 highlights a crucial dimension of the **Nyāya** inference—namely, the universal association (***vyāpti***) between "humanity" and "mortality." To return to the previous example, we see smoke, we invoke the putative universal association or invariable relation (***vyāpti***) between smoke and fire, and we conclude that fire is present. The term ***vyāpti*** means "pervasion," and in this case, the smoke is the "pervaded" and the fire is the "pervader." This is because wherever there is smoke, there is fire, but it is not the case that wherever there is fire, there is smoke; for example, a red-hot iron frame enveloped in flames generates no smoke. Given that knowledge of ***vyāpti*** is crucial to inferential reasoning, **Nyāya** philosophers devoted a lot of attention to fine-tuning this concept. While we perceive individual cases of smoke, we never perceive a universalization such as "*all* places with smoke are places with fire." One suggestion is to posit a generalization through enumeration—because all the occurrences of smoke that we have observed are associated with fire, we conclude that there is a co-extension between the presence of smoke and the presence of fire. To strengthen the conclusion, we add the contraposition "Where there is no fire, there is no smoke," and point to the clear surface of a lake with neither fire nor smoke. In other words, since smoke is posited as the "pervaded" of the "pervader," which is fire, in the absence of the latter, the former too should be absent.

In positing such generalizations between the "pervader" and the "pervaded," however, it is important to ask if they are mediated by any extraneous background conditions (*upādhi*). If I start standing at the bus stop at 9:45 a.m., and the bus always arrives at 10:00 a.m., I should not conclude that there is a ***vyāpti*** between my waiting for the bus and the arrival of the bus. There are various factors—such as a well-maintained bus, a timetable, and so on—that ensure that the bus arrives at 10:00 every morning. Likewise, I should not posit the generalization "Where there is fire, there is smoke," because it presupposes the conditional presence of wet fuel. Therefore, I cannot reason inferentially that "where there is fire, there is smoke; this is fiery; therefore, this is smoky," because the presence of fire is related not unconditionally to smokiness but only if the fuel is wet. However, such moves do not fully exorcise the specter of the "problem of induction," and a sceptic could retort that what has not been demonstrated is that *all* instances of smoke are associated with fire. Perhaps there is a region of space-time within or beyond our solar system where smoke arises spontaneously or without the kindling of fire. At this stage, a **Nyāya** philosopher may appeal to the causal structure of the world and point to the untoward implications of suggesting that there is smoke in the absence of fire. If smoke could be produced by something other than fire or without any cause at all, our everyday activities such as looking for food, which rely on or presuppose certain causal regularities, would be nullified.

In this way, we would gradually uncover the fabrics of the everyday world, which, according to Nyāya-Vaiśeṣika, is densely packaged with various kinds of things and where a property (such as red) is related to its substantive (such as a rose) as qualifier and qualified. In its realist understanding, perceptual experience does not construct or generate the world but illuminates its preexistent structures. For instance, the perception of a white sheet of paper on the table is to be explained in this way: the universal whiteness inheres in a particular instance of white, which inheres in the paper, and the paper is in contact with the eye. More generally, the content of a perception is a substantive, a qualifier, and a relation between the two, and all these entities are rooted in reality. The **Nyāya** analysis is opposed to the Buddhist claim that the world is composed of inexpressible and momentary point-instants (*svalakṣaṇa*), and general notions such as universals are subjective constructs (*vikalpa*) that are spread or projected on them by us. Just as a large collection of discrete houses can be categorized as a "village" even though there is no universal called village-ness, **Nyāya** universals such as white-ness and cow-ness too should be regarded as linguistic labels that are applied to evanescent events. The conclusion to draw from this deconstruction is not that a linguistic item such as "cow" should be banished from everyday discourse—this word is indeed useful in negotiating environments such as a farm in the countryside because it gives us a classificatory label with which to mark out some entities that populate them, such as cows. The error would be to think that "cow" picks out a basic thread in a preexistent fabric of reality. In truth, "cow" does not refer to anything out there but is a useful label with which to state, "That animal is *not* a non-cow."[3] Because we are unable to distinguish between the mind's imaginative activity of aggregating the point-instants and the point-instants themselves, we mistakenly believe that constructs such as white-ness refer to something really out there. This Buddhist rejection of universals is reflected in the terse definition offered by Dharmakīrti (c. 600 CE) of perception as free from conceptual construction and not erroneous. In other words, perception is a nonconceptual apprehension of *svalakṣaṇa*, and this apprehension becomes distorted when it is overlaid with categories such as "blue" and "cow."

ARE UNIVERSALS REALITY-ROOTED OR MIND-CONSTRUCTED?

In sum, the debate between **Nyāya** and Buddhism runs very deep—the former regards universals as reality-rooted structures, and the latter regards them as mind-constructed imputations.[4] According to **Nyāya** philosophers, verbal distinctions such as "cow" reflect objective features of the world, so that though the specific name given to a class-essence (Sanskrit: *gotva*, English: "cow-ness") is a linguistic accident, the class-essence itself is not a linguistic artifact. Reflecting this realist stance, *Nyāya-sūtra* 1.1.4 states that perception (*pratyakṣa*) is knowledge that arises from the contact of a sense organ with its object and that is not due to words (*avyapadeśyam*), unerring, and determinate. Perception is a cognitive episode that is generated by a causal interaction with an independently existing world. When I open my eyes in a brightly lit room, I have a sensory awareness that is judged to be that of "a painting on the wall, which is painted blue." My judgment is packaged with categories such as substance, quality, and universal, and this judgment is not a mental projection onto the world but re-presents its mind-independent structures. One may perceive something without being able to name it, and so it is meaningful to say *that* I perceive it even when I am not able to specify *what* it is. For **Nyāya**, perception is one of the four ***pramāṇa***, and the other three are inference, analogy, and reliable testimony. The key term ***pramāṇa***—often translated as "means of knowledge" or "knowledge source"—refers to the process through which episodes of veridical cognition (*pramā*) are generated. As to the objects of true cognition (*prameya*), *Nyāya-sūtra* 1.1.9 mentions the following: self (*ātman*), body, sense faculties, objects of the senses, cognition, mind, purposive action, reincarnation, fruit of action, suffering (*duḥkha*), and liberation.

Nyāya commentators regard perception (*pratyakṣa*) as preeminent among the four ***pramāṇa***, since inference, analogy, and reliable testimony are dependent on it. The word *pratyakṣa* literally means "before the eyes," which highlights the nonmediated aspect of perceptual experiences. Since perception is, as it were, our first point of contact with the world, it is crucial for **Nyāya** realism that this contact is an illumination and not a construction of the world. Following the reading offered by Vācaspati Miśra (c. 900 CE) of the term *avyapadeśyam*, perception is sometimes subdivided into two stages: nonconceptual perception, or indeterminate awareness (*nirvikalpaka*), and perception with concepts, or determinate awareness (*savikalpaka*). The first is the nondeterminate sensory presentation of an object before the object has been named and the second is the concept-structured perception of that object. That is, we apprehend an object as a *that* without classifying it as a particular kind of thing, and we then apprehend the object as belonging to a certain kind and as qualified by a specific color, shape, and so on. Suppose I am walking down the hallway of a friend's house, and I rush past what seems to me to be a pot. I stop and return to the object, inspect it carefully and exclaim, "Ah, what a fine specimen of Indian art!" In the first stage, what I perceived was a *that*, and in the second stage, the qualifiers of *that* are verbalized with concrete descriptions such as "blue inscriptions on a piece of red earth."

One way to understand this postulation of a *nirvikalpaka* stage before an object is grasped in its qualitative richness is to consider how a Buddhist thinker may analyze the perceptual process. The key point of dispute is this: Is the product of the second stage an authentic presentation, or is it a fundamental *mis*representation of the source apprehended in the first stage? From a Buddhist perspective, as we have noted, what is initially perceived are inexpressible *svalakṣaṇa*, and these are mistakenly aggregated with verbalized descriptions such as "blue inscriptions on a piece of red earth." In the **Nyāya** view, however, what I initially see somewhat unreflectively is just what I later see after careful examination; in applying to it qualifiers such as "clay" and "blue," I reveal its prelinguistic contours. More precisely, to name is to retrace one's moorings to the world.

Here is another thought experiment aimed at highlighting the epistemological significance of the first stage. Consider Sophie, who has lived all her life on a farm with cows in Lancashire. She is able to re-cognize cows whenever she sees them in the fields. If an animal were transported from India and placed in her farm, she would be able to say, "That's a cow too." In other words, she applies the description "cows" only to cows and not to goats, sheep, and sheepdogs. Let us say that she first encountered a cow (named Buttercup) when she was two years old. From a **Nyāya** perspective, although she did not then have the word "cow" in her lexical bank, she apprehended the mind-independent universal cow-ness and later learned to apply the word "cow" to different individuals who are indeed cows. That is, at the age of two, she apprehended cow-ness through a *nirvikalpaka* perception but did not apprehend Buttercup as qualified by cow-ness, which is why she could not make the predicative claim "This is a cow." Subsequently, through processes of language acquisition, she acquired the dispositional ability to correctly apply the word "cow" to

Buttercup, Bessie, and Brownie. In the process of repeatedly encountering cows, impressions of cows were registered in her as memory dispositions that shaped her *savikalpaka* perceptions of cows.

Crucially, error can emerge at this second stage when one has mistaken conceptions of what one perceives (returning to the example discussed in chapter 1, a rope is perceived as a snake when walking along a road that is poorly illuminated). In this case, a substantive entity is cognized, but the property attributed to it ("snake") is not what, in truth, qualifies it. In other words, error is a "mis-location" in the form of the misapprehension of one thing as something else (*anyathā-khyāti*). In contrast, a veridical cognition is targeted not only at the right object but also at that object as qualified by its property. Our cognitive processes generate true beliefs when they are characterized by a certain virtue (*guṇa*). For instance, in the case of perception, when I perceive a yellow flower, the eye is properly related to the flower and apprehends the yellowness that qualifies that flower. In contrast, a false belief is associated with a defect (*doṣa*)—perhaps I am suffering from jaundice, which is why I perceive a flower as yellow when, in fact, it is white.

To distinguish between cognitions as correct or erroneous, one tests them to see whether or not they lead to successful activity. The truth of a cognition is inferred through successful activity based on it so that the certification of a cognition is not intrinsic but extrinsic to it (*parataḥ prāmāṇya*). If I am uncertain whether what I perceive is indeed a pencil, I can try to inscribe a sentence with it on a sheet of paper; if I am successful, the perception of the object as a "pencil" is aligned with my immediate environment. This example highlights the **Nyāya** system's understanding of skeptical doubt as parasitic on true cognition. When I doubt whether what I see in front of me is a pen, I start writing on some paper; but am I justified in believing that what I see in front of me is *paper*? And what about all the other things that constitute the somewhat invisible background—the table on which the paper is resting, the room in which the table is located, and so on? According to **Nyāya**, we do not start in a condition of global skepticism, and everyday beliefs such as "this is paper" are justified until a doubt arises. Such doubts can indeed be generated in cases of inconsistency between different cognitions and disagreements with peers, and then proper investigation should be carried out into the causal chain that has produced that cognition. For instance, if I look at a post at the end of a road, I may mistake it for a human being because I observe only certain similarities and not the dissimilarities; likewise, if I am not paying careful attention, a lump of clay in the garden may seem to be a pigeon. Again, on a sunny day, I may see a patch of water on the road in front of me. In such cases, I should critically sift through the information and carefully assess the evidence in order to ascertain whether the content of the current cognition—a post, a pigeon, a patch of water—is part of the furniture of reality. However, such a reflective inquiry is possible because I already have certain concepts and the world is shaped by some real causal processes.

In short, the default position is not doubt but the inhabitation of a dense network of statements that are unreflectively taken to be true unless we have reason to doubt their truth. As *Nyāya-sūtra* 2.1.7 states, "Where there is doubt (*saṃśaya*), there should be meticulous examination." Provided that a cognitive episode is formed through a causal process that is reliable and hits the target of the object toward which it is directed, it is veridical (*pramā*), because it has been generated through the instrument of a ***pramāṇa***. Thus, as Vātsyāyana notes in the opening section of his commentary on the *Nyāya-sūtra*, cognitive success in mapping the world is integral to the pursuit of goal-directed action. Without a ***pramāṇa***, there is no proper cognition of an object, and without such cognition, successful action—directed at acquiring the object or getting rid of it—is not possible. This realist affirmation of a tie between cognition and action is reflected in his understanding of truth (*tattva*) as the notion of existence applied to something that does exist and as the notion of nonexistence applied to something that does not exist.[5]

THE MIND'S COGNITIONS AND THE WORLD'S TEXTURES

Stepping back for a moment from these philosophical debates over the relation between mind and world, consider a concrete example that highlights the central theme. Consider little Nora, who goes looking for herbs in the middle of a deep forest to prepare medicine for her deer who is sick. Now, not just any *kind* of herb will do—the herb has to belong to the *right* kind that possesses life-restoring properties. Because Nora has received instruction from her mother about how to identify medicinal herbs of the *sañjīvanī* kind and set aside poisonous weeds, she is able to promptly retrieve the healing plant, and her deer recovers within a few days. If Nora grew up to become a **Nyāya** philosopher, she would explain this foray into the heart of reality in this way: The Sanskrit name *sañjīvanī* ("reviver") is correlated with a mind-independent property of healing. Therefore, the reason why these and only these herbs have this property is because they share a class-essence. However, when Nora goes to the University of Sapientia, she meets a Buddhist philosopher who is not impressed with this analysis. The Buddhist standpoint is shaped by the criterion of reality that we indicated in chapter 1—namely, that which is real is what has causal efficiency. Entities such as timeless universals and timeless relations of inherence are lifeless abstractions that do not *do* anything, and because they are causally inert, they are not real. Therefore, the Buddhist argues that the name "reviver" does not refer to a mind-independent universal but is a pragmatically useful notion that helps herb hunters navigate complexly organized forest landscapes. In other words, the claim that the world is composed of *two* kinds of things—individual herbs and a class-essence called "reviver"—is too profligate, ontologically speaking. We should exercise austerity in our ontological schemes and work with *one* kind of thing—namely, innumerable particulars with life-restoring properties. These particulars are conveniently taxonomized with the label "reviver," which is just that: a label and not a mind-independent universal.

At one stage of her life, Nora becomes a florist who only stocks red flowers in her little hut at the edge of the forest. On three days of the week, she goes out into the middle of the forest and returns with baskets full of red flowers. A **Nyāya** philosopher would explain her success in this way: "Nora is able to identify certain flowers in her environment as red flowers because these flowers instantiate the nonrepeatable property of redness. The red in *this* red flower is distinct from the red in *that* red flower, but all these flowers are red because the universal *redness* inheres in them." A Buddhist philosopher may respond in this way: "The environment contains certain stretches of point-instants that are momentary, distinct from one another, and nonconceptualizable. They generate in Nora's sensorium certain fleeting cognitions that are clustered together with the conventional labels 'red' and 'flower.' With these labels, Nora is able to identify the flowers that she needs and separate them from the other entities." In short, the **Nyāya** philosopher sees Nora as a substantial self that endures through the processes of walking into the forest, retrieving flowers, and returning to her hut, and the Buddhist philosopher regards "Nora" as a useful name with which to refer to a causally connected stream of multiple psychophysical moments such as Nora $_{\text{walking}}$, Nora $_{\text{retrieving}}$, and Nora $_{\text{returning}}$.

Debating the nature of universals

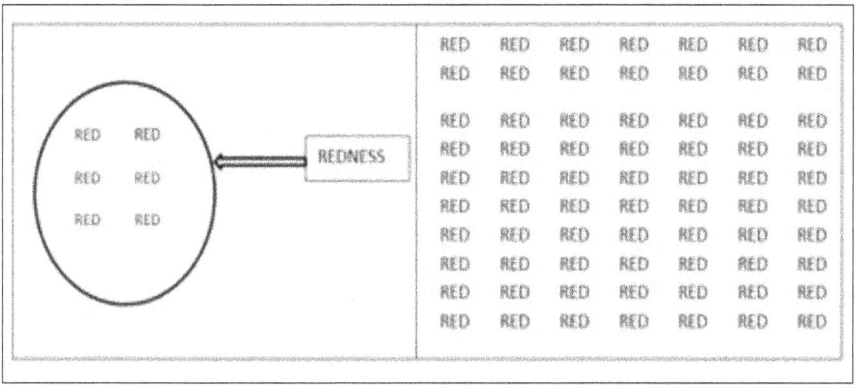

The Nyāya-Buddhist engagement is, then, a fundamental debate about how to balance the pulls of ontological simplicity ("Do not postulate more entities than what is necessary") and explanatory scope ("The entities that you do postulate should adequately account for what is observed"). The **Nyāya** philosophers argue that their outline of the world as constituted by universals that inhere in particulars has various theoretical virtues and explanatory powers, and one of them is an explanation of causal processes in terms of ***vyāpti***. The statement "A causes B" should be read as an objective regularity that obtains between particulars that belong to two universals—namely, A and B. Since A and B are natural features of the world, causation is not simply a set of psychological expectations that we have developed through inductive generalization by observing lots of A's along with lots of B's. We can be confident that statements such as "Where there is smoke, there is fire" and "Where there is humanity, there is mortality" express natural regularities. However, to return to the definition of perception at *Nyāya-sūtra* 1.1.4, it seems that we cannot, strictly speaking, perceive universals, since there is no contact of a sense organ with universals. This kind of perception is classified by philosophers in the **Nyāya** tradition, such as Jayanta Bhaṭṭa (c. 900 CE), as extraordinary (*alaukika*), and it is through this nonsensuous mode that we perceive the universal of "humanity" in every human being whom we meet. The reason why we declare that "all human beings are mortal" is not because we have painstakingly tested this statement with respect to every human being but because "humanity" dwells in all human beings, and through that extraordinary connection, we can safely conclude that an individual with the property of humanity also has the property of mortality.

At the same time, **Nyāya** philosophers laid down certain restrictions on identifying objective class-essences. The philosophical task is to find just those universals that meet the explanatory demands of our everyday linguistic discourses. For instance, we may accept "humanity" as a universal, but we do not need to invoke "bachelor" as another universal, because the latter can be built up from the former. One **Nyāya** criterion is that a universal is a simple property that is not resolvable into properties—thus, the phrase "brown cow" does not name a universal. Again, the relation between a particular and its universal must indeed be inseparable—thus, "cook-ness" is not a universal because an individual is only contingently related to the activity of cooking food. Moreover, it is generally agreed that universals cannot be "crosscutting." Thus, while "monkey," "elephant," "dog," and so on are universals, "beast-ness" (*paśutva*) is not a universal, since it is a linguistic construct that cuts across several natural kinds of animals.

In short, universals are not mind-generated but part of the furniture of reality. In our fallible attempts to ensure that our everyday vocabulary is properly synchronized with the texture of reality, it is vital to have a proper understanding of the relation between word and world. Thinkers in the **Nyāya** tradition considered three possibilities about the primary meaning of a word such as "cow." According to the first view, the word refers to an individual cow; according to the second, it refers to the configuration or shape of a cow; and according to the third, it refers to universal "cowhood." Commenting on *Nyāya-sūtra* 2.2.66, Vātsyāyana says that all three—universal, configuration, and individual—constitute the meaning of the word "cow." There is no specific rule about which of these should predominate: when we are interested in a specific object, it is the individual that is the primary meaning, and when we are speaking generally, it is the universal that is the primary meaning.[6] In the later development of **Nyāya**, the meaning of the word "cow" is said to be an individual as qualified by cowhood (*jāti-viśiṣṭa-vyakti*). Therefore, in understanding the sentence "The cow is in the barn," one grasps a certain object as qualified by cowhood and grasps this object as qualified by the property of occurring in a barn.

To return to a theme highlighted in chapter 1, while such philosophical debates may seem highly arcane and far removed from everyday concerns, in Hindu and Buddhist contexts, they are usually enfolded in the quest for liberation from the conditions of worldly suffering (***saṃsāra***). Thus, *if* the world consists of ineffable point-instants that are mistakenly aggregated into class-essences, then the postulation of mind-independent universals is another exemplification of the human ignorance that perpetuates suffering. Conversely, *if* the world is packaged with objective universals and particulars, which language reveals but does not construct, then the failure to orient one's existential compass toward this ontological texture reinforces human ignorance, which in turn generates and perpetuates misery. Against the backdrop of this dense intertwining of language, ontology, and liberation, **Nyāya** philosophers outlined various forms of pseudoreasons (*hetu-ābhāsa*) that indicate ways in which the compass point of reasoning, instead of being turned toward reality, has deviated from reality. Generally speaking, pseudoreasons do not embody one or more features such as these: the reason (the smoke) is a property of the inferential subject (the hill); the reason is present with the probandum (fire) in at least one instance (a kitchen); and the reason is absent where the probandum is absent (a lake).

In one type of erroneous reasoning, the reason is related to the existence as well as to the nonexistence of the thing to be proved. Thus, "the hill has fire, because it is knowable" is fallacious because the reason, "knowable," is related to fiery and nonfiery entities; in other words, it is related to both corroborative instances (*sapakṣa*) and negative instances (*vipakṣa*). In another type, the reason does not occur in the subject of the inference or the subject does not exist.

Consider these two argumentative patterns:

(A) Sound (subject) is a property, because it is visible (reason). Whatever is visible is a property.
(B) The sky lotus (subject) is blue, because it has lotus-ness (reason).

In the first, the reason (visibility) cannot be present in the subject (sound), and in the second, the subject (sky lotus) does not exist. In a more straightforward type of fallacy, the reason disproves the conclusion. Thus, in "sound is eternal because it is produced," the reason "a product" demonstrates not the eternality but the noneternality of sound.

Provided such erroneous forms of reasoning are avoided, inference can lead us from what is directly perceived toward the past and toward the future. In a *pūrvavat* inference, an unperceived effect is inferred from a perceived cause—thus, rain in the future from clouds in the sky. In a *śeṣavat* inference, an unperceived cause is inferred from a perceived effect—thus, rain in the past from a flooded river. These two types of inferences invoke ***vyāpti*** in the form of causal regularities relating to things like water and atmospheric conditions. In a *sāmānyatodṛṣṭa* inference, an unperceived entity or process is inferred on the basis of an analogy with everyday experience. Thus, after looking at the moon on different nights and noticing that it has different locations in the sky, we infer that it is a mobile entity, even though we do not perceive its motion. Just as in the case of terrestrial entities like animals, a change of place is associated with motion, so too is the moon inferred to have moved across the sky. Or, to take the crucial example of the self, just as we infer an unseen property bearer from a property (such as green), so too do we infer the unseen self from the properties of aversion, desire, and knowledge. In worldly experience, properties are not found floating in midair but are held together by some substratum, and on the basis of this observation, the self is inferred as a suprasensible substratum. In these ways, **Nyāya** inferential reasoning proceeds through a diagnostic study of individual cases to check if a particular case corresponds to a regularity, and such reasoning would be undermined by a counterexample. For instance, we may have concluded that the sign that something is earthen is that it can be scratched by iron, but when we find a diamond, we no longer defend an invariable association between being earthen and being scratchable by iron.

To summarize the discussion so far, for **Nyāya** philosophers the cognitive fields of epistemology ("how we know") and logic ("how we reason properly") are not distinct but mutually interrelated. It is not sufficient that the premises in an argument are logically interlinked in a "valid" argument; moreover, these premises should be true in a "sound" argument.

The following argument is valid but is not sound:

(C) All humans are immortals.
All immortals are birds.
Therefore, all humans are birds.

From a **Nyāya** perspective, such premises cannot be allowed in inferential reasoning because we cannot offer inductive support by pointing to real-world instances (*dṛṣṭānta*) of humans who are immortals ("*this* human") and immortals who are birds ("*this* immortal"). Thus, in (B) above, the inferential subject (sky lotus) is nonexistent, and the inference cannot proceed. In the example of perceiving smoke on the hill and inferring the presence of fire, the inferential sign (smoke) qualifies the inferential subject (the hill). However, in (A) above, the sign (visibility) is not present in the locus (sound).

To highlight another instance of this intertwining of logic and ontology, the Advaita argument outlined at the beginning of the chapter can be laid out in the following way, which indicates its **Nyāya**-shaped contours:

The finite world is ultimately unreal,
because it is different from *brahman*.
Whatever is different from *brahman* is ultimately unreal—for
instance, silver in a mother-of-pearl.

The debate partly turns on whether or not what is provided here—silver in a mother-of-pearl—is indeed a real-world illustration of the putative generalization. To return to the **Nyāya** notion of error as "mis-location" indicated earlier, the subjective feel of a silvery entity is to be explained in this way. I had once perceived a silvery object such as a silver bowl, and a memory-disposition (*saṃskāra*) of that silver is activated in the present because of some similarity between the silver bowl and the mother-of-pearl. I perceive a *this* in front of me through a sensory mode of perception, and I associate the silverness that exists elsewhere with *this* through an extraordinary mode of perception. It is crucial to note, therefore, that for **Nyāya**, the silver that I perceive is not a mental fabrication or projection because it truly exists somewhere. This analysis of error illustrates, once again, the realist tenor of **Nyāya**: the various middle-sized objects that populate our world—such as chairs, cats, and cups—are real, just as their atomic constituents are.

In this way, **Nyāya** philosophers give us a world structured with certain objective features, and human cognizers begin to know these features through various forms of fallible generalization that, in cases of doubt, have to be examined through reflective inquiry. To use their idioms, there is a structural correlation between knowledge sources (***pramāṇa***) and objects of knowledge (*prameya*). In the discussion so far, we have encountered the mechanisms of knowledge sources operating across worldly entities and processes. A topic of lively debate relates to whether the knowledge sources of perception and inference are sufficiently robust to take us from the finite world of pots, trees, mountains, and human beings on the one hand to the divine source of finite reality on the other hand. The phrase "divine source" refers, of course, to the concept of God—the transcendental cause, basis, and telos of the world. The Hindu philosophical literature operates with words such as *īśvara* and *brahman*, which may or may not be directly translatable with the word "God" as it is employed in Jewish, Christian, and Muslim contexts (we will return to this question in chapter 4). For now, we will carry on with our explorations into **Nyāya** logical territory by discussing their attempts to construct a rational theism in which they seek to infer, from the world, a personal deity (*īśvara*).

In characterizing this theistic perspective as "rational," what is highlighted is that it is based on ***pramāṇa*** that are accessible to all human beings as part of their human nature—for instance, perception and inference—and not on the exegetical details of a scriptural text. In a Nyāya-Buddhist dialectical setting, a **Nyāya** philosopher cannot abruptly invoke scriptural texts from the ***Vedas***, since the Buddhist interlocutor would not accept them as knowledge sources. Here the argument would have to proceed steadily through an examination of the perceptual evidence, the logical strength of the inferential edifice that is being raised on the bases of everyday experience, and so on. However, when a **Nyāya** thinker is working within a Hindu framework where Vedic texts are regarded as authoritative, scriptural proof-texting can be a vital aspect of the reasoning process. Along with **Nyāya**, the ***darśana*** of **Sāṃkhya**, **Yoga**, **Vedānta**, and **Mīmāṃsā** accept verbal testimony (*śabda*) as an independent ***pramāṇa***. Some **Nyāya** philosophers distinguish between two types of *śabda*—namely, divine and worldly, where the former refers to the infallible declarations of the Vedic scriptures and the latter to the statements of trustworthy individuals that are, however, fallible.

The triad of perception, inference, and scriptural testimony is marshaled by Udayana in his *Nyāyakusumāñjali* ("Flower Offering of Logic"), in which he works through various arguments for the existence of a personal deity (*īśvara*).[7] One form of reasoning developed by Udayana resembles the well-known "design argument" offered by William Paley in his *Natural Theology* (1802). When we look at a beautifully constructed watch and marvel at the intricate arrangements of its parts, we do not conclude that this structure was generated through sheer chance. Likewise, when we behold the harmonious operations of the natural world, we should conclude that it was created by a cosmic designer. In other words, the formal structure of arguments from design is based on an analogy between cultural "artifacts" that are the result of human productivity and "natural" entities in the spatiotemporal world.

Premise 1: From artifacts such as watches, we infer a human designer.
Premise 2: Artifacts such as watches resemble natural entities such as the human eye.
Conclusion 1: Natural entities such as the human eye are the products of *an* infinitely greater intelligence.
Conclusion 2: The world has *one* grand designer.

The key question is, of course, whether the analogy between *a watch* and *the world* is strong enough to establish the conclusion. Indeed, this argument has often been critiqued on two crucial points: premise 2 and the move from conclusion 1 to conclusion 2. Such criticisms were also levelled at **Nyāya** attempts to establish the existence of the divine reality through analogical arguments. Here, an analogy is proposed between an artifact such as *a pot* and *the world*, and it is claimed that just as the former is a product of human causes, so too is the latter a product of a divine cause. Another analogy is proposed between an artifact such as an ax, which is directed by a human agent, and natural entities such as atoms, which require a divine sentient agent for their operation.

The first argument can be schematized in this way.

1. Certain aspects of the world are qualified by product-ness.
2. Product-ness is invariably concomitant with an intelligent producer—for instance, a pot.

Generally speaking, Hindu ***darśana*** does not accept the notion of creation of the world out of sheer nothingness (ex nihilo), which is central to several schools of Jewish, Christian, and Islamic thought. For **Nyāya**, in particular, the deity does not create the world ex nihilo but supervises the operation of the substances of the atoms, space, time, ether, the mind, and the individual self. Moreover, **Nyāya** accepts the cosmological motif that the world goes through periodic productions and dissolutions, and an individual undergoes multiple reincarnations across these cycles (***saṃsāra***) on her spiritual trajectory toward liberation (*mokṣa*). This spiritual progression is structured by the moral principle of *karma*, which states that an individual will reap sometime in the future what that very individual has sown in the past. While there is no *one* doctrine of *karma* and reincarnation across the Hindu traditions, its minimal form claims that actions leave behind certain residues or potencies that lead individuals to experience happiness or suffering in future embodiments.[8] In the **Nyāya** view, the deity is the cosmic supervisor of the *karmic* mechanisms and ensures that human beings receive the fruits of their actions in the form of happiness or affliction. The deity is, in other words, the transcendental agent who directs the atoms and the individual selves such that living beings receive in the next world-order a new form of embodiment in accordance with their *karmic* merits and demerits.

Therefore, as indicated at 1, it is not the whole world but "certain aspects" of it that are qualified by product-ness or being-an-effect (*kāryatva*)—namely, composite wholes such as pots. The **Nyāya** commentators conclude that the maker of nonsentient entities such as trees, mountains, and oceans must be an omniscient and omnipotent being, since only such a being can discern and regulate the suprasensible individual selves and their *karmic* merits and demerits. Turning to 2, a crucial dimension of a **Nyāya** inference is—as we know—the concrete instance that should be acceptable to all parties in a debate. In the example of inferring fire on a hill from the perceived smoke, we do have an uncontroversial example—smoke in the kitchen. In the case of inferring the existence of the deity from the manifest world, the invariable relation that is postulated between "product-ness" and "an intelligent producer" becomes the site of dispute. A Buddhist thinker would agree that a pot is a product of human causes but claim that trees, mountains, and oceans do not have the characteristic of "product-ness" with respect to a transcendental deity. If the **Nyāya** philosopher proposes "product-ness" as the reason for demonstrating the existence of the deity, the Buddhist interlocutor charges that there are counterexamples to this putative relation—for instance, a tree in the garden. The **Nyāya** philosopher may respond that the Buddhist critic has not conclusively demonstrated that trees, mountains, and oceans are *not* produced by the deity—the complaint that the deity cannot be observed can be met with the reminder that the deity is, by definition, a suprasensible being. The dispute can be outlined in this way: "In pointing to a tree in the garden, have we identified a locus (tree) where the reason (productness) is present but the thing to be proved (intelligent maker) is missing?" While we do not observe an agent at work on the different parts of the tree, we cannot proceed straightforwardly from nonobservation to nonexistence: perhaps the agent is spatiotemporally far removed from us. There remains the question of whether one may justifiably move from the statement that trees, mountains, and oceans have *an* intelligent source (conclusion 1) to the statement that this source is *the* supreme deity (conclusion 2). Reason, it seems, is trying to overreach itself by straying beyond its empirical ambit. A **Nyāya** response at this stage could be that it is more reasonable to postulate *one* omnipotent and omniscient deity than an enormously large series of (possibly squabbling) demigods.

Once again, then, whether or not we have a good piece of reasoning is crucially dependent on what, in fact, exists. Moving to the second argument, its steps can be laid out as follows, following the commentator Uddyotakara:

> Primordial matter, atoms, and *karma* can function if they are directed by a conscious agent who is the efficient cause, because they are nonsentient—for instance, an ax.

This reasoning turns partly on the **Nyāya** understanding of causation in terms of a complex of conditions, which include, in the case of a pot and its potter, the substance of clay, the potter's conscious intentions, and the instruments used by the potter. More specifically, there is the "inherence" cause, which is the preexisting basis in which the effect such as a clay pot inheres; the "co-inherence" cause, which is a feature of the inherence cause such as the qualities in the clay; and the "efficient" cause, which includes agential features such as the potter and nonagential features such as the potter's wheel. Developing this argument that nonsentient entities need the regulation of a conscious agent, Uddyotakara also claims that the deity does not have a body because unlike our cognitive lives, which are limited to specific objects and are also dependent on psychophysical complexes, the deity's knowledge is unrestricted.[9]

REASONING TO THE ROOT OF REALITY

The debate over whether human reason can reach, or at least point toward, the deity indicates that epistemological debates are often entwined with ontological commitments. The accredited means of acquiring true cognition (***pramāṇa***) enable us to access and discern what there is in the fabric of the world (*prameya*). Therefore, in setting out to find what there is or is not in a certain region of space-time, one does not begin in an epistemological vacuum but by stating one's ***pramāṇa***. Suppose it is agreed that the Buddhist critic has won the day and the inferential argument is not cogent—a Hindu respondent could invoke the ***pramāṇa*** of scriptural testimony. Indeed, exegetes in the traditions of **Vedānta** usually claim that regarding supersensible entities such as the divine ground (*brahman*) of the finite world, Vedic revelation is the true source. Even more radically, suppose a critic denies that inference is a ***pramāṇa***—in this case, inferential reasoning from a pot to a maker of pots would not even get off the ground. Conversely, a certain interlocutor may not only accept inference as a ***pramāṇa*** but also propose one called postulation (*arthāpatti*), through which we put forward an unperceived fact to explain what is perceived, and one called noncognition (*anupalabdhi*), through which we know absences.

Crucially, in proposing a specific set of ***pramāṇa***, one has to argue that they are not interdefinable. For instance, **Vaiśeṣika** does not accept testimony (*śabda*) as an independent knowledge source because it views knowledge acquired through testimony as shaped by forms of inference. I may learn that the capital of Madagascar is Antananarivo by listening to a historian; I claim, therefore, that testimony is a knowledge source.

However, someone who rejects testimony would say that I am, in fact, arguing from the premises that the speaker is trustworthy, that trustworthy speakers communicate truth, and that I have understood the speaker's statements to the conclusion that Antananarivo is the capital of Madagascar. Similar debates apply to whether *arthāpatti* and *anupalabdhi* should be counted as independent knowledge sources. The standard example of the former is the process of reasoning from the statement, known through perception or testimony, "Devadatta, who is overweight, does not eat during the day" to the statement "Devadatta eats at night." The **Mīmāṃsā** commentators would argue that such reasoning cannot be laid out as an inference with an invariable relation between being overweight and eating at night. Moreover, one group of **Mīmāṃsā** commentators argues that absences—such as the absence of a lion in the room—are cognized through a knowledge source called noncognition, whereas others say that absences are known inferentially. The latter would argue in this way: "If there were a lion in the room, I would perceive the lion; I do not perceive a lion; therefore, there is no lion in the room." The former claim, however, that perception cannot generate an apprehension of negative facts, for perception works through sensory contact between a cognizer and positive features of the environment. Lastly, analogy (*upamāna*) is the cognition of similarity between a familiar object and an object that has not been previously perceived. Thus, Devadatta, who does not know what a bison is, may be told by a zoologist that a bison is similar to a cow. Later, Devadatta sees a bison on the prairies, cognizes its similarity to a cow, and says, "That is a bison." Once again, those who do not accept analogy as an independent ***pramāṇa*** may argue that it can be redefined in terms of perception and testimony.

The Different Knowledge Sources

Cārvāka: perception
Vaiśeṣika: perception, inference
Nyāya: perception, inference, analogy, testimony
Sāṃkhya: perception, inference, testimony
Vedānta: at least these three—perception, inference, testimony
Mīmāṃsā (Kumārila Bhaṭṭa): perception, inference, analogy, postulation, noncognition, testimony

Mīmāṃsā (Prabhākara): perception, inference, analogy, postulation, testimony

Although one knowledge source should not be reducible to another, the information about the world that I gain from one can support or reinforce the information that I acquire from another. This epistemic stance is generally enacted in everyday assessments. I say that I perceive some yellow flowers; you remark that what is on the table is, in fact, a bunch of white flowers that appear yellow to me because I am wearing yellow-tinted glasses; I look at the flowers carefully after removing my glasses and see that they are indeed white; and because I know that my niece does not like white flowers, I decide not to buy the bunch of flowers in front of me. To sketch a very different environment, I am walking through the forest when I perceive a lake in the distance. The sun is out in the sky, and I do not suffer from any optical defects. However, I remember being cautioned by my friend, who is an expert trekker, about mirages in certain parts of the forest. Doubting whether or not what I see in front of me is indeed a lake, I proceed in the direction in which I think there is water. I drink some of the liquid that lies stretched out in a vast expanse before me, and it indeed quenches my thirst. Thus, the initial cognition is certified as veridical through successful action, and this fit between cognition and world is supported by various interrelated facts such as the laws of the refraction of light and the properties of water. In other words, in our everyday lives, we operate with, and keep on recalibrating and refining, a map of coherence that gives us certain compass points for navigating the world.

From the **Nyāya** perspectives that we have been discussing in this chapter, such cognitive webs help us minimize a kind of global skepticism that may be generated by this thought: "A knowledge source (***pramāṇa***) such as perception generates veridical cognition (*pramā*). But how do I establish that perception is indeed a ***pramāṇa***? Perhaps I am moving inside a gigantic bubble and spinning out cognitions which are my own fancies." If I seek to address this skeptical scenario by declaring that perception is reliable, my reasoning would be moving in a circle—on the one hand, a cognition is said to be *pramā* when it is produced by a ***pramāṇa*** called perception but, on the other hand, this ***pramāṇa*** is said to be reliable because it produces a cognition that is *pramā*. Another way to articulate this concern is to say that while we can put a certain object on a weight balance and note that this object weighs forty-five kilograms, we may doubt whether the balance itself is properly calibrated, generating the question "Who will calibrate the calibrator?" If we invoke another calibrator, we seem to trigger an infinite regress unless we can access a supercalibrator that is self-calibrating.

More schematically, these two questions seem to be so deeply intertwined that in beginning to answer the second, one has already presupposed some answer to the first:

1. What do I know?
2. How do I know (what I claim to know)?

Thus, Madhusūdana Sarasvatī argues, from an Advaita perspective, that the definition of "real" as that which is the object of a true cognition is unacceptable. If "true cognition" is defined as cognition that has for its object a really existing thing, this definition presupposes the notion of real existence (*sattva*), which is precisely what we are trying to define.[10] A **Nyāya** philosopher may argue that in such cases, we should seek a rational equilibrium across the sets of information that we receive from different knowledge sources. Instead of declaring, "I *know* that the object weighs forty-five kilograms because I *know* that the balance is properly calibrated," I may begin with the fallible claim that the balance is properly calibrated and test its deliverances against different parts of my cognitive web. For instance, I can check whether the other weight balances constructed by several experts too yield the result "forty-five kilograms." Or I can reason in this way: "If the weight of this object is forty-five kilograms, then little Nora will not be able to lift it at all, and Timothy will just be able to do so." From this terrain of conjectures and refutations, a map of the world gradually emerges, and if this iterative projection helps us solve our everyday problems, we may tentatively endorse the truthfulness of the map.

Knowing what there is in the world is a central concern for **Nyāya**, because if we are not properly aligned with reality, we will also deviate from the highest good. Toward the beginning of his *Ātma-tattva-viveka* ("Determining the Truth of the Self"), Udayana writes that all individuals seek to overcome suffering and they begin to understand that knowledge of truth (*tattva-jñāna*) is indeed the means. This truth is the spiritual self (*ātman*), and Udayana will conduct an inquiry into its nature and will demonstrate that certain viewpoints about the nature of reality are erroneous.[11] In pursuit of this motif, we will turn our attention in chapter 3 to the cosmological backdrops of Hindu philosophical reasoning and explore how **Sāṃkhya**, **Yoga**, and some Vedāntic systems grapple with the question of the relation between the finite world and its spiritual root. With these traditions too, the definitions of crucial terms such as "being" and "error" play a vital role in building pictures of the world, as can be seen in Vijñāna-bhikṣu's response to Advaita. Advaita exegetes understand the notion of nondifference (*abheda*) in the strict ontological sense of an undifferentiated unity between *ātman* and *brahman*. However, Vijñāna-bhikṣu argues that statements of nondifference between the world and the divine foundation should be seen not as affirming complete identity but as affirming nonseparation (*avibhāga*). Vijñāna-bhikṣu understands "separation" as the manifested difference of characteristics (*abhivyakta-dharmabheda*) and "nonseparation" as the absence of difference of characteristics. These understandings allow him to state that in ***saṃsāra*** the finite selves are separated from *brahman*, while the liberated selves exist in a state of nonseparation. Further, he distinguishes between the common usage of the term "part" as a component or subdivision and a technical meaning that he offers—one criterion of being a part (*aṃśa*) of the whole is to be of the same class as the whole. Thus, the individual self is said to be a part of *brahman* because it falls under the class of selfhood (*ātmatva*) and of existence (*sattva*), which are also "properties" of *brahman*.[12]

Across these Hindu philosophical milieus, the proper understanding of the nature of the human self and the divine self and their interrelation is key to human flourishing within the world, and spiritual fulfilment across multiple forms of worldly existence. According to the worshippers of Lord Śiva in the **Śaiva Siddhānta** tradition, rooted in twenty-eight texts called Tantras or Āgamas, the term *advaita* should be understood not in Śaṃkara's sense of an ontological nonduality but in terms of the experience of a oneness in union with the divine ground. At the same time, Śaiva Siddhāntins seek to preserve the transcendent perfection of Śiva from any worldly imperfection. In the canonical texts, Śiva is the efficient cause (*nimitta-kāraṇa*) who generates the cosmos as the stage where individuals will overcome their worldly impediments, but Śiva is not the substantial cause (*upādāna-kāraṇa*), for the production of the world out of Śiva as its ontological foundation is said to implicate Śiva in the limitations of finitude. The spiritual essence of the individual self (*paśu*) is united with Śiva, but because it is presently encased in worldly bondage (*pāśa*), it is not aware of this deep communion. Śaiva poets such as Campantar (the seventh century CE) express their deep awareness of their own vileness in the presence of Śiva, whose praises they are unworthy to sing. Evoking the metaphor of conjugal union, they speak of Śiva as the bridegroom and the individual self as Śiva's bride and declare that the devotional love with which they seek communion with Śiva is itself generated and brought to fruition by the grace of Śiva. In this worldview, the path to liberation starts with ritual initiation (*dīkṣā*) through the imposition of mantras by a preceptor (*ācārya*). At this moment, some of the constraints on the self's innate powers of knowledge and agency are removed, and this process of recovery is to be carried on throughout one's life through various daily and occasional observances. With this regular performance, the substantial defects (*mala*) that keep individuals in worldly bondage are gradually diminished. For Hindu cosmological systems such as **Śaiva Siddhānta**, the process of returning to the root of the divine reality through the routes of ***saṃsāra*** is the subtle connecting thread running through all worldly states and processes.

3

Therapies for Liberation

On a summer evening, you are standing on the seashore and looking into the distance. There are thunderclouds in the sky, and you can smell the rain in the air. As the storm breaks, you begin to wonder if it is all sound and fury, signifying nothing, and that we human beings simply imagine that we can yet hear a haunting music through the whirlwind. Then you remember the words of your late grandmother, whom you remember fondly as someone who had the virtues of attentiveness, discernment, honesty, and reasonableness—she used to say that there is indeed some method to the madness and often asked you to look more carefully at phenomena for a cosmic reason informing them. The cold winds swirl around you, and you spontaneously see a swathe of arguments fleeting through your mindscape: it is superfluous to postulate a supersensible being when the world contains its own explanation, and at any rate, the presence of horrendous evil cannot be squared with the existence of an omnibenevolent deity.

These kinds of reflections, which form the core of what are called "arguments for and against the existence of God," are centered around the question of the epistemic reach of reason. If reason is a flickering candle in the encircling gloom of the world, we may disagree over precisely what we have seen and precisely what, if anything, lies undiscovered. If we were scientists working in a lab, we would regularly speak of arcana such as positrons, genes, and gravitational forces, which cannot be pointed to in the straightforward sense in which the cat on the mat can be pointed to. Therefore, if we declare that we should not postulate more entities than are necessary, we may be asked, "More than are necessary *for whom*"?

IS IT REASONABLE TO POSTULATE THE SUPERREASONABLE?

While many styles of ***darśana*** do affirm, on the basis of Vedic revelation, the existence of a cosmic source (*brahman*) of being, goodness, and value, forms of skeptical questioning can also be found across different discursive Indic milieus. According to one form, reasoning cannot extend beyond what is immediately perceptible in the spatiotemporal world, let alone beyond the empirical bounds of sense. Another, more mitigated form works within the parameters of Vedic visions and points to certain inconsistencies between everyday experiences and the concept of a deity. To pick up on a theme from chapter 1, these skeptical forms of thought again highlight the fact that Indic worldviews should not be monolithically characterized as variations on a strong idealism according to which everyday entities such as laptops, tables, and cars have no mind-independent existence. From around 800 CE, Vedāntic exegetical discourses begin to systematize the contents of scriptural texts such as the ***Upaniṣads*** and the ***Bhagavad-gītā***, and many of these worldviews are shaped by the type of common-sense realism that runs across the Nyāya-Vaiśeṣika system. From their distinctive lenses, these Vedāntic visions seek to work out the relation between the real world and *brahman*, who is the "cause of the world"—the source of its being and the reason for its continuing existence. Indeed, the *Śvetāśvatara Upaniṣad* 1.1 begins by saying that those who inquire into the nature of *brahman* ask questions such as "What is the cause?" "By what do we live?" and "On what are we established?" The ***Upaniṣads*** often speak with elliptical idioms and do not offer straightforward resolutions to the enigmas being articulated, and here too the next verse (1.2) goes on to outline causes such as time, intrinsic nature (*svabhāva*), necessity (*niyati*), chance (*yadṛcchā*), the natural elements, and the spiritual self (*puruṣa*). Two of these concepts—*svabhāva* and *puruṣa*—would have an especially long and complex history in Indian frames of thought. According to Buddhist systems, the fundamental misconception that the constituents of the world possess substantial existence generates rounds of suffering. For Vedāntic Hindu traditions, the deep-seated error (*avidyā*) is precisely the opposite—the failure to discern the enduring self that is the stable rock of being in the whirlpools of the world. Conversely, *vidyā* is the liberating knowledge that recenters us in the heart of reality and draws us away from our woeful immersion in the cycles of impermanence, ignorance, and suffering.

THE PLACE OF MIND IN THE MATERIAL WORLD

Notwithstanding certain crucial ontological divergences across Vedāntic Hindu and Buddhist worldviews, especially relating to whether there is a substantial self (*ātman, puruṣa*), they sketch vast cosmological vistas across which human beings progress through multiple lifetimes on dynamic trajectories of spiritual perfection. The moral motor of these trajectories is the principle of *karma* and reincarnation, according to which our actions in the present lifetime shape the nature of our future existences in cycles of reembodiments (***saṃsāra***). In contrast, the **Cārvāka**, or Lokāyata, traditions defend a resolutely naturalist standpoint according to which reality is constituted only of spatiotemporal entities, thereby rejecting all notions relating to *ātman*, ***saṃsāra***, and so on.[1] The views of the **Cārvākas** largely exist in the texts of their opponents, who tended to castigate them as a bunch of antisocial hedonists. One presentation is found in the *Sarva-darśana-saṃgraha* ("Collection of All Philosophical Systems") of Mādhava (c. 1400), where we read that they denied the existence of the self and affirmed perception as the only ***pramāṇa*** while developing critiques of inference.

Different constellations of ***darśana*** accept specific ***pramāṇa***, which are correlated with their ontological schemes. For Nyāya-Vaiśeṣika in particular, the arguments for the existence of the spiritual self (*ātman*) and the cosmic deity (*īśvara*) are partly based on the ***pramāṇa*** of inferential reasoning. In these reason-directed inquiries, we carry out an extrapolation from everyday occurrences such as memory and the production of pots to the existence of suprasensible entities. Success is, of course, not guaranteed in such inquiries into the fabric of reality—in framing conjectures about the relation between one class of entities and another class of entities, we may go wrong in various ways. For instance, looking at the field in front of my house on a wintry morning, I may claim to see some smoke rising in the distance and conclude that there is a fire somewhere. As it turns out, there is no fire in the field, which is shrouded in wisps of fog. In an alternative scenario, there is indeed a fire in the field that is foggy, and I have been lucky to somehow arrive at the right answer through a wayward route.

The **Cārvāka** view is that the invariable relation (***vyāpti***) that needs to be in place so that such inferences are warranted does not have robust epistemological credentials. For instance, since we cannot cognize every instance of smoke and every instance of fire, we are not able to reliably project a ***vyāpti***. Similar problems plague the postulation of a ***pramāṇa*** called testimony. When we take the words uttered by others to be truth-tracking, we are proceeding via the inference that the statements of a reliable authority should be accepted; however, this inference is unstable. With perception alone as our epistemic compass, we can navigate our way through a world with four perceptible elements: earth, fire, air, and water. Everything, including living organisms such as human beings, are composites of these elements or emergent products from them. For instance, consciousness is not the property of an immaterial self but is resultant from the constituents of the physical body in just the way that molasses become intoxicants when they are allowed to ferment. In other words, what people refer to as *ātman* is not an ontologically independent entity but the living body, which is conscious. We do not need to invoke a deity as a designer or supervisor, for the four elements are packaged with their inherent natures (*svabhāva*), and they interact with one another in accordance with these natures. There are no heavens or hells, and the rituals developed by Vedic priests are fabrications. Against those who may claim that all finitude is structured by suffering, which is why it must be rejected completely, the **Cārvāka** replies that joys and sorrows are interrelated poles of our fragile lives, and by learning to be prudent, we can increase the former and decrease the latter. In the pursuit of an impossible ideal of absolute happiness, we should not become like the individual who would not eat rice because it arrives in husks, not consume fish because they contain bones, or not grow crops because animals may destroy them.

In contrast, a **Cārvāka** such as Purandara seems to have endorsed certain types of inferential reasoning pertaining to this-worldly entities while affirming that, strictly speaking, perception alone is ***pramāṇa***. These two inferences—from smoke to fire and from pots to the deity—belong to two categorically distinct types in the sense that in the latter, reason needs a much longer epistemic leash to strike its intended target. While we can observe smokiness and fire on hills, we do not have straightforwardly empirical access to the putative deity of the world. The first inference ranges across entities within the same class, but the second inference seeks to move from entities in one class to entities in another. In accepting the former (that is, from smoke to fire), a **Cārvāka** would not also sanction the ontological packaging of substances, universals, relations of inherence, and so on; she would simply claim to follow what is established through worldly conventions (*loka-prasiddha*). Generally speaking, instances of smoke are associated with instances of fire and instances of fire are associated with instances of houses getting burnt down, and a **Cārvāka** would be happy to affirm such quotidian judgments for the purposes of negotiating complex worldly environments. Consider the notorious question that has given many philosophers sleepless nights: "How do I know that right now I am not in a dream?" A **Cārvāka** may reply that in the social milieus that she inhabits, individuals go about their lives by taking cups, chairs, and cars to possess an existence that is not dependent on their perception, and she is happy to approve these worldly ways. If we protest that the "unexamined life is not worth living," she might retort that the "overexamined life is not worth living either."

In several respects, the *brahman*-centered cosmology of Rāmānuja is opposed to the ontological naturalism of the **Cārvāka**. The source, basis, and telos of the finite world, which is ontologically real, is the supremely personal deity, Lord Viṣṇu-Nārāyaṇa. As a Vedāntic exegete, Rāmānuja develops his worldview by working with the scriptural data of the ***Upaniṣads***, the ***Brahma-sūtras***, and the ***Bhagavad-gītā***. Generally speaking, Vedāntic thinkers argue that human reasoning (*tarka*) should be guided by, or be conformable to, scriptural revelation (*śruti*). In the maelstrom of fluctuating opinions, scripture is invoked as the infallible lighthouse of truth. However, while reason is thus subject to revelational control, reason maintains its cognitive integrity in mundane milieus. These Vedāntic worldviews lay down a cognitive division of labor for the operations of ***pramāṇa***—finite entities such as cows, hills, and pots comprise the field for perception and inference, but the sole source of knowledge of supersensible beings is scriptural testimony. Thus, in his commentary on ***Bhagavad-gītā*** 18.66, Śaṃkara writes that even if a hundred scriptural texts (*śruti*) were to declare that fire is cold, they would not possess any justification (*prāmāṇya*) on this matter. If indeed such texts were found, we would have to read them in ways that do not contradict our perceptual experiences.[2]

Reflecting the motif that scripture is the sole ***pramāṇa*** that points toward the divine reality, Rāmānuja argues, in his commentary on ***Brahma-sūtra*** 1.1.3, that the arc of reasoning does not extend all the way to the Lord. Rāmānuja's presentation of some aspects of the prima facie viewpoint (*pūrvapakṣa*) can be outlined in this way:

> When we look at pots we infer an intelligent maker, and likewise when we encounter a royal palace for the first time we infer an architect from the intricate organization of its parts. So, when we understand natural entities in the world to be effects, we infer a cosmic person who possesses the knowledge of their constitution and the skill to produce them. Again, just as nonsentient entities such as axes cannot construct anything on their own but only when they are directed by a conscious agent, *karmic* merits and demerits, which are nonsentient, need to be operated by an intelligent principle. It will not do to claim, as a putatively more economical hypothesis, that individual selves regulate the world because the power of seeing things which are extremely subtle and spatiotemporally remote can belong only to a cosmic being.

In his conclusive statement, Rāmānuja rejects this inferential argument based on a relation between products and an intelligent maker by arguing that the two cases—namely, from many pots to one potter and from the world to the Lord—are not analogous. While we can infer a producer from observed artifacts, we cannot infer a single omnipotent and omniscient maker from the manifold features of the world. We observe that different pots are produced by different pot makers and at different times, and from such observations, we cannot conclude that the earth, oceans, and so on were produced at one time by a single producer.[3]

These patterns of analogical reasoning are shaped by two key questions: Is the world more *like* or more *unlike* a cosmic pot, and is the Lord more *like* or more *unlike* a human intellect? Given any two finite entities *x* and *y*, they are both like and unlike each other relative to different contexts of inquiry. Thus, insofar as a spider and a laptop are spatiotemporal entities, they are alike, and insofar as the spider is sentient and the laptop is nonsentient, they are unlike. In the case of the finite world and the nonfinite deity—where the latter, by definition, is not directly perceptible—proponents and critics of analogical reasoning would focus on similarities and dissimilarities to varying extents. Certain strands of **Sāṃkhya** highlight various dissimilarities between human producers and the producer of the world. According to the ontological scheme that the **Sāṃkhya** and the **Yoga** traditions share, worldly phenomena are a product of the association between nonsentient *prakṛti* and pure spirit (*puruṣa*). While *prakṛti*-shaped objects and processes are finite and temporal, the *puruṣa*, of which there are a multitude, is nonactive and unchanging. In a primordial state of stability, the three strands or constituents (*guṇas*) of which *prakṛti* is composed were in a condition of equipoise; somehow a conjunction (*saṃyoga*) took place between *puruṣa* and *prakṛti*, and this relation led to the dynamic evolution of *prakṛti* into the everyday world.

More specifically, the strands are purity (*sattva*), activity (*rajas*), and inertia (*tamas*), and all worldly phenomena—physical as well as psychological—are a result of their combination in different proportions. Thus, *sattva* is associated with subjectivity and consciousness, *rajas* with energy and movement, and *tamas* with materialization and reification. On this cosmological landscape, in addition to the principles (*tattva*) of *puruṣa* and *prakṛti*, there are twenty-three principles that unfold from *prakṛti*—moving through intellect (*buddhi*), egoity (*ahaṃkāra*), mind (*manas*), five sense-capacities, five action-capacities, five subtle elements, and five gross elements. The mind is a "material" entity, made of extremely refined *prakṛti*, and receives its cognizing capacity from *puruṣa*, the self-luminous self. So when Devadatta sits down at a table to write a letter and formulates the thought, "I will now write," the true referent of the word "I" is not the mutable psychophysical complex including his mind, physical body, and so on but, paradoxically, the immutable *puruṣa* that is not engaged in the unfolding activity and remains as its serene witness. However, because Devadatta does not discern the ontological distinction between *puruṣa* and *prakṛti*, he conflates his sense of worldly individuality with *puruṣa*. This process of the retrieval of *puruṣa* from misassociation with its *prakṛti*-layered body may require several lifetimes, and individuals with names such as "Devadatta" would progress toward this recovery through vast cosmological eons (*yuga*), which are structured by the principle of *karma* and reincarnation.

A key debate across these Hindu conceptual frameworks relates to whether one needs to invoke the deity—*īśvara*—as the governor of the *karmic* mechanisms. If the deity supported or supervised a world structured by regular patterns, it would seem that the deity was bound to follow these regularities. But if the deity contravened this orderliness, occasionally or frequently, we would inhabit a chaotic world. To reiterate a point from chapter 2, according to these systems of ***darśana***, the world is not created out of nothingness (ex nihilo) and is without temporal origination. That is, there is no one moment—say 13.8 billion years ago—when ***saṃsāra***, shaped by *karma* and reincarnation, began to exist. If that is so, someone could claim that we should take ***saṃsāra*** as a complete ontological package that contains its own internally consistent explanation and not invoke an additional factor called the deity as its superintendent.

IS THE DEITY BOUND TO THE DEITY'S WORLD?

Some strands of **Sāṃkhya** and **Yoga** are theistic, such as Patañjali's *Yoga-sūtras* (c. 300 CE), where we read about *īśvara*, who is a *puruṣa* untouched by the afflictions (*kleśas*), *karma*, the fruition of *karma*, and latent predispositions. Moreover, *īśvara* is omniscient and is the teacher of the ancients, since *īśvara* is not limited by time (1.24–26). The afflictions in which *īśvara* is never enmeshed are ignorance (*avidyā*), egoism (*asmitā*), desire, aversion, and clinging to life (2.3). As in the case of **Nyāya**, here too *īśvara* is not a creator God who generates the world out of sheer nothingness: *īśvara* is a special being who is never contaminated by the *prakṛti*-shaped objects and dynamisms that are full of worldly suffering. Some other strands express nontheistic viewpoints. For instance, commenting on some of the aphorisms in the *Sāṃkhya-sūtra* (c. 1500 CE), Aniruddha presents a series of viewpoints that state that the postulation of the deity is superfluous or inconsistent (5.1–9). If the Lord is truly an independent producer of the world, the Lord would not have to depend on *karma* as an auxiliary principle, but if such a principle is indeed necessary, it can do the work of producing the world without the Lord. Moreover, all activity is driven by either egocentric or altruistic motivations. The former is not possible in the case of the Lord, and we cannot attribute the latter to the

Lord, since this world filled with suffering (*duḥkha*) could not have been produced by a Lord who is compassionate. Again, activity is possible only in the presence of desire (*rāga*) as the dynamic motor, but there can be no such desire in the Lord who is never bound to the world.[4]

In other words, the Lord is an eternally free *puruṣa* with no association with desires, intentions, and so on, but precisely because the Lord does not possess any such *prakṛti*-structured capacities, the Lord cannot produce the world. Indeed, aphorism 1.92 does not hesitate to state enigmatically, "because of the nonestablishment of *īśvara*." An influential commentator, Vijñāna-bhikṣu (c. 1600), however, offers a distinctively theistic reading of the *Sāṃkhya-sūtras* and argues that declarations about the nonexistence of *īśvara* are to be read as concessionary statements or bold assertions that are directed at individuals who might seek to acquire lordliness.[5] For Vedāntic exegetes such as Śaṃkara and Rāmānuja, the moral of the story would be that human perceptual or inferential capacities cannot sketch a luminous line extending from the world to the deity. They argue that knowledge of the divine reality (*brahman*) can be obtained only from Vedic revelation (*śruti*) of which the divine reality is the transcendental author or source. Thus, *Muṇḍaka Upaniṣad* 2.1.4 says that the speech of the supreme principle discloses the ***Vedas***, and in *Bṛhadāraṇyaka Upaniṣad* 2.4.10, we read that it breathes forth the ***Vedas***.

An intriguing pathway through these terrains was forged by the **Mīmāṃsā** tradition, which argues that knowledge of suprasensible entities is available only from the ***Vedas*** but the ***Vedas*** do not have a personal author. The Vedic texts are to be regarded as a beginningless stream of "self-revealing" words that do not have a particular revealer as the transcendental guarantee of their authority. In other words, the authority of the ***Vedas*** does not need any external certification—they are self-certifying. Kumārila, one of the most important defenders of this tradition, critically examines various standpoints relating to the claim that the world is produced by a deity. In his *Ślokavārttika*, he asks how the deity, who is said to be without a physical body, could have any desire to produce a world. Given the independence of the deity with respect to any extraneous principle, it is not clear what could have motivated the deity to produce the world. He concludes that there is no proof to demonstrate that the entire world goes through productions and dissolutions; rather, such processes should be regarded as similar to everyday events such as the construction of a particular pot and its destruction.[6]

The crux of the matter is that on these conceptual landscapes, Nyāya-Vaiśeṣika is more willing than the other systems to reason from what is familiar (the human maker of pots) to the unfamiliar (the divine maker of the world). Having observed that pots are made by potters in a certain village, Devadatta goes to a nearby town where he notices that bracelets are made by jewelers, carts by carpenters, and trays by coppersmiths. One day he is sent to a dense forest, where he encounters a massive cave temple and infers a conscious maker who is presently unobservable. In the view of **Nyāya** philosophers, this arc of reasoning is properly extended from an everyday entity such as a pot to a relatively more uncommon entity such as a cave temple to the cosmos-producing deity. Thus, commenting on *Nyāya-sūtra* 4.1.21, Vātsyāyana says that *īśvara* is a particular self (*ātman*) with various qualities and that the nature of *īśvara* is akin to that of a self. However, *īśvara* is distinct from other selves—*īśvara* is devoid of delusion, possesses lordliness in the form of various yogic powers such as the ability to become as minute as an atom, and activates the *karmic* merit and demerit collected in all individual selves. When an individual is striving for a certain *karmic* fruit, *īśvara* actuates its realization; without the action of *īśvara*, human activity would not generate its result. Indeed, the relationship of *īśvara* to finite beings, Vātsyāyana tells us, is similar to that of a father to his children.[7] In short, *īśvara* is the universal efficient cause who operates not beyond but precisely through the *karmic* trajectories of individuals. Regarding the crucial question as to *why* the deity is operative in this way, Uddyotakara notes at 4.1.21 that it is the nature of *īśvara* to produce the world just as it is the nature of the earth to uphold things. However, it should not be claimed that someone whose nature is activity has to remain engaged in action at all times—*īśvara* is endowed with intelligence, and *īśvara* acts in accordance with the merit and the demerit of different beings.[8]

REASONING IN THE WORLD AND LIBERATION FROM THE WORLD

One way to review the discussion so far is to highlight the significance of analogical reasoning that is pivoted on everyday objects such as pots. Here is the formal outline of a Buddhist argument for radical impermanence (*kṣaṇabhaṅga*):

Everything is impermanent,
like a pot.

To begin with, we could query whether the pot is indeed a good example for the thesis. A pot in someone's kitchen seems to be a quite durable entity; moreover, in museums, one can see pots from ancient kingdoms. In response, a Buddhist philosopher may argue on the basis of the definitions of key terms such as *existence*, *causality*, *perception*, *meaning*, and so on that certain inconsistencies would result if we considered the pot to be a permanent entity. A Hindu respondent—say, a **Nyāya** philosopher—will argue, by offering alternative definitions, that no such untoward consequences follow if the pot is regarded as enjoying some kind of permanence. In this way, an entire universe of discourse, Hindu or Buddhist, is nested inside a mundane pot.

However, as a **Cārvāka** onlooker would claim, from a logical point of view, the inference-grounding universal generalization is shaky insofar as it proceeds from a few entities or one entity (this pot in my room) to all entities (everything that there is). Perhaps in a remote part of the Milky Way, there is a teapot that was not constructed by any conscious agent. Or perhaps this teapot is eternal and thus is a counterexample to the proposed relation between existence and impermanence. In such cases, a **Nyāya** philosopher may employ dialectical or suppositional argumentation (*tarka*), in which one's viewpoint is presumed to be correct although one is not able to offer conclusive evidence. One systematically works out the implications of hypotheses *x* and *y*, and if the implications of *x* are undesirable in the sense that they conflict with what is generally acceptable, then one may shift the burden of proof to the defender of *x*. As Vātsyāyana explains in his commentary on *Nyāya-sūtra* 1.1.40, such *tarka* is not a source of knowledge and cannot prove a thesis, which has to be supported through independent evidence. Later, Udayana would mention, in addition to undesirable consequence, four other types of *tarka*: self-dependence (proving A from A), mutual dependence (proving B from A and A from B), circularity (proving A from B, B from C, and C from A), and infinite regress.

THE HEART OF YOGIC MATTER

To return to a theme highlighted in chapters 1 and 2, such dense configurations of reasoned analysis are often enmeshed in a quest for liberation from the conditions of worldly finitude. Commenting on *Nyāya-sūtra* 1.1.2, Vātsyāyana writes that the supreme good of liberation (*apavarga*) is the spiritual peace in which all worldly miseries dissolve. With the attainment of knowledge of truth (*tattva-jñāna*)—relating to the self, *karmic* activity, transmigration, and liberation—there is absolute cessation of suffering (*duḥkha*).[9] In his commentary on *Nyāya-sūtra* 4.2.46 and 4.2.47, Vātsyāyana tells us that on the pathway to liberation, one should undertake self-purification through the means of yogic restraints and observances; instructions relating to breath control, withdrawal from the senses, and meditation (*dhyāna*); and the rules of yogic practice. One should acquire knowledge of the self (*ātma-vidyā*) through repeated processes of reading, listening, and reflecting, and also discussion with those who have this knowledge.[10]

Here Vātsyāyana invokes three fundamental concepts that recur through vast bodies of commentarial literature associated with **Sāṃkhya**, **Yoga**, and **Vedānta**: suffering, self, and purification of self. Their worldviews are shaped by a therapeutic program in which a certain diagnosis of the human condition is offered and a remedial pathway is laid down. Generally speaking, the diagnosis is that the embodied self is immersed in a deep-seated ignorance about its spiritual reality and the remedy is that worldly action has to be properly aligned with the correct understanding of the self. At present, we are out of sync with the deep structure of reality, and unless we become properly synchronized with it through specific spiritual disciplines, we shall continue to languish in the vales of worldly suffering across multiple reembodiments. For instance, I may mistakenly view my corporeal identifications (I am a human being with this laptop, these books, etc.) as exhaustive of my true identity and fail to discern the spiritual center that holds together, and subtly animates, all aspects of my worldly existence. However, regarding the two crucial questions of the nature of the self (*ātman, jīva, puruṣa*) and the nature of the self's liberation (*apavarga, mokṣa*) from the world, there is a significant diversity of viewpoints.

To begin with Nyāya-Vaiśeṣika, we encounter a fairly common view of the nature of human embodiment. If you believe that your material body is enlivened by an individual spiritual principle (called the "soul"), when you look at the flowers in the garden, you may regard this perceptual experience in terms of a psychophysical unit that thinks, feels, acts, and lives in the world. If you see little Nora walk into the garden, you regard her too as enlivened by such an individual principle. Moreover, consciousness is a contingent feature of this principle: you are conscious when you look at the flowers, and you are not conscious when you are sleeping. Reflecting such an understanding, Nyāya-Vaiśeṣika states that there is an ontologically real distinction between one self and another self—these selves are not aspects or manifestations of some "super self." Conscious events are specific properties of the self when the self is associated with a psychophysical complex of the body and the mind or inner sense (*manas*). Crucially, therefore, the state of liberation is the complete absence of consciousness so that the self experiences neither joy nor sorrow. This vision of the complete transcendence of pain as well as of pleasure is motivated by the claim that the latter is associated or commingled with the former so that suffering preponderates over happiness. Even occasions of joy are tinged with suffering: we may feel somewhat uneasy at the thought that our delights will pass away. Such an asymmetric relation between happiness and suffering indicates that suffering is a kind of steady background radiation that seeps into all our experiences and happiness is a fleeting respite. Thus, Vātsyāyana comments on *Nyāya-sūtra* 1.1.2 that the state of liberation is freedom from pleasure (*sukha*) and pain (*duḥkha*); pleasure is connected with pain, and this combination is to be avoided in the manner of food that is mixed with honey and poison.[11]

This motif of the universality of suffering is highlighted in Patañjali's *Yoga-sūtra* 2.15—to the one who discerns correctly, all indeed is suffering (*duḥkhameva sarvaṃ vivekinaḥ*). Because the embodied self is deluded about its true nature as pure consciousness, it remains entangled in the sorrowful streams of the impermanent world. The remedy lies in gradually learning to distinguish between one's self as the translucent witness (*puruṣa*) and the mutable states of the psychophysiological complex (*prakṛti*) so as to reach the destination of detachment (*kaivalya*) from nonsentient entities and processes. Thus, in a state of ignorance, Devadatta may say, "I, Devadatta, the son of so and so, possess these things in the world." Instead of mistakenly appropriating *prakṛti*-structured goods to himself in this manner, however, he should systematically cultivate the discriminating wisdom (*viveka*) that *puruṣa*, in its primordial purity, remains forever dis-associated from them. This appropriative mechanism is driven by egoity (*ahaṃkāra*)—literally "I-maker"—whose self-aggrandizing modes of acquisition structure conditions of worldly existence. An analogy that highlights this deep misconception is the white crystal that takes on the appearance of a reddish object when it is placed in proximity to a hibiscus flower. Just as the crystal never loses its intrinsic whiteness, the self-luminosity of *puruṣa* too only seemingly becomes obscured by the transformations of *prakṛti* but, in truth, remains completely untinged and untainted. Therefore, overcoming the spiritual ignorance in which he misidentifies the psychophysiological body with *puruṣa*, Devadatta should instead meditatively reflect in this way: "*I* am not this, *I* am not that."

In other words, worldly existence is driven by a form of misplaced identity: an individual such as Devadatta, who is a result of the conjunction between *puruṣa* and *prakṛti*, mistakenly thinks that he is of the nature of materiality. However, in his spiritual essence, he is not any product of nonsentient *prakṛti* such as the physical body, intellect (*buddhi*), and mind (*manas*, *citta*) but the self-luminous *puruṣa* that shines in its own light. When Devadatta sees a tree in the garden, a reflection of the tree is impressed on the visual organ and on the mind, which organizes such sensory imprints. Through this activity of the sense organ and the mind, the intellect takes on the form (*ākāra*) of the tree. The intellect is, in itself, nonconscious, but it receives the luminosity of the self-luminous *puruṣa*, and this process gives rise to Devadatta's perceptual experience of the tree. Crucially, this perception is not, as **Nyāya** philosophers would put it, an event in the self—it is to be regarded as a transformation in the intellect and not in *puruṣa*, which is beyond all association with mutability. The intellect undergoes a real modification, but this transformation should not be located in or attributed to *puruṣa*, just as when we see the moving reflection of the sun on the surface of a windswept lake, we do not ascribe these movements to the sun itself. When the intrinsic radiance of *puruṣa* is disentangled from the objects of *prakṛti* that it illuminates, *puruṣa* is established in its unalterable purity. In this way, a diseased individual may be led back to health through a route similar to the prescription of a medical system: a diagnosis is offered of the human condition as steeped in suffering, and a remedy that points toward wholeness is provided. Vyāsa's commentary on *Yoga-sūtra* 2.15 states that just as in medical science there are four parts—namely, disease, cause of disease, recovery, and medicine—so too does the quest for liberation consist of four components (namely, ***saṃsāra***, the cause of ***saṃsāra***, liberation [*mokṣa*], and the means of liberation). ***Saṃsāra***, which is full of suffering, is what is to be avoided, and the connection of *puruṣa* and *prakṛti* is the cause of what is to be avoided. The absolute cessation of this conjunction is the removal of worldly suffering, and the means of this cessation is proper discriminative knowledge.[12]

The distinction between the embodied self and the pure self

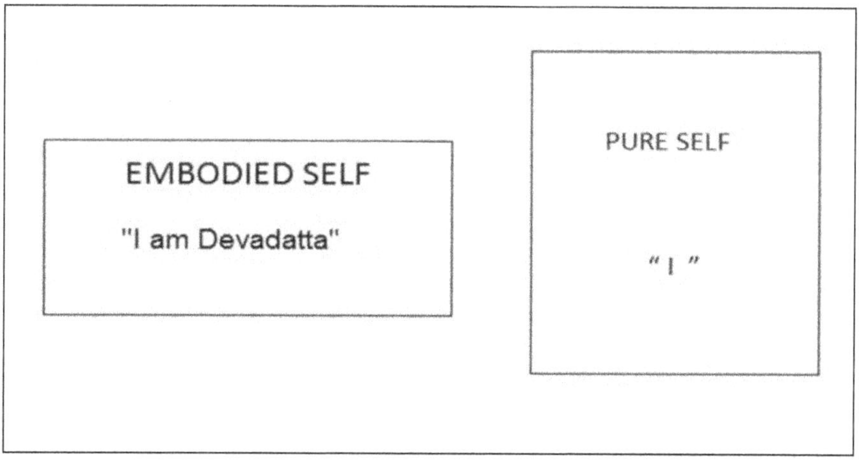

This therapeutic structure is announced at the beginning of the *Sāṃkhya-kārikā* of Īśvarakṛṣṇa (c. 400 CE), which states that because of the torment of the three types of suffering, there arises the desire to know the means to terminate them. These are the internal type, which is produced by an individual's psychophysiological constitution; the external type, which is produced by the physical world; and the cosmic type, which is produced by divine forces. As one gains insight into reality, one sees worldly existence as saturated with suffering, and to facilitate the deepening of this healing vision, *Yoga-sūtra* 2.29 lays down a set of techniques comprising eight steps or limbs: restraints (*yama*), observances (*niyama*), yogic postures (*āsanas*), breath control (*prāṇāyāma*), withdrawal of attention from the objects of the sense-organs (*pratyāhāra*), concentration on a particular object (*dhāraṇā*), meditative attentiveness to the object that is focused on (*dhyāna*), and awareness of oneself as pure witness (*samādhi*). These graduated steps would enable an individual to recover the transcendental purity of *puruṣa* by distinguishing it from the fleeting objects of the world. More specifically, the last stage of *samādhi*, when *puruṣa* returns to itself such that *puruṣa* abides in a reflexive awareness of itself, consists of two steps: the first involves conceptualization and focused attention on an external or internal object (*saṃprajñāta-samādhi*), and in the second, all *karmic* seeds or traces are eliminated, and *puruṣa* shines forth in its own form (*asaṃprajñāta-samādhi*). Through this transformation of self-understanding, there takes place the cessation of misidentification with the transient modifications of the mind (*citta-vṛtti-nirodhaḥ*), and the self-luminous *puruṣa* is restored to its pristine condition (1.2–3). This cessation is effected through strenuous practice that is continuously undertaken for a long time and through the cultivation of dispassion (1.12–14).

In other words, the spiritual summit of this process—namely, *samādhi*—is the state of pure witness in which the self (*puruṣa*) does not mistakenly project its spiritual reality onto any nonsentient objects, which are marked with mutability. Here, the self is completely free from any ignorance (*avidyā*), which is the seeing of what is eternal, pure, joyful, and self in what is ephemeral, impure, sorrowful and not-self (2.5). However, actions performed in a state of *avidyā* leave behind *karmic* traces, and these traces, when they bear fruit, generate suffering in this lifetime or in a future life. Given the conjunction between *puruṣa* and *prakṛti*, it is particularly difficult for the embodied self to discern their ontological distinctness. A conscious state shaped by the intellect, mind, and sense-organs is a consciousness *of* something. However, the self, which is pure consciousness, is not the consciousness of *this* or the consciousness of *that*, which illuminates discrete objects such as chairs, tables, and laptops; it is not any such world-directed light but rather light in its own effulgence. As an analogy, consider Nora who, at the age of eighteen, beholds the Mona Lisa for the first time at the Louvre. In the process of examining the different parts of the painting, she becomes so absorbed in the painting that she no longer has the sense of being a distinct "I" over and above that which she is observing. Her attention is initially directed toward the painting, and then the subject-object distinction fades away so that what remains is a moment of nondyadic awareness. From the perspective of the *Yoga-sūtras*, such a fleeting moment of this-worldly *samādhi* is a pointer toward the unchanging self, which is pure consciousness.

Therefore, one way to understand yogic practices is to see them as a form of "yoking" the psychophysiological self to the spiritual root from which it has become unmoored. Through the eight steps, it is realigned with *puruṣa* as it moves away from fragmentation in the mutability of the everyday world. By withdrawing from the dispersal of the mind (*citta*) across worldly objects that are as fleeting as the waves on the surface of an ocean, an individual becomes stabilized in the heart of reality. At 1.6–11, the *Yoga-sūtras* note five types of these modifications (*vṛtti*): the sources of knowledge (***pramāṇa***), which are perception, inference, and testimony; false cognition, which is not based on the nature of an object; conceptualization, which is not directed to a real object; sleep; and memory. To restrain these turbulences, an individual has to generate an uninterrupted continuum of thoughts centered on the immutable self so that through an intensified single-pointedness, the mind becomes not world-directed but self-oriented on a spiritual journey. This cultivation of the self is especially highlighted in the three "inner limbs" of *dhāraṇā*, *dhyāna*, and *samādhi*, which constitute a spectrum of progressive unification. In *dhāraṇā*, an individual tethers the mind to a particular object for a period of time. This focal point can be a mantra, a figure (*yantra*), or a symbolic diagram (*maṇḍala*). Awareness is deepened in *dhyāna*, and a steady stream of thought is directed to the object of meditation. In progressing toward the summit of *samādhi*, the sense of being an "I" cognizing an external object or mental object dissolves. While these transconceptual states are initially fleeting because of the countervailing force of the subliminal impressions (*saṃskāra*) generated by past *karmic* actions, through constant practice, such impressions are gradually effaced. The self then shines forth as the pure witness (*draṣṭā*) of the world without confusing its reality with that of the mutable world.

While the *Yoga-sūtras* are the textual template for a particular worldview with multiple cosmological, psychological, epistemological, and therapeutic strands, the term *yoga* is employed across the multiple forms of Hindu ***darśana*** in a broader sense to mean practices geared toward a reformation of the embodied self that leads to a discovery or recovery of one's true nature. The associations of yoga with integrity, equilibrium, tranquility, and pacification can be found in the ***Upaniṣads***, the

Bhagavad-gītā, and the epic narrative the *Mahābhārata*. Thus, we read in *Kaṭha Upaniṣad* 6.11 that yoga is the steadfast control of the senses and in *Śvetāśvatara Upaniṣad* 1.3 that those who follow the yoga of meditation (*dhyāna*) perceive the divine, the self, and power, all concealed by their own qualities. More concretely, *Maitrī Upaniṣad* 6.18 outlines a method for discerning the spiritual foundation that comprises the dimensions of *prāṇāyāma* (breath control), *pratyāhāra* (withdrawal of the senses), *dhyāna* (meditative attentiveness), *dhāraṇā* (concentration), inquiry (*tarka*), and *samādhi*. In the **Bhagavad-gītā**, we are offered a precise definition of yoga as "sameness of mind" (2.48), and the yogi is described as a lamp that does not flicker in a windless place (6.19). We read that while worldly actions are performed through the products of *prakṛti*, the self that is deluded because of its association with egoity mistakenly thinks, "*I* am the doer" (3.27). In a striking metaphor, individuals with a firmly established wisdom who draw their senses away from the objects of sense are compared to a tortoise who draws in its limbs (2.58). This motif of the meditative stabilization of the flickering mind through which one attains a state of unperturbed serenity is articulated in various places in the *Mahābhārata*. The sage is said to move among living beings in the way that a bird moves about on water but is not tainted by it, for such a sage, equanimous and free from envy, abides in one's inherent state (*svabhāva*) (12.194.47). These idioms relating to reining in the fluctuating dimensions of one's psycho-mental existence are structured by the cosmological account in the *Sāṃkhya-kārikā* of the generation of worldly experience. The term *sāṃkhya* also appears in several verses of the **Bhagavad-gītā**, where it refers to the cultivation of discriminative insight (2.39; 3.3; 5.4–5; 18.19). Again, throughout the chapters of the **Bhagavad-gītā**, one encounters the concept of yoga in connection with action (*karma*), knowledge (*jñāna*), and devotional love (*bhakti*), and the Vedāntic traditions interweave these paths in different ways in sketching their cosmological visions of the journey of the embodied self toward its divine destination.

One core theme from the **Bhagavad-gītā** that is resonant with the cosmologies and the disciplines of **Sāṃkhya** and **Yoga** is that spiritual progression involves the process of distancing oneself from the impermanent fruits of *karmic* action. And yet, the claim is not that one may simply spend their days sleeping on the sofa or under a tree but that one should become recentered in *puruṣa* by working through the densities of worldly existence. One remains active in the world, and one simultaneously cultivates an inner detachment from one's agential capacities in the manner of a lotus that grows on muddy terrain but remains untouched by impurities. For instance, an individual may renounce her sense of being an autonomous and independent agent and, by recentering this agency in the Lord, perform her worldly activities with the consciousness that it is the Lord, the supreme agent, who is working in and through them. This would be a paradoxical mode of "active nonactivity"—she is *acting*, and yet it is not *she* who is acting—through which she would become liberated from the transmigratory world of suffering. As we will see in chapter 5, action in itself is not ***saṃsāra***-binding; rather, egocentric acquisitiveness generates *karmic* merits and demerits through which individuals remain enmeshed in matrixes of suffering. Whether the "I" and its actions in the world, and the Lord to whom finite agency is surrendered, are to be regarded as real or not is, once again, at the heart of the ontological debate across different styles of **Vedānta**.

THE ONE OF **YOGA** AND THE ALL OF ADVAITA

The emphasis on cultivating meditative stability is reflected in some of Śaṃkara's exegeses of the ***Upaniṣads*** and the ***Bhagavad-gītā***, where such cultivation is directed toward removing obstructions in order to clearly grasp what is apprehended through scriptural reading. Throughout the milieus of Advaita spiritual life too, one encounters the repeated exhortation not to confuse the immutable self (*ātman*) with what is not-self—namely, the finite world of mutability, for this conflation is the driving motor of our enmeshment in the cycles of reincarnation. However, one crucial sticking point relates to whether there is an ontologically real multiplicity of *puruṣa* or whether this multiplicity is to be read as a pointer to the ontological nonduality (*advaita*) between the finite world and its transcendental foundation. At *Sāṃkhya-kārikā* 18, we find a clear affirmation of this multiplicity on the basis of our observation that different individuals undergo birth and death and their different modifications are shaped by the three strands (*guṇas*). In the commentary on *Sāṃkhya-kārikā* 18 in *Sāṃkhya-tattva-kaumudī* ("Moonlight on the *Sāṃkhya* Principles of Reality"), Vācaspati Miśra says that if *puruṣa* were accepted to be one in all bodies, when one individual is active, all other individuals would become active. This viewpoint is reflected in *Yoga-sūtra* 2.22, which states that when one individual reaches the highest spiritual goal, the world does not cease to operate for others. In other words, when one embodied self recovers its identity as *puruṣa* by withdrawing from the products of *prakṛti*, many other embodied selves remain engaged in the milieus of shared experience.

From an ontological perspective, a common Vedāntic critique of this picture is that it cannot provide a coherent account of how *puruṣa* and *prakṛti*—two distinct principles whose natures are essentially opposed—could have become associated in the first place. At *Sāṃkhya-kārikā* 11, we read that both the unmanifest state and the manifest forms of *prakṛti* are tripartite, nonconscious, and productive, while *puruṣa* is the opposite of these forms. The problem is only accentuated by the claim that *puruṣa* is always liberated and that it is neither bound to cycles of reincarnation (***saṃsāra***) nor involved in processes of attaining liberation. As *Sāṃkhya-kārikā* 62 notes, there is, in truth, no one who is bound, or released, or wanders—it is *prakṛti* that wanders, is bound, and moves toward liberation. Therefore, individuals who are trying to become liberated should develop the insight that they *are* pure spirit.[13] Thus, the *Sāṃkhya-kārikā* is structured by this dilemma: either *puruṣa* is eternally disengaged, or *puruṣa* seeks liberation through the matrices of the temporal world. On the first route, we have to explain why anyone would undertake an inquiry into the overcoming of affliction and also ask precisely who is engaged in this inquiry, while on the second, the claim that *puruṣa* is striving toward liberation is not consistent with the claim that *puruṣa* is immutable. A possible way through this dilemma is to say that the embodied self begins to understand that it is immersed in worldly suffering because of its lack of discernment. Thus, when Devadatta claims, "I am bound to the world," the "I" should be understood as pointing not to "I-as-*puruṣa*" but to "I-as-Devadatta," where the latter's psychophysiological capacities are somehow enlivened by the former. The charge of conceptual inconsistency relates to the "somehow"—if *puruṣa* is unchanging, how can it be the animating engine for the temporal evolution of *prakṛti*?

The text engages with this conundrum by speaking of the "appearance" (*iva*) of bondage and liberation; it appears to Devadatta that he has become bound and that he is in the process of becoming liberated, while in his spiritual center of gravity, he is always liberated. Thus,

Sāṃkhya-kārikā 20 states that due to the conjunction of the two principles, the nonconscious structure of embodiment appears as if (*iva*) it were conscious, while owing to the activity of the strands, the nonengaged *puruṣa* appears as if it were active. Various metaphors are employed to articulate the dense enmeshment between *puruṣa* and *prakṛti* that generates this reciprocal misattribution: nonsentient milk nourishes the sentient calf just as nonsentient *prakṛti* brings about the liberation of the spirit. The two principles are united in the manner of a blind person who can move but cannot see, and a lame person who cannot walk properly but can see. By cultivating a fine-tuned discernment of the distinction between *puruṣa* and *prakṛti*, Devadatta would understand that temporal processes such as bondage, reincarnation, and liberation do not truly qualify *puruṣa* and are only ascribed to *puruṣa* in the way that defeat and victory are ascribed to a ruler, while it is individual soldiers who are engaged in battle. Therefore, Devadatta would not speak of the liberation of *puruṣa* but of the liberation of his own *prakṛti*-shaped embodiment.

Advaita reflects certain dimensions of this cosmological picture and sharply diverges from some others. From the perspectives of Advaita too, the deep self is never bound to the world of ignorance, impermanence, and suffering, nor does it become liberated from worldly finitude. In a commentarial text, the *Bhāmatī*, Vācaspati writes that though the true self is not really defined by the limiting conditions posited by ignorance, it appears as if (*iva*) it is defined; though it is not an agent, it appears as if it is an agent; and though it is not an object, it appears as if it is an object of the concept "I."[14] In the ultimate analysis, *ātman* cannot be individuated as *this* self or *that* self, and *ātman* is ontologically nondual with *brahman*, which is beyond all qualities, features, and classifications (*nirguṇa*). To apprehend this nonduality, it is vital to remove from *ātman* the connotations of an individual cognizer and from *brahman* the connotations of a personal God with qualities such as world-production, world-preservation, and world-dissolution. As discussed in chapter 1, according to Advaita, the term "reality" is properly applied only to that which is intrinsically immutable and that which is utterly independent. Therefore, *ātman* should not be confused with the mutable embodied self (*jīva*); whereas the latter is conscious of *this* object or *that* object, the former is the pure consciousness that witnesses conscious states without undergoing any change. Advaita commentarial texts distinguish between the transient cognitions of empirical objects through specific mental transformations (*vṛtti-jñāna*) and the invariant witness of these variable cognitions. The nonsentient intellect appears to be a cognizer because of the superimposition of the self-luminous *ātman* on it, while because of the superimposition of the intellect on the *ātman*, the nonagential *ātman* appears to be engaged in cognitive processes. This mutual superimposition of self and not-self gives rise to claims such as "I know," "I hear," and "I am human."

When Devadatta says, "I see a tree in the garden," and after fifteen minutes, reports, "I now see a little dog sitting down under the tree," these temporally indexed cognitions are associated with the psychophysiological processes of the *jīva* and not the limitless *ātman*, which abides as the self-luminous background. As the crimson hues of the sunset fill the sky, Devadatta's sense of being *a* perceiver gradually fades away and he merges into the eloquent silence of the landscape. When his sister Śakuntalā walks into the room and asks him what he has been doing, he is shaken out of his reverie and says, "I have been observing the sky." From an Advaita perspective, this "I" ultimately points not to Devadatta as a finite *jīva* but to the indivisible *ātman* that is self-reflexive consciousness. So *ātman* is not an individuated awareness directed to *this* laptop or to *that* chair; *ātman* is awareness itself and is devoid of a subject-object dichotomy. That is, *ātman* is the contentless luminosity that illuminates cognitions of specific contents such as "trees," "dogs," and "skies."

The nature of pure consciousness

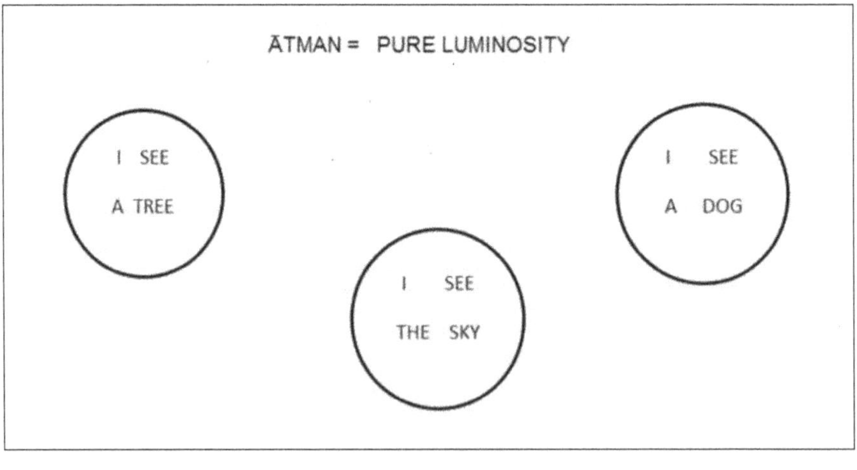

Again, *brahman* does not have any qualities such as the attributes of omnipresence, omnipotence, and omnibenevolence. If we wish to view *brahman* through the prisms of such features, we should use disclaimers on a pathway of negation—*neti, neti* ("not this," "not this")—which would remind us of the fallibility of our human concepts. In his commentary on ***Bhagavad-gītā*** 13.12, Śaṃkara says that *brahman* is not a genus (*jāti*) such as "cow," not a quality (*guṇa*) such as "black," not an action such as "cooking," and not a relation such as "possessing cows." Because *brahman* is utterly unique, qualityless, nonrelational, and nonobjectifiable, it cannot be described with any human-shaped word.[15] Therefore, regarding this unconditioned reality, we cannot say *what* it is, and we can only indicate, following scriptural revelation, *that* it is. From Śaṃkara's perspective, a statement such as "The great Lord moves across the sky on a fiery chariot" cannot be taken as a truthful account of deep reality, for *brahman* is beyond any transformation. Therefore, it has to be read allegorically as a reminder that the variegated skyscapes that unfold before the observer are ultimately directed toward *brahman* as their unmoving center.

Given the radical ineffability of *ātman* and *brahman*, the fact of nonduality cannot be articulated in conceptual categories; it is a form of holy silence in which *ātman-brahman* stands forth as the immutable reality. However, until this spiritual summit of liberation (*mokṣa*) is reached, the language of the "I" has to be used in an everyday world that is shaped with the idioms of difference. As discussed in chapter 1, Śaṃkara both defends and denies difference from two standpoints. Empirically speaking, the world is populated by individuals with names such as "Devadatta" who are seeking liberation from the cycles of reincarnation, but transcendentally speaking, these individuals are multiple names and forms who are essentially not-distinct from *brahman*. While Devadatta and Yajñadatta are empirically real human beings, any sense of being ontologically distinct categories is an expression of deep-seated ignorance (*avidyā*) about nondual reality. Devadatta and Yajñadatta are, in truth, *ātman*, which is nondual with *brahman*; it only appears to Devadatta and Yajñadatta, because of their ignorance, that they have become immersed in vales of suffering. Therefore, the state of liberation should be characterized not as the retrieval of the transcendental purity of *one* self and *another* self but as the realization that each self is ontologically nondual with the indivisible foundation of the world.

ADVAITA AND THE ELUSIVE MĀYĀ

And yet, even an individual on the pathway of Advaita cannot deny the subjective feel of inhabiting a world marked by difference. When she buys pasta for dinner, it is pasta and not chocolate that she will eat, and when she goes to Dover on holiday, it is to Dover and not to Normandy. Conceptually speaking, what Advaita needs is a principle of error that will make sense of why the indivisible ground of being seems (to us) to have become multiply divided into worldly beings, and this principle is *māyā*. To characterize *māyā* as a "principle" is already to entertain paradox, for like the snake in the rope-snake illusion, *māyā* is neither utterly unreal nor truly real. The difference between Dover and Normandy is not a complete hallucination—if General Eisenhower were a follower of Śaṃkara, he would still have taken this difference seriously in terms of spatiotemporal coordinates. However, he would have understood that such geophysical markers are multiple names and forms that are like the rolling waves on the English Channel that cannot touch the unperturbable heart of the ocean. A wave qua wave is contingently real, and its contingent reality is derivative from the reality of the self-existent ocean. Left to its own devices, the *māyā*-wave is neither here nor there, suspended as it is in an ontological limbo.

Reflecting this cosmological vision of a world whose mutable matrices are woven with threads of *māyā*-shaped precarity, the Advaita traditions can speak favorably of the practices of purification of mind that are associated with **Yoga** while rejecting the ontological duality between *puruṣa* and *prakṛti* that is outlined by **Sāṃkhya**. On the one hand, Śaṃkara highlights the conceptual instabilities in the **Sāṃkhya** standpoint. In his *Upadeśa-sāhasrī* ("A Thousand Teachings"), he notes that because *prakṛti* is nonconscious, it cannot render any service to *puruṣa*, while if action is admitted in *puruṣa*, then *puruṣa* becomes perishable.[16] On the other hand, in his commentary on the ***Bhagavad-gītā***, he affirms forms of yoga such as *karma-yoga* as means through which a finite self would develop the realization that it is not a worldly agent. However, these purgative processes simply remove impediments on the pathway toward the realization of nonduality; liberation is not an effect or a product of human effort, since *brahman* is always liberated. Thinking that you have misplaced your spectacles, you may spend an hour looking for them in the different rooms of the house until your friend points out that you are wearing them. So too is liberation the *re*covery of an established fact, the vision of which has become obscured due to the dust of human ignorance.

In short, notwithstanding their ontological divergences, the therapeutic regimes of Advaita, **Sāṃkhya**, and **Yoga** are shaped by a "paradox of practice." In truth, Devadatta and Yajñadatta *are* liberated, and yet it is from within the domains of worldly self-forgetfulness that this truth has to be uncovered. From Advaita perspectives, worldly differences can be cultivated as useful fictions toward the liberating insight of the nonduality of *ātman* and *brahman*. If tomorrow Devadatta receives initiation from a guru in an Advaita lineage, Devadatta may be instructed to undertake certain forms of yogic discipline. Such techniques are useful because they generate in Devadatta the meditative self-control that is necessary to realize the nonduality of *ātman* and *brahman*, but Devadatta should also understand that these techniques are ultimately fictions because they do not describe any immutable entities at the bedrock of reality.

In an Advaita context, this account raises the question of how liberation (*mokṣa*) from the world of ignorance, divisibility, and multiplicity is possible if the means—such as scriptural texts—are themselves enmeshed in this world. The Advaita traditions seek to resolve this paradox by claiming that when the human mind, which is a construct of *māyā*, undergoes a scripturally guided purification, it can become—on the analogy of using one thorn to remove another—the instrument that dissolves this *māyā* as well as itself. Thus, in a mind-bending moment, the individuated "I" itself dissolves and deep nonduality is recovered. The **Śaiva Siddhānta** traditions discussed in the previous chapter would oppose this claim of an undifferentiated unity. Here, the Lord Śiva, the individual self, and the world are distinct. As Sadāśiva, the Lord performs five functions: emanation of the world and its maintenance and absorption, self-concealment of Śiva, and self-revelation of Śiva through grace. The properly initiated individual undertakes a life structured by ritual, and through these activities, worldly impurities are gradually erased. Finally, in liberation from the cycle of reincarnations, the self becomes omnipotent and omniscient like Śiva but, crucially, remains ontologically distinct from Śiva. Through the daily enactment of such cosmic visions, the world becomes a human habitation, and its rootedness in the divine source is firmly realized in the life of the worldly individual.

4

Finding a Home in the World

Walking along the seashore on an autumn evening, Gārgī sees the sun slowly sink into the horizon. As she looks at the waves, she again feels intensely that the whole world is enveloped by and encapsulated in *brahman*. On the basis of her readings of the scriptures such as the ***Upaniṣads*** and the ***Bhagavad-gītā***, she articulates this experience in this way: even as *brahman* pervades all finite reality, *brahman* remains ontologically distinct from it. On returning home, she sees her brother, Janaka, meditatively weeding and planting in their small garden. From various discussions on the theme of the relation of *brahman* and the world, she knows that Janaka would speak about such an experience by saying that the innermost being of the human self is ontologically not-distinct from *brahman*.

The disagreement between Gārgī and Janaka is partly related to the exegetical question of whose reading of scripture properly reflects the meaning of the text. Perhaps when some scriptural texts declare *brahman* to be qualityless, this is a denial not of every attribute but only of human imperfections such as suffering, ignorance, and the like. Therefore, *brahman* should be seen as the abode of every supereminently perfect quality such as omnipotence and omniscience. Or perhaps such declarations should be read as the final word, and they sublate all depictions of *brahman* as having a specific form or quality. Therefore, descriptions of *brahman* as omnipotent or omniscient do not pertain to the essence of *brahman* but contingently characterize *brahman* as the originator or governor of the world. Such motifs constitute the focal point of many of the exegetical disputes between Advaita and the theistic forms of **Vedānta**; according to the former, *brahman* is the qualityless reality (*nirguṇa*) beyond all descriptions, and according to the latter, *brahman* is the supremely personal reality (*saguṇa*) without any worldly flaw.

CAN THERE BE A RELATION BETWEEN THE FINITE AND THE NONFINITE?

In addition to such interpretive tussles, there is the conceptual challenge of articulating the relation between the finite world, which is temporal and divisible, on the one hand, and the nonfinite center, which is eternal and indivisible, on the other hand. In response to the question "What is Nora's relation to him?" we say, "She is his daughter," and to the question "How is the cat related to the mat?" we reply, "The cat is on the mat." However, such relations—shaped by spatiotemporal markers—cannot apply in a straightforward sense between what is finite and what is not finite. One such relation that Vedāntic thinkers work with, in the light of scriptural texts, is the origination of the world from *brahman*. The word commonly used in Vedāntic texts for "creation" is *sṛṣṭi*, which has the connotations of sending out or projecting. Thus, the production of the world is the pouring forth of the world from the inexhaustible plenitude of *brahman*. Now, if there is a real relation between *brahman* and the world, *brahman* would seem to be contaminated by the world, just as when a liter of muddy water is poured into a beaker, the glass base becomes tainted by earthen deposits. Therefore, when *brahman* is said to uphold the world, this support has to be delineated in such a way that *brahman* is not sullied by the world's limitations. An entire galaxy of Vedāntic exegetes such as Śaṃkara, Rāmānuja, Madhva, and Vallabha grapple with this problem of articulating the motif that *brahman* is the transcendental basis of the world and *brahman* is not touched by any worldly defects. If product*ion* involves a change in the producer, someone could argue that *brahman* cannot be the substratum of such processes. Indeed, following his axiomatic equivalence between reality and immutability, Śaṃkara concludes that from the ultimate perspective, there is no product*ion* of a world of multiplicity out of *brahman*; all such descriptions are useful fictions that are meant to teach human beings that they are ontologically nondual with *brahman*. In contrast, Śaṃkara's critics, such as Rāmānuja and Madhva, develop resolutely theistic cosmologies in which the world is an ontologically real domain of temporality that is originated from and supported by its supremely personal and transcendent foundation.

THE DIVINE ROOT OF WORLDLY ROUTES

These Vedāntic disputes over the nature of *brahman* are worked out through commentarial texts on the ***Upaniṣads***, the ***Bhagavad-gītā***, and the ***Brahma-sūtras***, which, in turn, are regarded as containing the revelatory message of the infallible ***Vedas***. Central to Vedic cosmological imaginations is the notion of world-production through sacrificial ritual (*yajña*), which is a cosmos-generating and cosmos-stabilizing instrument. It is because of the orderly performance of ritual that the different types of regularities that we observe in the world are preserved. If sacrifices were not performed by ritual specialists, the harmonies that structure the world would gradually run down, and it would move toward chaos. This cosmic order is founded on a primordial sacrifice announced in a famous hymn in the *Ṛg Veda* (10.90), according to which the body of the person (*puruṣa*) was ritually dismembered into the natural elements, the heavens, animals, and so on. Another hymn sings with deeply enigmatic notes about the origin of the world:

> *There was neither non-existence* [asat] *nor existence* [sat] *then; there was neither the realm of space nor the sky which is beyond. What stirred? Where? In whose protection? Was there water, bottomlessly deep?*
> *There was neither death nor immortality then. There was no distinguishing sign of night nor of day. That one breathed, by its own impulse. Other than that there was nothing beyond . . .*
> *Who really knows? Who will here proclaim it? Whence was it produced? Whence is this creation* [visṛṣṭi]*? The gods came afterwards, with the creation of the universe. Who then knows whence it has arisen?*[1]

The authors of the *Brāhmaṇa* literature seek to explain the significance of the ritual, which, if properly understood and undertaken, can give its officiants power over worldly forces and ward off evil in this world and the hereafter. There exist deep equivalences (*bandhu*) between rituals, cosmic forces, and supernatural powers, and the comprehension of these connections enables their knower to maintain the sacred order. If entities and phenomena can be correlated with a specific number, they are homologous with it, so that, for instance, one can gain sevenfold the world of the gods or domestic animals with a hymn of seven stanzas; in a ritual, one supplies food to the deity Agni with four stanzas, which are equivalent to four-footed animals; and for the deity Prajāpati, who is seventeenfold, one should recite seventeen stanzas. These ritual motifs of Vedic poetry continue to be explored in the ***Upaniṣads*** with their multiple psychological, moral, and cosmological themes. One of the earliest ***Upaniṣads***, the *Bṛhadāraṇyaka* (c. 800 BCE), starts by elaborating the notion of *bandhu* between the ritual microcosmos and the macrocosmos: the dawn is the head of the sacrificial horse, the sun is its sight, and the wind is its breath. Some *Upaniṣadic* texts homologize aspects of the external world with physiological and mental processes so that the true sacrifice is that of the self. In the visions of the ***Upaniṣads***, often elaborated with cryptic idioms, the world is a densely woven web of crisscrossing threads, and an individual attains immortality by intuitively apprehending the esoteric homologies between the human realms and the cosmic realms. As Śaṃkara, Rāmānuja, Madhva, Vallabha, and others explore these cosmological-existential interrelations, a fundamental question that they grapple with is whether the connections should be understood in terms of identity or of resemblance. In particular, their exegetical and conceptual debates relate to those texts that tie together *ātman* and *brahman*, raising the question of whether this concordance is to be regarded as pointing to a union in an undifferentiated absolute (thus, Śaṃkara) or a communion in a differentiated unity (thus, Rāmānuja).

Of the two terms *ātman* and *brahman*, the latter is somewhat more straightforwardly translatable into English. As indicated in previous chapters, *brahman* refers to the divine source, basis, and telos of the world. Thus, *Taittirīya Upaniṣad* 3.1.1 declares, "That from which these beings are born; on which, once born, they live; and into which they pass upon death—seek to perceive that! That is *brahman*!"[2] Again, *Taittirīya Upaniṣad* 2.1.1 declares that those who know *brahman* attain the highest, and *brahman* is reality, consciousness, and infinite. The term *sat* ("being"), the present participle of the verbal root *as* ("to be"), is also often applied to the divine foundation of the world. In the *Chāndogya Upaniṣad*, *sat* is analogized to a lump of clay out of which different pots of clay are made, where their modifications pertain not to the underlying essence of clay but to their distinctive characteristics. Notwithstanding the different names that we give to pots of clay from different places, they are all clay at the substantial root from which they are produced, which is why to know the essence of clay is to know the constitution of each pot of clay. These projective dimensions of *sṛṣṭi* are highlighted in *Chāndogya Upaniṣad* 6.2.1–3: "In the beginning, son, this world was simply what is existent—one only, without a second. . . . And it thought to itself: 'Let me become many. Let me propagate myself.'"[3]

Across various Hindu traditions, *ātman* is the spiritual principle in the human person—namely, the conscious self that is the seat of cognition, volition, and agency. Across the ***Upaniṣads***, the terms *ātman* and *brahman* are often used in the senses of true nature, universal essence, or primary being, and they are sometimes correlated with each other. Thus, *Bṛhadāraṇyaka Upaniṣad* 3.4.2 seems to present *ātman* and *brahman* as synonymous: "Explain to me the *brahman* that is plain and not cryptic, the self (*ātman*) that is within all."[4] While *Chāndogya Upaniṣad* 6.2.1 says, "In the beginning, son, this world was simply what is existent—one only, without a second," *Aitareya Upaniṣad* 1 says, "In the beginning this world was the self (*ātman*), one alone."[5] At *Bṛhadāraṇyaka Upaniṣad* 2.5.15, *ātman* is invested with certain cosmos-ordering capacities: just as spokes are fastened to the hub and the rim of a wheel, so too in *ātman* are held together all beings, gods, worlds, and vital breaths. We are repeatedly told that *ātman* cannot be perceived in the way that mundane objects can be cognized. After indicating that *ātman* is discerned by individuals with a purified vision, *Muṇḍaka Upaniṣad* 3.1.7 declares that it "is large, heavenly, of inconceivable form; yet it appears more minute than the minute. It is farther than the farthest, yet it is here at hand; It is right here within those who see, hidden within the cave of their heart."[6]

Given the conceptual fluidity of *ātman*, the translation of *ātman* as "soul" can be somewhat misplaced in certain Vedāntic contexts, such as Advaita, that propound ontological nonduality as the message of the scriptures. To repeat some of our discussion in chapter 3, *ātman* is not a finite self (*jīva*) but ontologically nondual with *brahman*, the foundation of reality, and only seems to have become *a* discrete entity from our perspectives of worldly ignorance. Again, *brahman* is not a personal deity (*īśvara*) but the transpersonal and suprarelational absolute without any attributes. Just as the red color that is contingently acquired by a white crystal in the presence of a hibiscus flower is not intrinsic to the crystal but is a superimposition, the characterization of *brahman* as *īśvara* is not essential to *brahman* but is a superimposition through our worldly prisms. From the standpoint of *māyā*, *brahman* somehow appears to human beings—who are themselves products of *māyā*—as *īśvara* with names and forms such as Viṣṇu or Kṛṣṇa or Śiva, but *brahman* is the ineffable reality beyond all such descriptive categories. When our human conceptual frames are transcended in the state of liberation, *ātman-brahman* shines forth, and the pristine nonduality is uncovered from its worldly encrustations. The entities of the world cannot be logically encompassed with realist categories; like the snake in the rope-snake illusion, they are inscrutable because they are neither unequivocally real nor utterly unreal (*anirvacanīya*).

Theistic forms of **Vedānta** dispute these meanings of the key concepts of *ātman*, *jīva*, *īśvara*, and *brahman*. The ***Upaniṣads*** are not scholastic exercises in systematic world-building, and their verses and passages—often shaped with symbolic idioms—are amenable to multiple readings. For the likes of Śaṃkara, Rāmānuja, and Madhva, the exegetical enterprise involves the weaving together of seemingly discordant scriptural texts so as to demonstrate that they have a singular purport. If *Chāndogya Upaniṣad* 6.2.3 declares, "And it thought to itself: 'Let me become many. Let me propagate myself,'" which seems to be an affirmation of multiplicity, *Bṛhadāraṇyaka Upaniṣad* 4.4.19 is a clear denial of multiplicity: "There is no diversity here about anything." As Vedāntic exegetes interweave the concepts of unity and plurality, the gnomic phrase "You are That" (*tat tvam asi*) becomes one central textual site upon which their worldviews are developed. In a narrative in the *Chāndogya Upaniṣad* 6.12, a father instructs his son Śvetaketu about the imperceptible essence that underpins finitude by asking him to cut the seeds of a fruit from a banyan tree into progressively smaller pieces. After some iterations, the son replies that he cannot see anything, and the father declares, "That which is the subtle essence, this whole world has for its self. That is the true. That is the self. That art [you] Śvetaketu."[7] Reading the "that" as referring to *brahman* and the "you" as referring to *ātman*, the conceptual task is to explicate the grammatical link—the "are"—in such a way that worldly limitations are not ascribed to the divine ground. In quotidian statements such as "You are an Englishwoman" and "You are a translator," the predicates qualify the finite being who is addressed. However, in contexts of worship, one would not address the divine being with statements such as "You are mortal" and "You are fallible."

Again, when *Chāndogya Upaniṣad* 3.14.1 declares, "*Brahman*, you see, is this whole world,"[8] if the "is" is read as playing the predicative role that it does in statements such as "This laptop is old," worldly defects would be attributed to *brahman*. The challenge of articulating the continuity between *brahman* and the world while preserving the transcendental perfection of *brahman* can be highlighted by pointing to *Muṇḍaka Upaniṣad* 1.1.7: "As a spider spins out threads, then draws them into itself. . . . So from the imperishable all things here spring."[9] On a straightforward reading, the relation between *brahman* and the world is analogous to that between a spider and its web. The spider generates the web out of itself without relying on any extraneous implements, and likewise, *brahman* produces the world without having to work with any finite materials that are independent of *brahman*. However, while a spider is directly affected by transformations in its fragile web, *brahman* somehow remains the imperturbable center in the world-web that it has spun through its own cosmic power.

As Śaṃkara, Rāmānuja, and Vallabha grappled with the conceptual problem of navigating the continuum between *brahman* and the world while maintaining the ontological integrity of *brahman*, they worked with a causal theory that states that the effect is substantially preexistent in the cause (*satkārya-vāda*). This theory is effectively a denial of creation of something out of sheer nothingness (ex nihilo) and is motivated by the observation that in seeking yogurt, we go to milk and not to grass, wood, or sand. There is a substantial continuity between the effect and the cause, so that the effect is not a temporally new origination but a modification of the causal base. Now with respect to yogurt and milk and, in the earlier example, the web and the spider, a key dispute relates to whether we are enumerating *two* ontologically different kinds of being or whether we should ultimately speak of *one* pure being. It seems that *satkārya-vāda* can be read in two somewhat divergent ways—someone could argue that because yogurt is different from milk in terms of solidity, taste, and so on, two distinct beings should be counted, while someone else could claim that because yogurt is substantially the same stuff as milk, there is only one being here. Again, when *Muṇḍaka Upaniṣad* 2.1.1 declares, "As from a well-stoked fire sparks fly by the thousands, all looking just like it, [s]o from the imperishable issue diverse things, and into it, my friend, they return,"[10] the sparks are numerically distinct from one another and yet, as constituted of one fiery luminosity, they are also substantially continuous with the fire.

Against the backdrop of these Vedāntic inquiries are two other texts, the ***Bhagavad-gītā*** and the ***Brahma-sūtras***. The ***Bhagavad-gītā*** ("Song of the Lord"), structured as a dialogue between Kṛṣṇa and Arjuna, brings together various cosmological, ritual, and experiential threads from the ***Vedas*** and the ***Upaniṣads***. Presenting Kṛṣṇa as the cosmic Lord and Arjuna as his disciple, the text speaks of different forms of yogic discipline relating to selfless performance of action (*karma*), contemplative knowledge (*jñāna*), and devotional love (*bhakti*). Across the chapters of the ***Bhagavad-gītā***, the relation between *ātman* and Kṛṣṇa can be read through distinct lenses. On the one hand, *ātman* is said to be eternal, all-pervading, unchanging, immovable, unmanifest, unthinkable, and immutable (2.24–25). On the other hand, Kṛṣṇa declares that he is the self (*ātmā*) seated in the hearts of all creatures and is the beginning, the middle, and the end of beings (10.20) and that a part of him has become a living self (*jīva*) (15.7). Thus, if in some verses, *ātman* is depicted with divine attributes, in others, a distinction between the human person and Kṛṣṇa is highlighted. Such ontological puzzles recur through the ***Brahma-sūtras***, which are a collection of 555 cryptic aphorisms. The text starts with the statement "Then therefore the enquiry into Brahman" (1.1.1),[11] and both Śaṃkara and Rāmānuja devote several pages of commentary to the words "then" and "therefore." In his commentary, the *Śrī-bhāṣya*, Rāmānuja sketches at 1.1.1 an outline of the Advaita understanding of the self as auto-luminous consciousness, develops various critiques of Advaita standpoints, and offers his distinctive readings of some key scriptural passages.

THE STRUCTURE OF REASON AND THE SHAPE OF REALITY

For Śaṃkara, whatever is not immutable and not self-existent is ultimately unreal. Therefore, the various pots of clay in the potter's shed and, by extension, all finite entities are ultimately unreal. Thus, according to Śaṃkara, the statement "*tat tvam asi*" is to be read as indicating that the true referent of the "you," not the mutable ego but the indivisible *ātman*, is nondual with the referent of the "that"—*brahman*, which is timeless, impartite, and qualityless. One of Rāmānuja's central claims is that the term *brahman* refers not to an undifferentiated unity but to the supremely personal Lord Viṣṇu-Nārāyaṇa, who essentially has a bodily form and supports the finite world as the divine body (*śarīra*). For Rāmānuja, the world of mutability is ontologically real, and it is also existentially dependent on its transcendental source.[12] In this theological worldview, there are three distinct ontological categories: the Lord, the finite conscious self (*cit*, *ātman*), and physical objects (*acit*). While *prakṛti*-structured objects, such as the human body, are subject to mutability, the conscious selves are imperishable. The Lord transcends all imperfections of ***saṃsāra*** and is ontologically distinct from *cit* and *acit*, which remain dependent on the Lord for their proper nature, subsistence, and activity.

IS EVERY DETERMINATION A LIMITATION?

From an Advaita perspective, *brahman* is said to be completely undifferentiated on the grounds that if something has a property, it becomes limited by this property. Thus, in the statement "John is a translator," the attribute "translator" is a limiter. Since in Rāmānuja's system, the world qualifies the Lord as the Lord's *śarīra*, it would seem that because of this predicative function of the world, the imperfections of the world would mar the Lord's ontological perfection. In engaging with this conceptual problem, Rāmānuja precisely defines the word *śarīra* as any substance that a conscious being is capable of completely controlling and supporting for its own purposes and whose essential form is to be the accessory of that being.[13] This definition becomes the conceptual pivot of an analogy of being between, on the one hand, the embodied human self (namely, the psychophysiological "I") and, on the other hand, the divine self (namely, the personal Lord who is embodied in the world). As in the case of the human person—where the physical body is animated, supported, and controlled by the imperishable self (*cit*)—so too are all finite selves and physical entities (*acit*) animated, supported, and controlled by the Lord. Again, just as in a blue lotus, the blueness is possessed by the lotus, which is its substratum, the finite world of *cit* and *acit* too has a structured existence because it is possessed by the Lord, who is its immutable foundation. Thus, the Lord, who is the supreme self and the abode of illimitable qualities, is the inner controller of the world, which is the *śarīra* of the Lord.

This interplay of divine transcendence and divine immanence shapes Rāmānuja's understanding of the production of the world out of the Lord. As discussed earlier, in the cosmologies of Hindu ***darśana***, the world is without a distinct temporal origination (*anādi*), and it goes through a series of productions and dissolutions as individuals progress toward liberation (*mokṣa*). In Rāmānuja's theological system too, the world is beginningless, and it has always existed, whether in a subtle form or in a manifest form, as the body of the Lord who is the divine reality (*brahman*). The Lord is both the substantial (*upādāna-kāraṇa*) and the efficient cause (*nimitta-kāraṇa*) of the world, which is ontologically distinct from the Lord. The claim that *brahman* is the substantial cause is also a negation of the ontological dualism in **Sāṃkhya** and **Yoga *darśana***, according to which the world is manifested through the conjunction of the finite spiritual self (*puruṣa*) and nonsentient matter (*prakṛti*). One scriptural template for Rāmānuja's cosmological account is *Chāndogya Upaniṣad* 6.2.1–3, which is to be read as indicating that *brahman* is both the causal basis of the world and the efficient cause in the production of the world. There is no ontological chasm between *brahman* and the world, and the latter, following *satkārya-vāda*, is the effect of the former. However, unlike cases of worldly production, where the substantial cause (such as the clay) and the efficient cause (such as the potter) are distinct, in *brahman*, uniquely, the substantial cause is congruent with the efficient cause. Though *brahman* always has *cit* and *acit* in the divine body, these finite entities do not always exist in specific forms that can be characterized with names. In a state of cosmic dissolution, they exist in an extremely subtle condition in which they cannot be designated as different from *brahman*, and this is known as the "causal condition" of *brahman*. With the intention "May I be many!" *brahman* produces beings with name and form, and this state is known as the "effected condition" of *brahman*. In this state, the finite selves are embodied in different kinds of physical bodies in accordance with their *karmic* merits or demerits.

While for Śaṃkara, a state such as the "effected condition"—marked by temporality and divisibility—would be only conventionally real as a useful fiction, Rāmānuja views it both as ontologically real and as ontologically nondual with *brahman*. This simultaneous affirmation—*both* that the world is an ontologically real qualifier of the Lord *and* that the world is ontologically nondual with the Lord—is encapsulated in the term *viśiṣṭādvaita* (nondualism of the qualified), which is often applied to Rāmānuja's worldview. It is through the lens of *viśiṣṭādvaita* that we should read the crucial dictum "You are That"; the "you" refers to the embodied self, which, as part of the body of the Lord, is a real qualifier of the "that" that refers to the Lord. The crucial connective "are" is to be understood in terms of the notion of inseparability (*apṛthak-siddhi*), which relates two entities that are distinct and yet inseparable. This exegesis is guided by Rāmānuja's understanding of the grammatical rule of coordinate predication (*sāmānādhikaraṇya*) as the application of several words, with different grounds for their occurrence, to one object. In a Sanskrit expression in the form of coordinate predication, the attributive words are predicated of the same substance that is internally differentiated. Therefore, "You are That" intimates that *brahman* is truly differentiated with an ontologically distinct body, namely, the world.

At the same time, it is vital to outline certain disanalogies between statements such as "The Lord has a body" and "I have a laptop." While the "I" is inflected in multiple ways by the finite conditions of its corporeality—such as illness, birth, death, and ignorance—the Lord is not touched in any way by the world, which is the divine body. Moreover, the "I" derives certain worldly benefits through its embodiment, but there is no assistance that the Lord obtains or seeks to obtain from the world, which the Lord supports through the divine will. Again, the "I" is productive by relying on extraneous elements—such as canvas and paint for an artist. But the Lord, who possesses powers that cannot be fathomed by the human mind, does not depend on the world when producing it at the beginning of each world-order. Thus, invoking *Bṛhadāraṇyaka Upaniṣad* 3.7.3, "this self (*ātman*) of yours who is present within but is different from the earth, whom the earth does not know, whose body is the earth, and who controls the earth from within—he is the inner controller, the immortal,"[14] Rāmānuja writes that while the Lord supports the existence of finite entities, the Lord is not subject to them.

Although the world is the *śarīra* of the Lord, not all embodied selves are able to comprehend this truth because of their spiritual ignorance (*avidyā*) about the nature of reality. Thus, Devadatta may say, "I am just my psychophysiological body made of *prakṛti*," or, "I am not existentially dependent on the Lord." Such statements would be expressions of *avidyā* in which an individual fails to discern the spiritual reality of the finite self (*cit*) and apprehend its dependence at all times on the Lord. However, in the light of scriptures such as the ***Bhagavad-gītā***, such individuals will gradually move away from the turbulences of the world shaped by *prakṛti*, become stabilized in the self, and realize that the self and the physical body are the body of the Lord. In this way, they begin to cultivate a deep devotional love (*bhakti*) of the Lord and see the finite realm as enfolded in and pervaded by the Lord. In his commentary on the ***Bhagavad-gītā***, Rāmānuja writes that they will seek refuge in the Lord with the understanding that it is the Lord who is the supreme agent motivating their exercises of finite agency. They are graced by the Lord's assistance (*prasāda*), and as they are increasingly suffused with *bhakti*, they envision the whole world as the glorious body of the Lord. To assist individuals on their pathway to the divine root, the Lord assumes different *avatāras* (literally "descent") in the world. The transcendental form of the Lord is inaccessible to human thought, and the Lord shapes this form, without any change in the essential nature, into the likeness of different beings and descends to their worlds to grant them their desires. As the reliever of the distress of supplicants, the Lord compassionately becomes a refuge for all, and by surrendering themselves to the Lord, devotees can progress toward liberation from the sorrows of ***saṃsāra***.[15]

According to Śaṃkara, such scripturally shaped descriptions of the divine reality are associated with *avidyā* or *māyā*, and *ātman-brahman* somehow appears as a personal deity (*īśvara*) who is involved in the world. We should read these descriptions as allegorical accounts that are intended to draw individuals away from the multiplicities of the mutable world and toward nondual reality. However, Rāmānuja does not accept Śaṃkara's conceptual equivalence between reality and immutability. He argues that it is not contradictory to assert that an object that exists at one spatiotemporal location does not exist at another, and therefore, the nonpersistence of an object across these locations does not demonstrate that it is unreal.[16] The temporal world subject to mutability is ontologically real, and it is the body of *brahman* who is the personal Lord. In the footsteps of Rāmānuja, Vedānta Deśika (1268–1369) would argue that we should distinguish between destruction (*vināśa*), which means that an object that exists at one time is nonexistent at another, and negation (*bādha*), which means that an object does not exist even when it is perceived. While an effect is subject to origination and dissolution, this does not imply that *it* does not exist in its own time, and hence it cannot be regarded as illusory.[17]

Over the centuries, the *viśiṣṭādvaita* tradition has developed several lines of criticism of Śaṃkara's Advaita, whose defenders have sought to rebut the charges and clear the ground toward the realization of undifferentiated nonduality between the human self and the divine self.[18] Śaṃkara usually characterizes *avidyā* as an epistemic defect, whereas for some of his followers, it becomes the material cause (*upādāna*) from which perceptual errors or illusory cognitions (*mithyājñāna*) emerge. That is, *avidyā* is quasi-materialized by these followers into a cosmic power that is, however, characterizable neither as real nor as unreal—it is "more" real than utter nonbeing, and it is also "less" real than *brahman*. One recurring critique relates to the precise location of *avidyā*—it would seem that Advaita cannot provide a coherent account of how *brahman* is associated with *avidyā*. On the one hand, *brahman* cannot be the locus of *avidyā* because *brahman* is beyond all imperfections and also because *brahman* is propertyless and cannot be the substratum of any quality. On the other hand, *avidyā* cannot exist in the "I" because the individuated "I" arises from *avidyā*. Therefore, if *avidyā* were to reside in the "I," which itself is a product of *avidyā*, we would have the fallacy of reciprocal dependence. To the second option, Advaita exegetes may reply that the relation between *avidyā* and the "I" should be understood not as chronological but as logical. Just as in the case of a lens, neither the concave surface nor the convex surface is temporally prior to the other, but the concept of concavity is implicated in the concept of convexity, and vice versa; likewise, neither *avidyā* nor the "I" is chronologically antecedent to the other, but each conceptually implies the other. Both *avidyā* and the "I" are mistakenly superimposed on *brahman*, and with the establishment of deep insight into nonduality, they are both dissolved, leaving *brahman* in its primordial purity. In a mind-bending paradox, the "I" that overcomes the constraints of *avidyā* is itself a product of *avidyā*, just as a prisoner may use the tools present inside a jail to break down this very jail and realize that the jail was an artificial constriction in boundless space. Regarding the first option, Advaita exegetes may argue that to say that *avidyā* has *brahman* as its locus is to affirm not that *avidyā* is a real qualifier of *brahman* but that individuals mistakenly project multiplicity onto *brahman*. Just as clouds can temporarily obscure the sun without extinguishing the luminosity of the sun, human misconceptions are directed to *brahman*, but they cannot diminish the self-luminosity of *brahman* in any way.

Many of these inter-Vedāntic disputes are shaped by dense patterns of analogical reasoning. From an Advaita perspective, one may argue that even unreal entities can be the cause of real effects. For instance, individuals who mistakenly fear that they have been bitten by a poisonous snake may actually suffer death. This analogy is aimed at defending the claim that scriptural statements, though they are ultimately unreal, can produce an intuitive realization of *brahman*, the absolutely real. However, Rāmānuja, who does not accept the Advaita distinction between "only empirically real" and "ultimately real," argues in his commentary on the ***Brahma-sūtras*** that the two cases are not analogous, for the representation of the imagined poison by the individual is real, and it is this real cognition that is the cause of the individual's death. In the case of dreams, too, on waking up what is sublated is not the dream-cognition but the dream-objects. Again, if it is claimed that the web of worldly misconceptions is analogous to the spell cast over an audience by a magician, Rāmānuja notes that their conscious states of fear, love, and other emotions are real.[19]

DIFFERENCE IN THE WORLD AND DEPENDENCE ON THE DIVINE

Both Śaṃkara and Rāmānuja affirm the continuum of nonduality between *brahman* and the world, but they disagree over whether this nonduality implies that the world is ontologically real or ultimately unreal. However, Madhva rejects this motif of a continuum, and by working his way through the scriptural texts, he concludes that *brahman*, who is the absolutely independent Lord Viṣṇu, is not the substantial cause of the world but only the efficient cause. The world is ontologically dependent on the Lord, and this dependence is articulated with the metaphor of reflection: the Lord is the prototype and as the reflection that is ontologically distinct, the world remains dependent at all times on its source. Liberation from ***saṃsāra*** is effected through the reception of divine grace, which is the motivating factor in human activity including acts of worship. Crucially, according to Madhva, the dictum "You are That" should be read as "You are *not* That." Indeed, the world is shaped by five types of differences, between (1) Viṣṇu and finite selves (*jīva*), (2) Viṣṇu and material entities (*jaḍa*), (3) *jīva* and *jaḍa*, (4) one *jīva* and another *jīva*, and (5) one form of *jaḍa* and another form of *jaḍa*.[20]

The realist tenor of Madhva's thought is evident throughout his *Viṣṇu-tattva-nirṇaya* ("Ascertainment of the True Nature of Viṣṇu"). He states that scriptures that are in conflict with direct experience cannot be regarded as authoritative. Whatever is established through perception cannot be dismissed as erroneous simply through logical reasoning, and inferences that are opposed to perception and other ***pramāṇas*** are fallacious. The Advaita view of nonduality is not only opposed to the scriptures but also opposed to one's own experience, for no one experiences oneself as omniscient, omnipotent, and free from empirical defects. The differences that structure the world are known and maintained by the Lord, and hence these cannot be illusory constructs. Turning to the scriptural text "through the knowledge of one the many are known," which Advaita often invokes in defense of its thesis of ontological nonduality, Madhva offers three alternative readings: first, when the most important individual in a group is known, the others are said to be known too; second, when the cause is known, its effects too are said to be known; and third, by knowing one individual, we can know others that are similar to the first. Again, the world is sometimes compared to a dream not to suggest that it can be sublated but only to emphasize its noneternity, mutability, and dependency on the Lord.[21]

In sum, the worldviews of Śaṃkara, Rāmānuja, and Madhva are three distinctive styles of engaging with this problem: if the world emerged out of *brahman*, it would seem that *brahman* becomes implicated in mutability. For Śaṃkara, the world only seems to have emerged from *brahman*; for Rāmānuja, the world is the divine body such that worldly changes are in the body of *brahman* and not in the essential nature of *brahman*; and for Madhva, the world is utterly dependent on *brahman*, who is its supreme controller. A fourth pathway is found in the Caitanya Vaiṣṇava traditions, centered in Caitanya (1486–1534), where *brahman* is the supremely personal reality, Kṛṣṇa, who is the possessor of numerous powers (*śakti*), but the worldly modifications that are effected through these powers cannot alter the spiritual form of Kṛṣṇa. Through *jīva-śakti*, Kṛṣṇa manifests the empirical selves (*jīva*), and through *māyā-śakti*, Kṛṣṇa produces the non-sentient physical world. Crucially, *māyā-śakti* is not an illusory principle but a real cosmic power that is rooted in Kṛṣṇa. Because the finite selves, which are manifested by *jīva-śakti*, are inclined toward the world produced by *māyā-śakti*, they tend to forget that their true nature is spiritual, but through the cultivation of single-pointed devotional love (*bhakti*) they can return to Kṛṣṇa.[22]

The relation between this finite world of empirical selves and physical matter, which is dependently real, and Kṛṣṇa, who is independently real, is that of difference and nondifference (*bhedābheda*), and this relation is suprarational and inconceivable (*acintya*). That is, questions such as how changes brought about by the divine powers do not effect a change in Kṛṣṇa in whom they are located, how the indivisible Kṛṣṇa can generate a multiplicity of ontologically real finite selves, and so on cannot be given a rational explication. As the commentator Jīva Gosvāmin (1513–98) notes in his *Tattva-sandarbha*, the finite self (*jīva*) is a portion (*aṃśa*) of *brahman* and is manifested by one of the inconceivable powers of *brahman*. The text "You are That" has to be understood as teaching oneness between the self and *brahman*, and this oneness is an identity of form (*samānākāratā*) because the self shares *brahman*'s conscious nature. Jīva develops an involved critique of a standard Advaita move to explain the appearance of multiplicity through the motif of the reflection of the one sun in contingent adjuncts such as the water contained in different pots. Jīva argues that if these limiting adjuncts are objectively real (*vāstava*) and not the product of ignorance, *brahman* cannot be subject to delimitation by them because that which is attributeless, all-pervading, and indivisible cannot have any reflection. But if these limiting adjuncts are unreal, the delimitation and the reflection that they supposedly effect must also be unreal, and these processes cannot take place.[23]

The cosmic vision of Vallabha (1479–1531) resonates in certain respects with that of the Caitanya traditions. Here too, *brahman* is the Lord Kṛṣṇa who is reality (*sat*), consciousness (*cit*), and bliss (*ānanda*) and is self-dependent and devoid of all empirical defects. This worldview is known as *śuddhādvaita*, or "pure nondualism," where the Lord is nondifferent from a world that is ontologically real.[24] Just as gold, without suffering any intrinsic change, becomes fashioned into different types of ornaments, so too the immutable Lord, without undergoing any essential transformation, manifests the finite selves (*jīva*) and the physical world. Only *sat* of Kṛṣṇa is expressed in the physical world, but *cit* and *ānanda* are concealed here, and in the finite self both *sat* and *cit* are manifested, but *ānanda* is concealed. According to Vallabha, the selves (*jīva*) enjoyed, before their manifestation on the empirical plane, the six attributes of Kṛṣṇa—namely, majesty, strength, fame, fortune, knowledge, and freedom from attachment. When Kṛṣṇa manifests the *jīvas* through his cosmic productivity (*līlā*), these attributes become concealed in the *jīvas*, which are subject to ignorance (*avidyā*). Because of this ignorance, the *jīva* forgets that its true nature is as a part of Kṛṣṇa and its fulfilment lies in rendering devotional service (*sevā*) to Kṛṣṇa.

While according to Vallabha, only nondifference between *brahman* and the world is real, according to Nimbārka, both difference and nondifference are real.[25] To complicate the continuum even further, Nimbārka takes the difference as well as the nondifference to be equally real and equally natural (*svābhāvika*), but according to Bhāskara (c. 900 CE), the difference and the nondifference are both real, but the difference is conditioned (*aupādhika*), and only the nondifference is natural. The same sea appears different with reference to the waves, which are the manifestations of its own powers, and the same fire appears different in its powers of burning and illumination. There is a formless causal state of *brahman* without any internal differences, and this becomes the effected state of *brahman* that has a real form and is both different and nondifferent from the world. The self is different and nondifferent from *brahman* only in the state of worldly reincarnations, and not when it is liberated. According to Nimbārka, however, there is no such purely nondifferent form of *brahman* who always has differences. The self is always different and nondifferent from *brahman*. The commentator Śrīnivāsa notes that there is nondifference between the finite self, which is a part (*aṃśa*) of *brahman*, and *brahman*, for the finite self has no existence and activity apart from *brahman*, and also difference, because the finite self possesses distinctive qualities such as ignorance that do not characterize *brahman*.[26]

For all these Vedāntic systems, the goal of human existence is to return to *brahman* through the multiple vales of ***saṃsāra*** across numerous reincarnations. On the basis of a foundational scriptural text, the *Bhāgavata-purāṇa* (c. 1000 CE), the Caitanya and the Vallabha traditions especially characterize these routes with aesthetic idioms, subjectivities, and experiences. In the tenth book of this text, we read about the cowherd women (*gopīs*) who leave behind their worldly concerns to dance with Kṛṣṇa, and they are presented as the exemplary devotees. Exegetes in the Caitanya tradition read this scriptural narrative as a window into the eternal dance between Kṛṣṇa and the powers, who are manifested on earth as the *gopīs*. Human beings too should emulate the supreme *bhakti* of these women who loved Kṛṣṇa selflessly and spontaneously without seeking anything in return. On the journey toward this spiritual summit of unalloyed love that is devoid of all egocentric concerns (*prema*), their lives would be structured by the cultivation of *vaidhi-bhakti* and *rāgānuga-bhakti*. The former is developed by following specific scriptural injunctions such as resorting to a spiritual guide, following the ways of saintly people, renunciating worldly enjoyment for the sake of Kṛṣṇa, residing in places of pilgrimage, going round an image of Kṛṣṇa, and so on. It is a stepping stone to the latter, which is a spontaneous attraction and wholehearted attachment to Kṛṣṇa and involves emulating the actions and the feelings of Kṛṣṇa's attendants such as the *gopīs*. For the cultivation of this *rāgānuga-bhakti*, a devotee vicariously participates in the sentiment of a particular attendant of Kṛṣṇa, by adopting the dress and the habit of that dear one. By constantly keeping in mind the *līlā* between Kṛṣṇa and the attendants, the devotee constructs oneself as the beloved of Kṛṣṇa and experiences the sentiments of these attendants for Kṛṣṇa. The devotee has to view the whole world as a dynamic stage on which the chief hero (*nāyaka*) is Kṛṣṇa, and they have to play out their parts by relating themselves to Kṛṣṇa. In this way, the devotee actively participates in the dramatic worlds of Kṛṣṇa and moves from their corporeal identity to their true body (*siddha-rūpa*), which is similar to the bodies of the companions of Kṛṣṇa. The *siddha-rūpa* is the meditative body that the practitioner inhabits while participating in the *līlā*, and it is also the eternal spiritual body that they will possess in the hereafter.[27]

This discipline of reenacting the supreme love (*prema*) of the cowherd women is encased in the idioms of aesthetic enjoyment (*rasa*). The abiding emotions (*sthāyī-bhāva*), according to the poetics of *rasa*, lie dormant in the mind as subliminal impressions, and these can be activated through certain types of stimuli such as the characters in a play, the words and the gestures of the characters, and the settings of the play. The *Nāṭya-śāstra* mentions eight abiding emotions: *rati* (love), *hāsya* (gaiety), *śoka* (pathos), *krodha* (anger), *utsāha* (enthusiasm), *bhaya* (fear), *jugupsā* (disgust), and *vismaya* (astonishment). To these correspond eight *rasas*: *śṛṅgāra* (erotic), *hāsya* (comic), *karuṇa* (pathetic), *raudra* (furious), *vīra* (heroic), *bhayānaka* (terrible), *bībhatsa* (disgust), and *adbhuta* (marvelous). According to the template of these aesthetic concepts developed by Rūpa Gosvāmin (1489–1564) and Jīva Gosvāmin, the abiding mood of love (*rati*) for Kṛṣṇa is transformed into the *rasa* of devotion (*bhakti*) through the appropriate excitants, auxiliaries, and so on. This *bhakti-rasa* appears as five different kinds—*śānta*, *dāsya*, *sakhya*, *vātsalya*, and *mādhurya*. The first is the mental equipoise that results from an identification with the transpersonal *brahman*, which, according to the Caitanya Vaiṣṇava traditions, is not the ultimate reality but a partial manifestation of Kṛṣṇa. There is an element of *bhakti* here, though it is inferior to the supreme *bhakti* because it does not involve any personal relationship between the devotee and the Lord. The second is the service of the devotees who view Kṛṣṇa as their eternal master and themselves as his servitors. The third is the loving devotion of individuals who regard Kṛṣṇa as their friend and their equal, and the fourth is the parental concern that a devotee exercises toward the infant Kṛṣṇa. The highest state of *mādhurya-bhakti* is the completely unalloyed and self-effacing love of the *gopīs* for Kṛṣṇa.

According to Rūpa, some of the characteristics of this supreme *bhakti* are the capacity to remove suffering, which may be due to sin (*pāpa*), the seed of sin, or ignorance (*avidyā*); the capacity to bestow auspiciousness; and the capacity to attract Kṛṣṇa.[28] Worldly selves who are currently overpowered by *māyā-śakti* would have to steadily progress toward this spontaneous love of Kṛṣṇa, who is the ideal connoisseur of *rasa* and the transcendental enjoyer of relish. Unlike human beings who can enjoy *rasa* only infrequently, Kṛṣṇa's life is one of infinite bliss and ultimate beauty. Caitanya Vaiṣṇava commentators emphasize the superiority of devotees who seek to realize this sweetness (*mādhurya*) of Kṛṣṇa to those who meditate on Kṛṣṇa's majesty (*aiśvarya*). The emotional attachment of the *gopīs* is therefore superior to that of the inhabitants of planes where only Kṛṣṇa's majesty is manifested.

Some of these motifs are present in the worldview of Vallabha too. Vallabha argues that the reason why the Lord Kṛṣṇa graciously engages in *līlā* with the cowherd women is because they are his friends.[29] He puts forward constant devotional service (*sevā*) of the Lord as the means through which individuals can overcome the pride that separates them from their Lord. A vital theme in the devotional life of the Vallabha tradition is the *puṣṭi* type of devotion. The commentator Bālakṛṣṇa defines *puṣṭi* as devotion that is caused by the special grace of the Lord and is characterized by the absence of desire for any reward other than the Lord.[30] He distinguishes between four types of *puṣṭi* and states that those who cultivate the fourth type remain engaged, with deep love, in acts such as serving the Lord, singing the glories of the Lord, and so on. In short, human subjectivities are transformed by the grace of Kṛṣṇa, and Kṛṣṇa becomes progressively expressed in the lives of the devotees. When human emotions are reoriented toward Kṛṣṇa as their ultimate object, and the senses are purified through service to Kṛṣṇa, deep levels of intimacy would develop between the devotees and Kṛṣṇa.

These Kṛṣṇa-shaped motifs relating to the dynamism of the deity are partly reflected in **Kashmiri Śaivism**, whose ontology is more aligned in some respects with the nondualism of Advaita. The term "**Kashmiri Śaivism**" refers to three traditions—Trika, Spanda, and Pratyabhijñā. Although these are distinct in some aspects, important figures such as Abhinavagupta (c. 1000 CE) wrote commentarial texts on all of them and synthesized diverse aspects of Tantric symbolisms and practices. In these traditions of nondual Śaivism—as developed by Somānanda (c. 900 CE), Utpaladeva (c. 950 CE), and others—the divine reality and the world are ontologically not-distinct, and the world is a manifestation of universal and dynamic consciousness (*saṃvit*). This divine principle is the union of Śiva and Śiva's cosmic energy (namely, Śakti), and it projects the world of finite selves and material objects, which do not exist independently of the divine root. The divine foundation is not utterly immutable, as is the case in Advaita, but a dynamic triad of pure awareness, action, and will, and it manifests the finite subjects and the finite objects of everyday experience. The aim of the initiate is to ascend from one's individualized consciousness to the supreme consciousness, understanding that a sense of duality pertains only to the lowest degree of the self-expression of *saṃvit*. This process is structured by the purification of the body through the imposition of mantras, inner worship through a visualization of Śiva's presence, and external worship with a symbolic diagram. Through these ritual practices, the initiate would realize their identity with pure consciousness, which consists of an oscillation (*spandana*) or interplay of two inseparable moments: awareness of objects (*prakāśa*), which corresponds to Śiva, and reflexive awareness (*vimarśa*) of oneself as an experiential subject, which corresponds to Śakti. Here *prakāśa* is the universal light that is the ground of all beings and the cause of their manifestation, and *vimarśa* is the essential nature of this light that is always aware of its manifestations. Thus, when I perceive a blue pot, even if I am not consciously articulating the thought "Here I am looking at an antique in a museum," I am implicitly aware of *I* observing *this*.

Broadly allied to the Trika cosmos are forms of ritual that are structured by a homology between human cognition and divine creativity. Just as an ordinary cognitive state reaches out to an object, becomes attentively focused on it, and draws it into oneself in self-awareness, the divine principle generates the world, preserves it, and withdraws it into the transcendental root. In a meditative contemplation of divine productivity and its microcosmic instantiation, an individual ascends to the point where all distinctions between subject and object have dissolved. This ascent takes place from within the cosmos, which is a "contraction" or solidification of the supreme consciousness in graded levels, such that the solidification is denser in each succeeding level. The human body, which is such a contraction, implicitly contains the universe and is nondual with Śiva of whom it is a projection. An individual's experience is shaped by their location at a particular level; an unenlightened individual will identify themselves exhaustively with their *karma*-shaped body, and liberation is the purificatory "expansion" of this limited perspective to the horizon of nonduality. Through the meditative worship of various female deities, an individual breaks out of the bonds of the "I" with the recognition (*pratyabhijñā*) that one is, in truth, not-distinct from unbounded consciousness by saying, "I am Śiva and the world is my self-expression." This is the perfect "I-ness" (*pūrṇāhaṃtā*) that the practitioner attains through realizing nonduality with Śiva, and in this transfigured vision, the world is seen to be a dynamic manifestation of the supreme freedom (*svātantrya*) of Śiva.[31]

COGNITIONS IN TIME AND THE FORMS OF CONSCIOUSNESS

In sum, across these systems of ***darśana***, the self is the site of the return to the divine root. A key question is whether the self is intrinsically conscious, and their philosophers minutely examine the structure of a cognitive episode. To take a specific example, when I look in the direction of the table at the other end of the room, I am aware *that* there is a vase, but am I also aware *that* I am aware that there is a vase? To rephrase: is every event of awareness accompanied by self-awareness? According to defenders of self-illumination or reflexivism (*sva-prakāśa*), there is a deep form of self-awareness that is nondyadic in the sense that it is beyond the subject-and-object structure of everyday awareness. They claim that this dimension of depth supports my intuitive feel that it is *I* who is going through my everyday business in my nonreflective moments. According to defenders of other-illumination or reflectionism (*para-prakāśa*), however, the luminosity of consciousness is to be understood in terms of its ability to illuminate, without a concomitant self-awareness, specific objects such as a vase on the table.

CAN I BE TRUE TO MY OWN SELF?

An analysis of our everyday perceptual experiences would seem to suggest that both reflectionists and reflexivists have captured some of their key dimensions. When Devadatta is walking through a marketplace and trying to decide which pots to buy, he is not consciously thinking, "Here I am walking out from this shop; now I am walking toward the next shop." And yet Devadatta is not an automaton—he has a prereflective awareness of moving about in the marketplace, and it is such a nonthematized awareness that marks the distinction between Devadatta and nonsentient objects such as pots. Again, a cognitive state such as a toothache seems to be self-intimating in the sense that it announces itself without having to depend on a distinct cognitive state for its illumination. In our everyday lives, we usually go through the world in the manner of Devadatta—for instance, when we go shopping for pots, the content of our cognitive state is "this is a pot" and not "*I* see a pot." If Devadatta has been driving home from his office for twenty years on a specific route, he is able to easily navigate the different roads without an introspective awareness that it is *he* is who is sitting in the driver's seat. In other words, there is a distinction between being aware of a pot without explicit self-awareness and being aware of one's awareness of the pot.

According to defenders of reflectionism such as the **Nyāya** philosophers, a cognitive state (C) is directed toward objects such as a tree, and this state is revealed by a distinct metacognition (C*) or apperception (*anu-vyavasāya*). When I look at the tree, the content of the cognitive state is "a tree"—I am aware of its height, structure, and so on. This cognition is subsequently apperceived by C* with the content "I perceive a tree." However, there may be cases where a C is not followed by a C*: for instance, when I am looking at a painting on the wall, my attention may be abruptly drawn away by a loud noise in the corridor. In contrast, Advaita defends a form of reflexivism where the luminosity of consciousness is similar to the radiance of a glowing lamp, which does not need any extraneous light to become illuminated. Consciousness is self-revealing in the sense that it reveals itself in the process of revealing the painting. Since Advaita views *ātman* as nondual with the immutable *brahman*, here *ātman* is to be understood not as the "I" but as the self-identical and self-luminous witness consciousness (*sākṣin*) that remains still while transient cognitions appear and pass away. Advaita claims that changes of or in consciousness can be perceived only by something that is not itself subject to change—that is, by something that stands as their witness through the triad of waking, dream, and deep sleep. Therefore, in a perceptual experience, not only does the subject apprehend the object, but also this apprehension is simultaneous with the apprehension of the apprehension. That is, the perceptual judgment "This is a table," which is due to the cognitive apparatus, is accompanied by the knowledge *that* I know that this is a table, and this knowledge is due to the *sākṣin* that apprehends the cognitive state. In short, consciousness illuminates its objects and also itself, and its ability to illuminate objects is grounded in its ability to illuminate itself. This understanding of the self-luminosity of *ātman* shapes Advaita's analysis of the state of dreamless sleep. When an individual wakes up and reports that they were earlier not conscious of anything, it is in the light of the *sākṣin* that they say, "I did not know myself then." The immediate referent of the "I" cannot be *ātman* because the same entity cannot be the conscious subject and remain unaware of itself; therefore, the referent is the empirical self that was earlier quiescent. That is, what is denied is the presence of a cognized object in that state but not the pure seeing itself, which is the *sākṣin*.

For Rāmānuja, the finite self (*ātman*) is of the form of consciousness, and also, consciousness is a quality of the finite self. The relation between the *ātman* and awareness can be analogized to the light of a lamp. While the lamp illuminates other objects, it is also self-luminous, and its luminosity is not derived from anything external to its flame. Now the material of the flame (*tejas*) can be regarded both as a substance and as a quality, in the form of the flame and its light respectively, and an analogous relation holds between consciousness and its substratum, the conscious subject. Just as *tejas* is self-luminous and does not depend on an external source of light in illuminating itself, the *ātman* has consciousness as its essential nature. Again, just as light is a quality of *tejas*, acts of consciousness are the qualities of the finite self, which is their substratum. In this form of reflexivism too, the *ātman* is always present to itself and does not require a subsequent awareness to apprehend itself as the conscious self. In the statement "I did not know myself then," the referent of the "I" is indeed the *ātman*, which is only indistinctly aware of itself in the state of dreamless sleep, and the statement should be read as "I did not know myself as qualified by certain characteristics in that state." Thus, the ontological divergences across the ***darśana*** of Śaṃkara and Rāmānuja are reflected in their divergent accounts of the constitution of our conscious lives.

The two groups of **Mīmāṃsā** philosophers, the followers of Prabhākara and of Kumārila, hold differing views on this topic. The former argue that in a cognitive event, all three—the cognizer, the tree, and the cognition—are revealed together. That is, a cognitive event reveals not only the tree but also itself and the cognizer. The latter argue that a cognition cannot be its own object and a cognitive process should be analyzed in this way: when a tree is cognized, the tree becomes characterized by the property of being cognized, and on the basis of this property, it is inferred that there is cognition of the tree. That is, I become aware of perceiving the tree through a metacognition of the "cognized-ness" of the tree. Here the metacognition is directed toward the tree, while for **Nyāya** philosophers it is directed toward the perceptual cognition of the tree. They argue that cognitions are formless (*nirākāra*) and refer to objects that lie outside them. A diametrically opposed view is held by some schools of Buddhism according to which cognition does not apprehend an object directly but through the intermediary of an aspect or form (*ākāra*) that is an imprint on the mind of the object. The blue color of the vase that I observe is a specific *ākāra* that is a feature of awareness; crucially, awareness takes on this *ākāra* and also reveals it. Therefore, every moment of awareness is intrinsically reflexive (*svasaṃvedana*) and does not need a distinct awareness to reveal it. More concretely, awareness has an objective aspect, which is the form that the mental state assumes, and a subjective aspect, which is the experience of the objective aspect. A mental state consists of both these aspects—one world-directed and the other self-directed—so that it is reflexively aware of itself in being aware of an object. In other words, self-cognition is not a higher-order cognition but an intrinsic feature of a cognitive event: it is the basic awareness of the subjective dimension and the objective dimension of this event.

A related question is whether in a cognitive event C, the awareness of the truth of C is intrinsic (*svataḥ*) to C or extrinsic to C (*parataḥ*). According to **Mīmāṃsā**, when C is cognized, it is also cognized as true, and its falsity may be ascertained through unsuccessful activity. According to Kumārila, the capacity of being truth-conducive is intrinsic to a cognition and is not derived from extraneous reasons. We do not usually go around checking if our first-order cognitions are reliable by depending on a second-order cognition that indicates that the object of perception has pragmatic efficacy. This reliability is obtained through the cognition, and unless some overriding cognition presents itself, the initial cognition is taken to be veridical. In other words, they hold the view that truth is intrinsic to a cognition and falsity is extrinsic to it. According to **Nyāya**, as indicated in chapter 2, we ascertain whether a cognition is true or false through successful or unsuccessful activity that is based on it. In other words, **Nyāya** philosophers hold the view that both truth and falsity are extrinsic to a cognition. Whether or not a particular cognition is truth-targeted has to be methodically established through careful inquiry. To take an example from a specialized field, if little Nora wishes to become a gemologist, she has to be apprenticed to a jeweler who will teach her that the property of having a rainbowy gleam is what marks out a ruby as genuine. Subsequently, she affirms a natural relation between "rainbowy shine" and "a genuine ruby" by discerning the presence of this property in many genuine rubies and its absence in many fake rubies and also ruling out any background conditions (*upādhi*).

For all these Hindu worldviews, getting the right answer is crucial not only for everyday cognitive transactions but also for learning to become properly related to fellow human beings, the world at large, and the foundations of reality. If Devadatta thinks of himself entirely as a psychophysiological entity, it may be the case that he would associate the goal of human existence with the accumulation of material objects in a self-aggrandizing manner, without any concern for the interests of his neighbors. In contrast, if Devadatta gradually becomes recentered on a horizon of relationality, it may be the case that he would learn to extend his moral vision to include the concerns of others and even undertake the arduous discipline of seeing one's own self as densely continuous with the self of another.

5

Multiple Modes of Morality

Grieving for a loved one who has recently passed away, on a gray winter evening, you walk a few feet into the sea. The water is cold, but even its iciness cannot touch your numb soul. The frayed threads of your existence have unraveled, and now they lie dispersed across the sea. Everywhere you look, you see vastness, but it is only the hollow vastness of a vacuity. Your mind is racing in a hundred different directions that seem to be as disconnected as the waves lashing at your feet. Perhaps Macbeth was right: life is a narrative full of sound and fury, signifying nothing. Then you remember the elderly Hindu guru whom you had once met in Brighton on a bright spring morning. She had peered into your eyes and, with an enigmatic smile, said to you softly, "The world is woven on the warp and weft of *dharma*. When *dharma* is preserved, *dharma* will preserve you. This whole world is the battlefield of *dharma*—shake off your despondency and be victorious!"

A leitmotif running through roughly two millennia of Hindu ***darśana*** is that an integral dimension of the recovery of *ātman*—irrespective of how its ontological status is understood—is the cultivation of the discipline of seeing oneself as another. The fundamental concept is *dharma*, which is a polyvalent term encompassing connotations such as order, basis, stability, essential nature, duty, and proper way of living. In short, *dharma* is the unshakeable center that holds things together and is the cement of the world. If fire naturally rises upward and unsupported stones naturally fall downward, such movements are encoded in their *dharma*, and if human beings should cultivate self-control, truthfulness, benevolence, and altruism, such self-cultivation is a constitutive element of their *dharma* in the world.

IS MORALITY A SUBJECTIVE INCLINATION OR AN OBJECTIVE ORDER?

First enunciated in the *Ṛg Veda* (c. 1500 BCE), the theme of *dharma* is reworked across the multiple ***Upaniṣads***, the *Manusmṛti* (c. 200 CE), the ***Bhagavad-gītā***, the *Rāmāyaṇa* (c. 400 CE), the *Mahābhārata* (c. 400 CE), and other texts. As discussed in the previous chapter, we read in the *Ṛg Veda* that the symbiotic synergies across the universe are dynamic expressions of the order-establishing ritual sacrifice (*yajña*) of a cosmic person (*puruṣa*). This cosmogonic instrument has generated structure-sustaining *dharma* across multiple ritual, ethical, and social domains. The worldly *dharma* is not an already established fact but is a constantly repeated performance. Thus, the *Jaiminīya Brāhmaṇa* narrates that a battle went on for years between Prajāpati, the lord of all finite beings, and Mṛtyu, death personified, since both were equally strong, and neither could overcome the other. Finally, Prajāpati had a vision of the symbolic connections between meters, melodies, and verses, and with this knowledge-shaped power, he defeated Mṛtyu. In other words, the Vedic cosmos is poised on a knife-edge balance between life and death, order and chaos, and good and evil. It is the dynamism of the ritual that injects the rejuvenating power of being into the universe's structures threatened with dissolution. In some strata of the ***Upaniṣads***, this cosmos is reenvisioned allegorically so that the sacrifice is understood, through a psycho-cosmic mapping, not as an external ritual performed with physical implements but as an interiorized offering of the individual's cognitions, breaths, and volitions into the purgative "fires" of self-inquiry.

This vision of cosmos-structuring *dharma* is codified by the male Brahmin composers of the *dharma*-treatises such as the *Manusmṛti*, and their hierarchical classifications often reflect their own socio-elitist and androcentric presuppositions. In these voluminous compositions, the ***Vedas*** are presented as the foundation of the socio-moral duties (*dharma*) of individuals that are layered on hierarchically structured planes of gender and caste (*varṇa*). For instance, the *dharma* of a woman, of a man from the priestly (*brāhmaṇa*) or the servant (*śūdra*) caste, of a warrior in the stage of life (*āśrama*) of a student, and so on are meticulously outlined in this vision of an ideal *dharmic* polity. In these texts, *dharma* is the ethno-cultural demarcator of the way of life of a particular group of people who are descended from the primordial *puruṣa* and whose social systems are to be defended against foreigners (*mleccha*). Their dwelling is the sacred ground where *dharma* is to be cultivated with the refined language—namely, Sanskrit—and they must avoid transactions with *mlecchas* (*Manusmṛti* 1.31; 1.87; 2:17–24; 10:44–45; *Vasiṣṭha Dharmasūtra* 6.41).

This ecosystem of *dharma* structured by *varṇa* and *āśrama* is said to be eternally etched on the canvas of reality—thus, the proper fulfilment of worldly *dharma* expresses, and also stabilizes, the cosmological *dharma*. According to this socio-cosmic mapping, individuals maintain *dharma* by discharging their own *dharma*-shaped obligations. Thus, in the ***Bhagavad-gītā***, when Arjuna refuses to participate in a battle against his kinsmen, Kṛṣṇa sets out various reasons why Arjuna should go forward into the heat and dust of this worldly struggle. One of the directly *dharma*-rooted reasons is that Arjuna is a warrior (*kṣatriya*), and for him, there is no *dharma* that is higher than fighting in a righteous battle (2.31). The implication is that if Arjuna, as a member of the *varṇa* of warriors, were not to fulfil his this-worldly *dharmic* responsibilities of protecting the cosmological *dharmic* order, the fabrics of reality would gradually unravel, and chaos would ensue on diverse ontological, moral, and social planes.

Across the multiple tapestries of Vedāntic Hindu cosmologies, these exhortations to enact a world-structuring *dharma* exist in a somewhat uneasy tension with the quest of a world-transcending sublation of finitude. The milieus of *dharma*, which give structure to worldly living, are immersed in impermanence, divisibility, and suffering, while the *ātman* is the unshakeable citadel of permanence, indivisibility, and bliss. A crucial theme that Śaṃkara, Rāmānuja, Madhva, and others develop is the dialectic between the embodied self currently embedded in *dharmic* systems and *brahman* beyond all finitude. In some contexts, this relation is expressed in terms of the four goals of human life (*puruṣārtha*): the "this-worldly" triad of *dharma*, *artha* (material prosperity), and *kāma* (pleasure) and the fourth "trans-worldly" destination of liberation (*mokṣa*). One great debate across Vedāntic spaces is over whether the emphasis should be placed on the continuities or on the *dis*continuities across the four *puruṣārtha*. For the exegetes of Advaita, the triad pertains to existential dimensions that are, in the ultimate analysis, illusory, whereas for exegetes from theistic standpoints, these dimensions are ontologically real. Their distinctive articulations of the significance of social engagement in the here and now embody their divergent visions of reality.

The dialectic can be outlined as follows:

As embodied self, *ātman* is hierarchically inscribed into *dharmic* spaces of *varṇa* and *āśrama*, where the *dharmic* obligation of the *śūdra* lower castes is to serve others, and the *strī-dharma* of women is to be dutiful to their menfolk. In this "vision of austerity" (VAU) configured by male priests, structure is to be maintained in a precarious world that is poised on the dynamic borderlines where the antagonistic forces of *dharma* and anti*dharma* (*adharma*) collide.

As essential self, *ātman* is limitlessly free in spiritual spaces without hierarchical constraints. In this state of liberation, where *ātman* recovers its true identity, there are no *dharma*-structured differentiations relating to gender, caste, region, or ethnicity. In this "vision of abundance" (VAB), the world is pervaded by a spiritual egalitarianism encompassing all beings. On this horizon of transcendental peace, the universal *dharma* cannot be refracted differentially with respect to different groups of human beings.

Throughout the centuries, Hindu living has been shaped by the copresence of VAU and VAB. In some milieus, we find a "gradualist" understanding of their relation—if individuals fulfil their VAU-structured duties (*sva-dharma*) in the present lifetime, they will ascend, across multiple reincarnations, to the realization of the universal sameness of VAB-rooted equalities. This realization presupposes a certain form of spiritual preparedness that is to be cultivated from within multiple social domains marked by difference. In some other milieus, however, we find a more "immediatist" conceptualization. Individuals must concretize VAB-inspired cosmologies in the here and now and also override, if necessary, any VAU-informed constraints. Here the motif is "Become what you are"; if you *are* the spiritual self, which is not marked by any social constraints, *become* an enactor of this transcendental sameness in everyday life in this world.

In milieus shaped by this dialectic, human flourishing is concurrent with the cultivation of certain values, excellences, and virtues that are prescribed by the traditional lineages (*sampradāya*) of Vedāntic exegetical interpretations and also encoded in moral exemplars from epic narratives such as the *Mahābhārata* and the *Rāmāyaṇa*. The ***Bhagavad-gītā*** directs individuals to develop unswerving devotion, which is associated with virtues such as humility, nonviolence, patience, constancy, self-restraint, and the absence of egoism (13.8–12). A focused set of virtues (*dharma*) appears in Vātsyāyana's commentary on *Nyāya-sūtra* 1.1.2, which states that the virtues of the body are charity (*dāna*), protection of others, and service (*paricaraṇa*) to others; the virtues of speech are truthfulness, beneficial words, gentle speech, and Vedic study; and the virtues of the mind are kindness, indifference to material gain, and piety (*śraddhā*).[1] For these worldviews, the ***Vedas*** are central to moral deliberation because they provide the normative criteria for reasoning about what is to be done. In sociocultural contexts where sacrificial ritualism was denounced by Buddhists and others, defenders of Vedic visions routinely claimed that ritual killing is, in fact, not violence, because it has Vedic sanction. As *Manusmṛti* 12.106 states, only they who use forms of reasoning (*tarka*) that do not contradict the teachings of the ***Vedas*** know *dharma*.[2] More expansively, *Manusmṛti* 2.12 describes the fourfold mark of *dharma* as the ***Veda***, the scriptural texts attributed to specific authors (*smṛti*), the conduct of the good, and what is dear to oneself. Moreover, *Manusmṛti* 2.14 notes that when there are two contradictory statements on a topic, both are *dharmic* according to *smṛti*, because the wise have pronounced both of them to constitute *dharma*.[3]

In short, the question "What is my *dharma*?" does not have a straightforward answer. In one immediate sense, the answer is *sva-dharma* or one's own *dharma*, such as the *dharma* of Arjuna, a member of the warrior *varṇa*, which is to fight in a righteous battle. However, in addition to the particularized *dharma* that applies to individuals of each *varṇa*, texts such as *Manusmṛti* 10.63 point to the generalized *dharma* that applies to every *varṇa*: the virtues of nonviolence (*ahiṃsā*), truthfulness, not stealing, purity, and mastery of the senses. To complicate matters further, the *Mahābhārata* is filled with instances of moral conflicts where *dharma*-shaped imperatives collide at crucial existential junctures. The ***Bhagavad-gītā***, included as part of the epic, starts with a famous crisis generated by conflicting *dharmic* demands—an implication of the *sva-dharma* of Arjuna is that he has to slay his own kinsmen. Again, in the eighth book of the *Mahābhārata*, we encounter a form of this dilemma: "You are a truth-telling person. Devadatta is being chased by a murderer, and he rushes past you while you are sitting under a tree and contemplating the mysteries of human existence. Devadatta implores you, 'Please don't tell anyone that I am going toward the Vindhya mountains.' Soon the murderer arrives and asks you, 'Did you see a man go this way?' You could tell a lie and send the murderer in the direction of the eastern sea, or you could speak the truth and possibly bring about the death of Devadatta." One way to read such narratives that are built into the framework of the *Mahābhārata* is as a reminder that even as we may seek to encode *dharma* into a series of dos and don'ts, no absolute code can be laid down that will resolve every existential ambiguity, contradiction, and dilemma. In this sense, living one's life, and trying to live it well, is an art involving ongoing negotiation and not an algorithm yielding a straightforward resolution.

RETURNING TO THE CENTER OF REALITY

Some of these complexities are reflected in Śaṃkara's Advaita where VAU-*dharma* struggles to rise to the equalizing heights of VAB-*dharma*. Many premodern Advaita cosmologies affirm that those who see difference in this world remain entangled in the round of reincarnation; at the same time, they declare that women and groups such as *śūdras* shall not access the Vedic scriptures through which liberation is possible. This simultaneous affirmation of transcendental equality and sociological hierarchy generates a volatile nexus across multiple Hindu cultural systems. A galaxy of Hindu thinkers and social activists such as Swami Vivekananda, Mahatma Gandhi, and Sarvepalli Radhakrishnan radicalized certain scriptural worldviews and claimed that the cultivation of other-regarding virtues directed toward socioeconomic reconstruction on the one hand and the quest for liberation from the world on the other hand are not intrinsically opposed but are two dialectically interrelated moments.

On their modernist trajectories, they skillfully reworked the notion of liberation in the state of embodiment (*jīvanmukti*) as articulated in some traditional templates. According to Advaita, if the *ātman* is always liberated in its transcendental core, and the perception that *ātman* is afflicted is a misconception from *māyā*-shaped perspectives, it is possible for a sage to shake off this sense of egocentric individuation in the here and now and become a living embodiment of the universality of the *ātman*. A good source of these motifs is the *Viveka-cūḍāmaṇi*, which is sometimes attributed to Śaṃkara. Worldly bondage is not located in structures of reality and when the mind overcomes its false sense of separation from the world, the indivisible *ātman* becomes expressed. Therefore, an aspirant for liberation should diligently cleanse the mind by moving away from enmeshment in sensual pleasures and by exercising careful discrimination between what is self and what is not-self. In this way, one develops the understanding that worldly distinctions relating to caste (*jāti*) are false superimpositions on the transcendental purity of the *ātman*, which stands beyond their limitations. Through yogic discipline, one will continue to focus the mind on *brahman*, the limiting adjunct of the "I" fades away, and one becomes established in *brahman*. They who have become stabilized in the bliss of *brahman* are not touched by social markers, and worldly trials and tribulations do not perturb them. Such an individual is the *jīvanmukta*, who looks everywhere with an eye of equality in a world that is full of elements with merits and demerits. They delight in the *ātman* and maintain an attitude of equanimity through pleasant and painful experiences. They are magnanimous individuals who are ever doing good to others, and having crossed the frightful ocean of birth and death, they help others do the same, without any self-centered motive. Their very nature is to seek, of their own accord, to remove the weariness of other people, just as the moon cools the earth that is parched by the flaming rays of the sun.[4]

Even as some strands of Advaita emphasize yogic forms of meditative exercise, Śaṃkara and his disciple Sureśvara are insistent that such activities should be regarded not as possessing the causal power to generate liberation but only as removing obstacles by purifying and stabilizing the mind. Sureśvara writes that knowledge of *brahman* and action cannot exist as equal partners because they stand to each other as contradictor and contradicted; the sphere of knowledge is the highest reality, while the sphere of ignorance is the unreal.[5] Against **Mīmāṃsā**, Advaita argues that no ritual action can generate the supreme good, which is eternal. The realization of *brahman* is dependent on the apprehension of nondifference, while the performance of ritual activities is dependent on the apprehension of difference. Thus, there can be no combination (*samuccaya*) of the two. The establishment of *ātman-brahman* involves not a change in the individual in a real world but only a cognitive shift from within a *māyā*-shaped world. One does not "attain" liberation in the sense in which one visits the museums in a new city by traveling to it or constructs a new building with different materials. Rather, one wipes away the layers of dust encrusted on a gem and lets its natural luster shine forth. If the attainment of *brahman* were a subsidiary of the performance of ritual actions and liberation were accomplished by that which is to be done, *brahman* would be noneternal. However, *brahman* is deathless, self-effulgent, all-pervading, pure, and never bound to the world, and liberation is the realization of this deep truth. Sureśvara writes that the individual who sees the same self in the friend, in the enemy, and in her body cannot feel anger toward them, any more than she could do so against the limbs of her own body.[6]

Reflecting this quest for the unshakeable center from which altruistic motivations spontaneously radiate outward, the *Avadhūta-gītā* (c. 1000) states that the sage is steady and not assailed by desires, gentle, friendly to all, compassionate, nonviolent, forbearing, purehearted, the same to all, and beneficent to all.[7] Again, the *Aṣṭāvakra-gītā* notes that with peaceful minds, the sages sit, sleep, move, speak, and eat contentedly in the affairs of the world. They feel no distress when they are engaged in practical life, and they remain undisturbed like a great lake with their sorrows extinguished. They move about in a childlike manner without desire in all their undertakings, and they have no attachment even in the actions they are performing.[8] In the Advaita traditions, the guru is often presented as such a sage who, through supreme compassion, assists the disciple in the realization of nonduality, which is liberation from the matrices of suffering. However, the state of *jīvanmukti* would seem to be deeply contradictory—the sage is liberated, and yet the sage remains a participant in worldly matters. In response, it is argued that with the arising of liberating insight, the sage ceases to wrongly associate one's psychophysiological complex with the true self: the sage perceives *ātman-brahman* nonduality in all worldly dualities. However, until the exhaustion of the *karmic* momentum that has generated this complex, the sage remains embodied and continues to be a teacher to disciples. That is, the sage lives in and passes through the world without foregrounding the "I" (*jīva*) as cognizer, agent, and experiencer, for this "I" has become decentered from its worldly moorings and recentered in *ātman*. Various metaphors are marshaled to make sense of how the sage lives *in* the world but is not *of* the world. Just as a snake that has sloughed off its skin would not identify its being with that skin or a pot on a potter's wheel continues to revolve for a while with its acquired impetus after the potter has moved away, the sage remains engaged in the world without associating herself with its ways of ignorance.

However, this account presents an intriguing problem relating to the object of other-regarding virtues. If the language of "I" and "you" is effaced at the spiritual apex, toward *whom* does an individual cultivate benevolence? One response is that the guru knows that the "I" who regards themselves as *an* ontologically discrete self is in a state of deep misconception (*avidyā*), and it is to this "I" that the guru compassionately offers the therapeutic teaching of nonduality. Each "I" is a fleeting vortex that develops within a cosmic tornado, and when one particular "I" realizes that each vortex is not-distinct from the tornado, this enlightened vortex may convey the liberating truth to other vortices. When a guru teaches Devadatta, the guru is a useful fiction as much as Devadatta is a useful fiction; "fiction" because neither guru nor Devadatta turns up in the inventory of being from the ultimate standpoint (*pāramārthika*) but "useful" because through the use, from the empirical standpoint (*vyāvahārika*), of these names and forms, the medicine of *advaita* is dispensed. To turn to Hollywood, in *The Matrix* (1999), Neo is awakened by Morpheus, and Neo works through the useful fiction of a computer simulation to reach the other side.

A related query is whether the Neo-like aspirant can do just what they please on the spiritual ascent because the "I" and the "you" are ultimately not ontologically real. Śaṃkara's Advaita outlines four interrelated virtues that the disciple should possess: first, the ability to discriminate between what is eternal and what is not eternal; second, the detachment from an egocentric enjoyment of the fruits of action; third, the perfection of six practices, which are control of the mind, control of the sense organs, a state of repose in which one overcomes agitations, forbearance, faith in scripture as taught by the guru, and focused attention; and fourth, the intense desire for liberation. Thus, from within the *vyāvahārika* domain, Devadatta would generate a meditative stability in the *ātman* through the six practices, and it is along this pathway that he discerns the one indivisible self in all beings whom he had earlier egocentrically regarded as radically other. This correlation between rootedness in the divine basis and cultivation of altruism is reflected in *Bṛhadāraṇyaka Upaniṣad* 4.4.23: by knowing the nature of *brahman*, an individual is not tainted by evil action (*pāpa*), and by becoming calm, self-controlled, unperturbed, patient, and focused, they see *ātman* in themselves and they see all things as *ātman*. If someday Devadatta himself becomes a guru with five disciples, he will engage (patiently and attentively) with the distinctive dispositions, capacities, and inclinations of each of these disciples whom he would not regard as ontologically other. He will not harbor self-directed thoughts such as "If *I* teach them, *I* will get the prize for the best teacher" and "*I* will gain 500 virtue points this week." He perceives the light of *advaita* illuminating the existence of each student, and he teaches them in a self-effacing manner by regarding them as multiple social personae that are rooted in the indivisible *ātman*.

In short, while the *jīvanmukta* such as a guru does undergo experiences such as a toothache or a headache, they do not tether this experience to the "I." While I may loudly claim, "It is *I* who am thirsty, and *I* demand a glass of water at once," a *jīvanmukta* would patiently observe, "Thirst has arisen in this *jīva*, and water is drunk to satiate this thirst." That is, the *jīvanmukta* knows that a fleeting event such as thirst does not touch the *ātman*, and properly discriminating between what is eternal (*nitya*) and what is not eternal (*anitya*), the *jīvanmukta* does not superimpose this temporal stage on the *ātman* but ascribes it to the psychophysiological complex. For Śaṃkara, the life of the wandering ascetic seems to be the path par excellence for the attainment of such liberating knowledge.[9] The term *saṃnyāsa* refers to the rejection of rituals and the various implements associated with the performance of rituals such as sacred fire, sacrificial string, and mantras. The *āśrama* system, which began to emerge around the fifth century BCE, sought to incorporate the renunciatory ideals of early Buddhism and Jainism. The *Dharmasūtras* view the *āśramas* as voluntary institutions that can be adopted by different people on the basis of whether they wish to follow the *dharma* of action (*pravṛtti*) or the *dharma* of nonaction (*nivṛtti*). They seek to provide a legitimization for celibate modes of living by including them in the sphere of *dharma*. The *dharma* of action is for people who move within social spheres, and the *dharma* of nonaction is for those who seek to transcend sociality. However, the later texts often see the *āśramas* not as four alternative styles of living but as obligatory forms that are sequentially applicable to four stages of life: celibate student, married householder, retiree to social peripheries, and renunciant. In texts where the *āśrama* of the ascetic is outlined, we read that those who have moved beyond social bounds have become selflessly transparent to the world. The *Nārada-Parivrājaka Upaniṣad* notes that a sage feels neither elation nor revulsion at what they hear, touch, see, taste, or smell. They bear harsh words patiently and have no hostility to other living beings. They do not direct anger toward people who are angry with them, and, in fact, they bless those who curse them. Their only marks are a begging bowl, a place of residence at the foot of trees, a ragged garment, a solitary life, and impartiality toward all. They are tranquil and show kindness toward all beings.[10]

RECENTERING SELF AND WORLD

The theistic Vedāntic traditions, generally speaking, argue that such styles of world-renunciation are not a prerequisite for liberation. This claim is often based on the ***Bhagavad-gītā***, which they read as affirming that what matters is not one's physical migration to a remote cave or a secluded island but the internal offering to the Lord Kṛṣṇa of the "I"—that is, one's sense of individuated and ego-centered agency. If an individual gradually becomes detached from her actions and from the fruits of these actions by regarding Kṛṣṇa as the supreme agent, such detachment is itself the renunciation where one becomes like the lotus that grows on swampy land but remains uncontaminated by the mud. This motif is encoded in the enigmatic verse 4.18, which states that those who see action in inaction and inaction in action are truly wise among human beings.[11] On the one hand, because their center of agency has been shifted from the "I," they embody action in *in*action, but on the other hand, they remain active in this meditative displacement and continue to perform *action* through inaction.

Therefore, while it may seem that only spiritual virtuosi living in hermitages on mountaintops are capable of effecting such an inner transfiguration, Hindu devotionalism claims that worldly individuals too can resituate their world-bound "I" in the divine person. When Devadatta attends to his beloved Śakuntalā, who is convalescing in a hospital, it is without a conscious sense that it is *he* who is spending sleepless nights at her bedside; his labor of love is, paradoxically, performed effortlessly. From the perspective of the ***Bhagavad-gītā***, Devadatta's single-minded devotional self-offering becomes a quotidian performance of Vedic ritual sacrifice (*yajña*). Through the purgative fires of his meditative focus, the dross of worldly individuality is burnt away, and the transfigured Devadatta begins to hold the world together through his this-worldly existence. If a householder can thus become oriented toward *brahman* and attain the structured spontaneity of living in *brahman* and living with *brahman*, social existence becomes a moral stage for simultaneously cultivating ego effacement and *brahman*-centeredness. While Śaṃkara presents the pathways of ritual action (*karma*) and devotional love (*bhakti*) as pointers to the intuitive realization (*jñāna*) of nonduality—such that after the arising of *jñāna*, *karma* and *bhakti* cannot directly contribute to liberation—Rāmānuja argues for a much tighter interweaving across these pathways. The supreme devotees of the Lord understand that the fruits of sacrificial action are limited and impermanent, and only devotional centering in the Lord leads to the highest goal of liberation from the world of reincarnations.[12] Devotional knowledge, which is synonymous with meditative worship (*dhyāna*) of the Lord, is to be continuously practiced by a householder, and it can destroy accumulated *karma*. The due performance of the socioreligious works prescribed in the ***Vedas*** helps in the origination of this devotional knowledge. Just as a horse that is used for transporting people needs to be groomed, so too devotional knowledge, which is itself the means of liberation, has to be accompanied by various works.[13]

DOES ALTRUISM INVOLVE THE ERASURE OF THE "I" OR THE REORIENTATION OF THE "I"?

In other words, ontology and the shape of moral living mirror each other. Since in Rāmānuja's worldview, reorientation to *brahman* involves a real change in the embodied self, temporal processes such as ritual action and devotional worship are directly charged with liberating power. Different technologies of the self are sketched across Hindu worldviews, where the journey to the spiritual summit and the development of other-regarding virtues are often densely enmeshed. The commentary of Vyāsa on *Yoga-sūtra* 1.12 states that the river of the mind flows in two directions:

toward the good (*kalyāṇa*) and toward evil (*pāpa*). The river that flows in the direction of discernment (*viveka*) flows toward the good, and the river that flows in the direction of non-discernment flows toward evil. The flow toward objects can be weakened through detachment (*vairāgya*), while by the habitual practice of discernment, the flow of discernment is increased.[14] The commentary on *Yoga-sūtra* 1.33 states that one should cultivate friendliness (*maitrī*) toward all beings who have attained happiness, compassion toward those who are suffering, joy toward those who are engaged in meritorious acts, and indifference toward those who are engaged in nonmeritorious acts. Through such cultivation there arises pure *dharma*; thereafter, the mind becomes clear and it attains steadiness.[15]

As discussed in the previous chapter, many of the devotional forms of Hindu ***darśana*** emphasize the active practice of self-effacement in which an individual recenters their sense of finite agency in the divine agent. Thus, in the Vallabha tradition, a devotee cultivates the sense of belonging to the Lord alone by offering up one's own self to the Lord and seeking refuge in the Lord. Through the cultivation of single-minded devotion in which they become lovingly attached to the Lord without any self-interest, they become even-minded with friend and foe. For the devotees who live in the area of Braj in northern India, the entire region is envisioned as a cosmic stage of Kṛṣṇa's manifest *līlā*, and by dwelling there and traveling to the various sacred sites, they imaginatively participate in this *līlā*. During theatrical reenaction of the *līlā*, audiences can become powerfully affected and drawn into the dramatic narrative, so that they begin to sing, laugh, and dance. They seek to experience a self-forgetfulness through their participation in the emotions that are expressed toward Kṛṣṇa by the actors on the stage.[16]

In these Hindu devotional streams, surrendering one's worldly subjectivity to the Lord is the way to gaining power to live fully in the world. The **Mīmāṃsā** vision of ego-effacement is opposed, in several respects, to such theocentric accounts. Here the ritual specialist is one node in an intricate matrix of sacrificial rituals that are oriented toward the supersensible *dharma*. Jaimini's *Mīmāṃsā-sūtra* 1.1.2 says that "*dharma* is a goal defined by injunction (*codanā*)," and so the good life is to be shaped by the injunctive texts in the ***Vedas*** that enjoin the performance of specific rituals. A ritual is to be performed not primarily because of certain fruits that the officiant may receive but because it *ought* to be performed. Thus,

Vedic injunctions enjoin the addressee to continually bring into being a world that is vitalized through Vedic sacrifice, on a ritual horizon that transcends the perspective of an individual sacrificer. At the same time, human desires are not negated outright, and it is accepted that they constitute the motivational impetus for undertaking sacrificial action. Some Vedic commands apply to sacrifices that are to be performed throughout one's life (*nitya*) or on specific occasions (*naimittika*), while some apply to optional sacrifices that are to be performed for desired ends (*kāmya*) such as cattle, material wealth, and so on. Such a prescriptive understanding relating to "what has to be done" is obtainable only from the ***Vedas*** and not from worldly means—from the latter, we learn about things that are already established (such as cows, utensils, and sticks), while the former teaches us about what is to be realized through ritual. In their attempts to delineate rules for various ritual contexts, **Mīmāṃsā** exegetes reject appeals to a divine foundation such as *brahman* or to special yogic powers. In this sense, **Mīmāṃsā** is pervaded by an uncompromising this-worldly realism. Indeed, in this "demythologizing" program, the Vedic deities enter the sacrificial picture not as beings with ontologically robust existence but as grammatical datives—that is, as names unto which offerings are made. At the same time, **Mīmāṃsā** defends, against Buddhist philosophers, the existence of a spiritual self and the infallibility of the ***Vedas***, which are taken as a mine of injunctions for specific rituals. Additionally, they accept a special power (*apūrva*) that preserves the efficacy of the rituals that are performed; this potency remains in the individual self and generates the fruits that are enjoyed by the self in favorable conditions.

Thus, in a world with mind-independent objects, a real subject of experience will enjoy the fruits of action across lifetimes and finally gain release from the cycle of reincarnations. This ritual imagination is reflected in their interpretive strategies for reading Vedic texts. In a sentence, the causal situation (*bhāvanā*), which is expressed by the verb, is the predominant element, and the meanings of the other words are subordinated to this element.[17] The sentence forms a meaningful unit because these words qualify the *bhāvanā* by telling us what is to be brought into being, and the requisite means and procedures for this production. For instance, in the injunction "One who desires heaven should sacrifice with the jyotiṣṭoma," heaven is the thing that is to be brought into being, the performance of the particular sacrifice named "jyotiṣṭoma" is the means, and various sacrificial materials and mantras constitute the procedure. Some of the details relating to the preparation of the sacrifice have to be gathered from contiguous sentences, and all these sentences have to be read as connected in such a way that the text expresses a singular meaning—the sacrificial result for the performer of a complexly organized ritual. Even declarative statements, which seem to state facts about things in the world, have to be read figuratively as praising elements of the sacrifice. So when we are told, after reading some sentences that ask us to offer an animal dedicated to the deity Vāyu, "For Vāyu is the swiftest of all deities," the proper way to understand this sentence is as an encouragement to perform the sacrifice and not as a descriptive account of the powers of Vāyu.

In the multiple systems of Tantra and the Nāth yogis, we find a somewhat different way of harnessing cosmic power—by immediately becoming that power. The Nāth yogis sought worldly expressions of sacred power such as a perfected body, liberation in life (*jīvanmukti*), the elixir of immortality (*amṛta*), and becoming an adept (*siddha*) or a wizard. The visions of Tantra too are oriented toward the goals of autonomy, omniscience, superhuman powers, and bodily immortality in a world that is envisioned as the manifestation of the divine reality, Śiva, and the locale of human self-realization. The term "Tantra" refers to a diverse range of teachings and practices that begin to flourish sometime around the middle of the first millennium CE and are oriented toward the acquisition of power (*śakti*). The universe is a unified system that pulsates between effulgence and reflection of the supreme consciousness, so that the body of the practitioner is the stage for the return of the absolute that has descended into the phenomenal world.[18] The practitioners of Tantra were regarded as possessing supernatural powers with which they could exorcise demons, treat poison, bring about longevity, cause rain, and so on. Between the seventh and the twelfth centuries, Hindu kings sought initiation (*dīkṣā*) with special mantras from Tantric gurus who would consecrate their earthly domains as circles of royal power. These gurus claimed that such rituals gave their receivers worldly power over their enemies and ensured the vitality of their reign and the material prosperity of their kingdom. In return for the Tantric legitimation of their rule, the kings would build monasteries (*maṭha*) for the Tantric orders, give them land grants, and promote their interests in the kingdom. These *maṭhas*, which were established in the centers and the peripheries of kingdoms, became seats of learning and sites of meditation; many of them were autonomous units for collecting revenue, and some even maintained military forces. Some of the gurus acquired enough land and wealth to set up temples, reward poets, and establish new monasteries.[19]

Over the last one hundred years or so, such vigorously this-worldly styles of social engagement have been configured by other Hindu figures whose cosmic visions are shaped by certain dimensions of Advaita. Swami Vivekananda developed a "Practical Vedānta" on the site of the Vedāntic dictum "You are That" (*tat tvam asi*): each individual is centered in *ātman*, and our love for the neighbor is actuated by a vivid sense of this ontological continuity. Thus, he argued, "The Vedānta philosophers . . . discovered the basis of ethics. . . . Why should I not injure my neighbor? . . . Each individual soul is a part and parcel of that Universal Soul, which is infinite. Therefore in injuring his neighbor, the individual actually injures himself. This is the basic metaphysical truth underlying all ethical codes."[20] One aspect of the realization of such a Vedāntic vision of spiritual sameness would be the institutionalization of programs of selfless service of the poor. In helping the afflicted, Devadatta is in the process of erasing his egocentric "I," and therefore he would not be filled with a self-righteous pride—rather, he would regard others as embodiments of the divine reality. For Swami Vivekananda, service of the world and a transpersonalism shaped by Advaita are deeply interrelated: indeed, only through liberation from egoism, attachment, and fear can one be truly involved in assisting those whose lives are filled with various forms of suffering. Thus, he often spoke of a "Practical Vedānta"; unlike the earlier forms of Advaita, which he claimed had been lived out only on the spiritual planes by monks in forests, his socially oriented **Vedānta** would be enacted in the multiple domains of everyday living in the world. In a similar vein, by working with some scriptural templates from the ***Bhagavad-gītā***, Sarvepalli Radhakrishnan argued that the ***Bhagavad-gītā*** does not ask individuals to retreat to a mystical solitude but urges them to remain engaged in this-worldly activity, so that the world becomes a moral stage on which one would overcome centeredness in the ego.[21] Radhakrishnan sought to develop the nation-state's commitments to liberal democracy, social justice, universal education, secularism, and scientific modernization through the lens of a Vedāntic vision of the ontological affinity of all beings. His reformulated **Vedānta** was a highly creative tapestry in which he interwove *Upaniṣadic* material with contemporary European idioms of creative evolution, axiology, and spiritual progress.

The social activism of Mahatma Gandhi too was pivoted on the ***Bhagavad-gītā***, which he read as an allegory of an ongoing conflict within every human self. According to him, *ahiṃsā* ("not-violence") is not simply the passive condition of avoidance of harm to others but is a positive state of loving, and doing good to, those who hate us and commit evil deeds. He believed that we respond to violence with brute force because we have not cultivated soul-force (*ātma-śakti*). We overlook the fact that retributive viciousness only generates another spiral in a feedback loop within which we, the oppressed, and they, the oppressors, become even more deeply enmeshed. Instead, we have to train ourselves toward the state of the *sthita-prajña* indicated in ***Bhagavad-gītā*** 2.54: the individual who overcomes hatred, greed, and fear through the spiritual surgery of excising the acquisitive ego. Like an Arjuna who would rise above enmity precisely on a battlefield, Gandhi's "soldier of the spirit" (*satyāgrahī*) would effect the (higher) violence on the ego and thus end the (lower) violence directed at the world. However, since moral sensibility has become eclipsed in the oppressors, it is the oppressed—as the *sthita-prajña*—who must vicariously undertake the arduous task of awakening it in the oppressors with a suffering love enacted through fasts, long marches, and civil disobedience. In Gandhi's VAB-vision, we are all interconnected units of a spiritual whole, and the *satyāgrahī* would attempt to bring about a moral transformation by appealing to the dormant core (*ātman*). Therefore, in Gandhi's moral utopianism, *svarāj* ("self-rule") meant not simply the end of British rule but also the regeneration of humanity across all divides. When in September 1947, Gandhi began a fast in Calcutta torn apart by Hindu-Muslim conflict, many people laid down their weapons and wept at his bedside. While Lord Mountbatten, the last viceroy of British India, claimed that Gandhi had succeeded where 55,000 soldiers had failed in the Punjab, Gandhi himself saw in this "heart-transformation" a confirmation of his conviction that soul-force is more powerful than brutal retaliation.

To summarize our discussion so far, the social locations of Hindu ***darśana*** are shaped by a volatility across two dimensions: one rigidly hierarchical and the other implicitly egalitarian. The first can be found in the *dharma*-treatises such as the *Manusmṛti*, which lay down certain socio-ritual structures. The groups at the apex of the social pyramid—namely, the Brahmins—are to be served by those at the bottom, and this is the template, implemented across large parts of the subcontinent, that B. R. Ambedkar (1891–1956), the chairman of the Indian Constitution Drafting Committee, described as a system of graded inequality. The second is the refrain of Advaita **Vedānta** that all empirical distinctions are ultimately illusory. Consequently, all hierarchical categories are conventional designations that lack substantial reality. The intriguing question, of course, is why styles of Hindu ***darśana*** that are shaped by such idioms and subjectivities did not traditionally draw on this ontological thesis to develop social worlds free from the discriminations of caste and gender. While Advaita milieus in premodern India viewed the categories of caste and gender as useful fictions to be discarded on the path toward liberation, they did not usually develop programs actively directed at dismantling such categories in the here and now. In this way, much of Vedāntic thought provided a sacred canopy over social exclusions by consigning them to the "conventional" level, which, on the one hand, had to be transcended through a liberative insight at the "ultimate" level but, on the other hand, had to be maintained for the sake of social cohesion until this insight was attained.

Nevertheless, the presence of the second dimension along with the first constituted an uneasy tension across Hindu life-worlds: the second, which pointed to ultimate reality as beyond all empirical distinctions and social exclusivities, lingered as an irritant in a body politic structured by the first. One set of movements that did seek to destabilize, if not actually eliminate, hierarchies of caste (*jāti*) was the devotional *bhakti* traditions, which spoke of the equality of all individuals. However, the equality in question was predicated on the spiritual community of devotees, and these movements, with some major exceptions, lacked a programmatic framework for systematically eradicating worldly discrimination. Some holy individuals (*sants*) such as Kabīr (c. 1500 CE) rejected notions of scriptural revelation, image worship, and caste hierarchies, and their ethical views emphasized nonviolence, humility, compassion, and reverence for all. They sometimes used Vaiṣṇava names of the deity such as Rāma, Hari, and Govinda for the formless (*nirguṇa*) deity and declared that liberation is accessible to all individuals. However, these movements should not be viewed as subaltern proto-communist uprisings, for they did not usually seek to institutionalize social egalitarianism but rather viewed notions of caste as an obstacle in an individual's spiritual progress.[22] The Caitanya traditions too grappled with the translation of the affirmation that Caitanya was the divinity who had descended to the world to rescue women, the lower castes, and sinners into a direct engagement with socioeconomic asymmetries. By and large, the early devotees accepted certain social restrictions of *varṇa-āśrama-dharma*, such as devotees of different castes not intermarrying or interdining with one another.[23] For a more straightforward repudiation of all vestiges of social codes enshrined in the *dharma*-treatises as well as a rejection of gradualism in place of an emphasis on the here and now, we can turn to the songs of the wandering minstrels of Bengal, the Bāuls, who direct the attention of the listener, somewhat in the style of Kabīr, to the "I" that is beyond all distinctions of caste. The Bāuls believe that within the human body lies the divine essence as the "man of the heart," which cannot be encapsulated in hierarchical notions, social mores, and cultural conventions.[24]

Therefore, the question of whether the contemporary liberal democratic notions of civil rights, equality, and social justice were present in the premodern social milieus of Hindu ***darśana*** can only receive a qualified affirmative; the traditions contain themes that were sometimes employed in the direction of respect for persons, though these socially egalitarian strands were usually rewoven into the tapestry of caste hierarchy. Figures such as Swami Vivekananda would later develop activist modes of confrontation with social inequalities as a mediate process through which individuals may progress toward spiritual perfection. They speak of *jīvanmuktas* as liberated beings who are altruistically engaged in such activism for the sake of the preservation of world order (*loka-saṁgraha*), while they are themselves without any egocentric desires.[25] Thus, Radhakrishnan argues that "activity . . . is not inconsistent with the truth of non-dualism. The liberated, even when alive, are lifted above the sense of egoity, and so above the sway of the law of karma, and they act, filled with the vision of the most high."[26]

FROM SUFFERING TOWARD FULFILMENT

A fundamental constituent of these accounts of human transformation and flourishing is the doctrine of *karma* and reincarnation, according to which individuals are bound to cycles of reincarnation (***saṃsāra***) until they begin to move toward liberation, whether this "movement" is understood as a temporal shift in a real world or as a cognitive reorientation in an ultimately unreal world. This doctrine—which appears in a developed form in Śaṃkara, Rāmānuja, and others—can be traced to the notion of sacrificial action in the ***Vedas*** and the *Brāhmaṇas*. It is present in a cryptic form in *Bṛhadāraṇyaka Upaniṣad* 3.3.2, where Ārtabhāga asks Yājñavalkya some questions about death and the afterlife. He wishes to know what happens to the person (*puruṣa*) when the speech of the dead enters into the fire, the breath into the air, the eye into the sun, and so on. Yājñavalkya tells Ārtabhāga that they should not discuss this matter in public, leads him away, and declares, "A man turns into something good by good action and into something bad by bad action."[27] Occasionally, the ***Upaniṣads*** spell out the dynamics and the consequences (*karmaphala*) of reincarnation. At death, after the physical body is dissolved, the subtle self (*liṅga*), comprising an individual's stock of *karmic* merits and demerits, is reincarnated, and it goes to the object to which the mind is attached. In the *Manusmṛti*, some chains of *karmic* causality across lifetimes are spelled out. For instance, the stealers of specific objects attain specific rebirths: by stealing deer, one becomes a wolf, and by stealing a horse, a tiger (12.55–68). The long-range operation of moral causation is delineated with quasi-mathematical precision in *Bhāgavata-purāṇa* 6.1.45 (c. 900 CE): the same person enjoys the fruits of the same meritorious or demeritorious act in the next world, and in the same manner and to the same extent according to the manner and the extent to which that act has been performed in this world.

While birth and death constitute the fibers of worldly existence, individuals can break through this chain along different pathways such as self-inquiry, forms of asceticism, devotion to the divine reality, death at a place of pilgrimage (*tīrtha*), and so on. Thus, in *Mahābhārata* 1.1.186–90, Sañjaya advises King Dhṛtarāṣṭra that he should not grieve over death because nobody can escape the decrees of time, which produces and destroys all beings. Indeed, every major character in the epic suffers a violent death or survives a great war only to live out their remaining days in a state of grief. Running through various other strands of art and literature is the theme of the utter impermanence and vanity of human existence. At *Yoga-vāśiṣṭha* 1.14.1, for instance, we read that human life is as fragile (*bhaṅgura*) as a drop of water dangling on the tip of a leaflet and as momentary as the rolling waves in the sea and the fleeting clouds of autumn. At the same time, various teachers, texts, and traditions point human beings toward horizons where they would conquer death. Thus, in the *Kaṭha Upaniṣad* a young boy called Naciketas overcomes death through his knowledge of *brahman*. He arrives at the house of Death (*mṛtyu*), and Death tells him to ask for three boons. Death readily grants him the first two that he seeks. Then Naciketas demands to know what happens to the departed—Death says that the afterlife is a subtle matter that is not easy to understand and requests Naciketas to ask for a different boon. Naciketas remains undeterred, and Death teaches him about the self hidden in the cave of the heart that can only be discerned by those of tranquil minds who have moved away from the transient desires of the world. Again, in the *Viṣṇu-Purāṇa*, we read about Prahlāda, the supreme devotee of Viṣṇu, who is trampled upon by elephants and thrown into a fire but remains untouched by these dangers because his mind remains immovably fixed on Viṣṇu. The Lord Śiva is often portrayed as performing a cosmic dance of destruction on a cremation ground. The ritual practices of the Śaiva groups such as the Pāśupatas, the Kāpālikas, the Aghorīs, and others are centered on the cremation ground, which becomes the soteriological space where an individual, surrounded by the signifiers of death such as skulls and bones, ritually dies to the fleeting world in the process of returning to Śiva. This motif of the emptiness of worldly possessions is articulated by the eighteenth-century Bengali poet Rāmprasād, a devotee of the goddess Kālī. In his compositions, he exhorts the fickle mind to awaken and take the name of Kālī, who will rescue him in these evil times which, according to Hindu mythic chronologies, are the *kali* age. By constantly keeping in mind Kālī, an individual can overpower Death: "When Death shall seize me by the hair, then, Mind, do thou cry Kali, Kali, and vain will be Death's purposes."[28]

In this way, a tough-minded acceptance that life is often nasty, brutish, and short is concurrent with exhortations to seek an immutable center of gravity that lies beyond our fragile fabrics that are suffused with suffering. The key concept here is the richly polyvalent term *duḥkha*. It encompasses, among others, the senses of pain, frustration, anxiety, distress, and a deep-seated dissatisfaction with the limitations of worldly existence. Across the worldviews of Hindu ***darśana***, we encounter various attempts to make sense of the *why* in the questions "Why suffering—at all—in a world rooted in *brahman*?" and "Why me, in particular?" The thin red line of suffering weaves crisscrossing patterns, at times in a seemingly gratuitous manner, through the golden tapestry of being, and Vedāntic scriptural commentaries can be read partly as conceptual exercises in grappling with the gnawing *absence* at the heart of foundational *presence*. In this context, we may speak of a "problem of evil." The ultimate basis of ***saṃsāra*** is the transcendental plenitude beyond all human imperfections—namely, *brahman*, which raises the question of whether *brahman* is unwilling to eliminate worldly evil or wishes to eradicate it but does not have the power to do so. One way of engaging with this problem is to argue that the world is oriented toward a "soul-making" goal so that the instances of suffering currently undergone by an individual are shaped by a *karma*-guided vector. Each individual can strive, with the conviction that there is no deep randomness in the moral universe, for their spiritual development that unfolds across many lifetimes.[29]

In other words, there is no radical evil, and *duḥkha* should be understood as charged with teleological directionality toward liberation from the fragmentations of finitude. On these cosmological landscapes, Vedāntic exegetical systems expound a set of aphorisms from the ***Brahma-sūtras*** (2.1.32–36) in engaging with the question of the origin and the telos of *duḥkha*. These aphorisms grapple with the theme that *brahman* cannot be the ultimate cause of a universe in which various types of inequalities and imperfections are expressed. Rāmānuja notes the claim that the merciful Lord would not produce a world filled with evils of various kinds but produce one that is completely happy. In his commentary on 2.1.33, he argues that the Lord produces the world as an expression of nonnecessitated and superabundant productivity (*līlā*). Though the Lord is ever self-satisfied and has no desires that are unattained, the Lord may find a certain activity delightful not because the Lord can gain something from it but simply because it is delectable. However, while the Lord's production of the next world-order is not constrained by any necessity, it follows the *karmic* results of the actions of individuals. Therefore, the Lord cannot be charged with partiality or cruelty with respect to the differential forms of suffering of individuals.[30]

In sum, *karmic* processes should not be regarded simply as a juridical matter of recompense: individuals undergo, in and through the retributive systems of *karma*, a reformation in the direction of the divine reality. However, the conceptual coherence and the moral plausibility of a *karma*-structured engagement with evil have been questioned from various perspectives.[31] First, one of the most significant critiques is the seeming lack of proportionality between the horrendous forms of *duḥkha* that we often witness in the world and the claim that the *duḥkha* of an individual is causally related to actions performed in the past. Entire populations have been wiped away in natural disasters, and in various other contexts, the existential gravity of *duḥkha* has crushed an individual rather than ennobled them. A possible response is that a *karma*-centered explanation is not an empirically verifiable statement that can be immediately put to the test with respect to each instance of *duḥkha* but a cosmic vision that offers the hope that *duḥkha* will retrospectively be seen to have been charged with liberating telos, if one is patient enough. From the vantage point of the ultimate destination, not currently accessible to human intellects, it will be understood that the proportionalities are sustained by the Lord who is the guardian of *karmic* mechanisms. Second, it has been argued that the claim that moral regeneration can be sustained through *karmic* processes is not coherent because individuals do not usually recall their putative past lives, and therefore, they cannot be regarded as morally culpable for instances of wickedness that they cannot remember. In response, it has been argued that while we indeed do not usually have such memories, this absence in itself does not falsify the ontological claims relating to a reincarnating self. We do not conclude that our early infancy did not exist simply because we do not recall it, and likewise, we should not claim that our lack of memories relating to previous lifetimes conclusively disproves their existence. Conversely, one encounters the claim that an individual gradually gains, on the path of spiritual perfection, the ability to discern the chains of *karmic* causality running through the universe. Third, it has been charged that if an individual's life is simply an unfolding of their *karmic* merits and demerits, we are living in a fatalistic universe. However, in various forms of *karmic* understanding, the "simply" is not read in terms of strong determinism: while certain aspects of one's current embodiment are inherited through *karmic* chains, an individual is said to possesses some volitional elbowroom to work against vicious dispositions and cultivate virtuous styles of living. Because individuals can exercise some measure of moral agency, this cosmological vision should not be read as supporting styles of amoralism, for various scriptural texts exhort individuals to cultivate other-regarding virtues such as benevolence, compassion, and others.

Thus, while a *karma*-focused vision is often offered as a rational explanation for *duḥkha*, this explanation itself is embedded in clusters of various truth-claims about the nature of reality, the epistemic reach of human reason, and so on. The explanation for why an individual is undergoing *duḥkha* is couched in terms of *karmic* deserts, but if we push the explanatory chain backward and ask *why* there is a *karmic* order in the first place, one answer is the Lord's joyful creativity (*līlā*), which is not cognitively comprehensible. The world is suffused with the "excess" of *līlā*, but for reasons that are not transparent to us, this ontological surplus is shot through with the dark densities of *duḥkha*. However, as an individual begins to re-envision the finite world as an outreach of divine *līlā* and inhabit its *duḥkha*-ravaged matrices, she may become so saturated with a sense of the divine that she perceives the divine as much in suffering as in joy. In this active rewiring of one's cognitive-experiential subjectivities, *karma* and reincarnation constitute not so much an *explanation* for why there is (a particular instance of) suffering as an *invitation* to become more strongly centered in *brahman* by trustfully accepting that, in the ultimate analysis, there is no gratuitous suffering. For instance, the *Bhāgavata-purāṇa* is replete with narratives where worldly loss is initially perceived by individuals as *duḥkha* but is subsequently reevaluated as Kṛṣṇa's gracious action through which Kṛṣṇa has reorientated them toward Kṛṣṇa (11.23.28; 10.88.8). This motif is clearly articulated at 1.8.25: "O guru of the world [Kṛṣṇa], may there always be calamities everywhere and may we have a vision of you [in those calamities], so that we do not have to see worldly existence again" (my translation). In other words, the ideal devotee of Kṛṣṇa does not shun *duḥkha* but actively seeks its purgative fires, which would burn away the empirical dross encrusted over the "I."

In recent times, this therapeutic note was struck by the mystical figure Ramakrishna Paramhangsa (1836–86). In his discourses with disciples, the spiritual pathway is often presented in terms of the practice of becoming reorientated to the divine in and through the crucibles of suffering, so that such individuals would overcome egoistic absorption in themselves and see the divine *in* everything. Crucially, while the divine *līlā*—which graciously projects, enfolds, and draws back the world—may be experienced by novices as the frivolous cruelty of the divine, those who are undergoing the discipline of surrendering the acquisitive "I" to the divine will are able to affirm that in the end, all is *līlā*. Such adepts learn to reenvision their *duḥkha* as the purgative stigmata of the ongoing perfection of the world in which nothing is irredeemably evil, so that gradually the "problem of evil" becomes not so much solved as *dis*solved. In other words, through the *karmic* processes of moral purgation, some individuals may become so progressively fine-tuned to the all-environing divinity that they receive even, or perhaps especially, their worldly suffering as a concrete instantiation of the divine presence that is reforming their finite existences.

Conclusion

Reorienting the Mind's Compass

Over the last five chapters, we have pursued some trails of problem-solving across the worlds of Hindu ***darśana***. To return to our characterization in the introductory chapter of ***darśana*** as "structured vision," we have encountered various understandings of the human person, social structure, and the world at large, and these understandings are meticulously worked out through different modes of systematic inquiry. For some forms of Hindu ***darśana***, the ***Vedas*** constitute the transcendental horizon of modes of reasoning that proceed through careful exegesis. Themes relating to the nature of the human self and the nature of the divine self, the interrelation between the human self and the divine self, the structure of ritual agency, the significance of worldly action, and so on are methodically worked out by writing commentaries on some scriptural urtexts. Many of these themes are also extensively debated by other forms of Hindu ***darśana*** where the ***Vedas*** appear only as a remote horizon; the scriptural authority of the ***Vedas*** is not necessarily denied here, but it is also not necessarily a crucial player in developing arguments about the ontological constitution of reality, the epistemic reach of reason, the structure of language, and the shape of consciousness.

One field of inquiry where, in different contexts, Vedic motifs can be crucial to an argument or an argument can be formulated without the direct invocation of Vedic motifs is philosophy of language. Consider the question "Why does the word 'cow' mean what it does mean—a domestic bovine animal?" We may say that some English-speaking human beings met one morning to set up a convention where by pointing to lots of animals of a certain kind in the fields, they declared, "Those guys out there we shall call 'cows.'" However, this sentence can bring about a sociolinguistic state of affairs only if the listeners understand the individual words in it—that is, if at some point in the past somebody had already defined "those," "guys," "out" and so on through additional conventions. It would seem that we are swimming in, or even submerged in, an open sea of conventions and can never get out of it and reach dry land. So according to Kumārila, the relation between words and their objects should be understood as primordial in the sense that meanings are not laid down by groups of human speakers. The connection between the word "cow" and real-world cows is not established through human construction or stipulation. Such a word-world relation cannot be fixed through a social contract because speakers can agree on conventions only if the meanings of at least some words have already been established. A transaction about what meanings are to be assigned to words has to take place *within* linguistic milieus where some meanings have already been fixed before the transaction. Kumārila is also a defender of *abhihitānvaya-vāda*, or the theory of "the connection of what has been expressed," according to which each word in a sentence indicates its specific meaning, and the combination of these meanings is the sentence meaning. According to the opposing view—namely, *anvitābhidhāna-vāda*, or the theory of "expression through what has been connected"—the meaning of each word is qualified by the meanings of the other words in the sentence meaning.

These two theories of how words generate meaning in a sentence can appeal to different sets of our intuitions about how we understand sentences. In support of *abhihitānvaya-vāda*, it can be argued that we are able to understand complex sentences because we apprehend the meanings of individual units, and these are arranged to generate an intelligible unit. So when I hear the sentence "The beautiful sweetly singing flamingoes moving about near the lake seem to fly," I successively grasp the distinctive meanings of the individual words and thus grasp the meaning of the sentence. It is not the case that the word "lake," for instance, has one meaning in this sentence—namely, a body of water—and another meaning elsewhere (say, a Martian visiting earth). However, defenders of *anvitābhidhāna-vāda* argue that a word such as "cow" is not sufficient to convey information, and it is only a collectivity, such as "bring a cow that is pink-eyed from the market," that is meaningful. The word "cow" designates its specific meaning by designating the sentence meaning along with the other words. The meaning of each word is qualified by the sentence taken as a whole, and so the word "cow" is to be understood in different ways in these two sentences—"Bring a cow for the sacrifice" and "Do not let them cow you into eating that pizza."[1]

In contrast to the **Mīmāṃsā** view that linguistic communication takes place through audible sounds that are combined in some manner to generate meaning, Bhartṛhari develops a more cosmologically intricate theory involving the notion of the indivisible *sphoṭa*, which is a singular whole. For Bhartṛhari, language is not simply a social transaction that facilitates everyday living but a cosmogonic power. He begins his *Vākyapadīya* with the statement that the objects of the differentiated universe are expressions of the fundamental word-principle (*śabda-tattva*), which is the imperishable *brahman*. Through its powers (*śakti*), this unchanging basis seems to have become multiplied.[2] According to Bhartṛhari, the world is word-rooted and word-shaped, and there are no nonverbalized cognitions. Even infants possess subtle word-traces that they have inherited from previous lives, and these potencies guide the subsequent development of their linguistic abilities. The word has three aspects: the manifest (*vaikharī*), which is the collection of sounds produced through vocal instruments; the middle (*madhyamā*), which is the mental image before it is enunciated; and the seeing (*paśyantī*), which is the state of utter undifferentiation. The *paśyantī* is the foundation of the other two such that the meanings and the articulations of ordinary language are enfolded in the primordial word.

Therefore, the proper understanding of language is not simply a grammatical or linguistic exercise but also the pathway to liberation. The true word is the *sphoṭa*, which is not a divisible entity such as the word "word," which is composed of four letters, or a sentence such as "This is a short sentence," which is composed of five words. Written words on a piece of paper or audible sounds are to be distinguished from the *sphoṭa*—the former serve to reveal the latter. The partless *sphoṭa* is manifested when distinct words are uttered in a temporal sequence by a speaker to a listener. When Devadatta walks into a lecture room and hears the professor declare, "Today we shall revisit the vexed topic of the relation between the worldviews of Bhartṛhari and Śaṃkara," Devadatta grasps the meaning of the entire sentence in a flash (*pratibhā*), without having to build it up in a piecemeal manner from the meanings of the individual words. However, while the sentence is an indivisible meaning-unit, someone who is beginning to learn English may have to take apart the words—"today," "relation," and so on—and inspect them individually.

All these forms of ***darśana***—centered around the ***Vedas*** or not—are developed through dense dialectical engagements with rival styles of inquiry across the milieus of **Nyāya**, **Vaiśeṣika**, **Mīmāṃsā**, and others. As indicated in the introduction, ***darśana*** is both visionary exploration and doctrinal establishment, and these two dimensions can be seen in the development of *sūtra*-based philosophical inquiry. The aphorisms provide gnomic pointers to the nature of reality, and as philosophers from traditions such as **Nyāya**, **Vaiśeṣika**, and **Sāṃkhya** began to comment on them and respond to rival viewpoints, they developed systematized bodies of statements (*siddhānta*). The *sūtras* can seem to be mere compilations of lists and intriguing bits of information; the job of the commentator is to weave a conceptual tapestry within which this content is meaningfully connected through rational threads. A significant amount of intellectual traffic takes place across the somewhat osmotic borderlines of these systematized presentations: for instance, while the **Nyāya** notion of inherence (*samavāya*) as a distinct ontological category is rejected by different traditions of **Vedānta**, these traditions usually accept the **Nyāya** delineation of inferential reasoning as structured by invariable concomitance (***vyāpti***).

In these concluding remarks, we will highlight some of these borderlines by discussing three interrelated motifs: (1) the relation between descriptive accounts and revisionary accounts of what exists, (2) the role of cognition in revealing or constructing the world, and (3) the relation between philosophy and emancipation.

Sometimes, there is a conflict between what we perceive with the senses and how we characterize, more reflectively, these perceptual cognitions. Looking at the sky on a summer afternoon, I declare that I see a shining disc that is around three inches wide. However, in the light of my knowledge of celestial mechanics, I correct myself and say that what I am observing is a spherical mass that is several thousands of miles in diameter. Again, looking at the distant horizon at dawn, little Nora says that the sun is rising in the vast emptiness of the orange sky, but her mother knows that a more adequate way of characterizing this phenomenon is in terms of the earth's rotational movement on its axis. Shifting to microscopic dimensions, an individual would need to undergo a significant amount of highly specialized training in fields such as quantum physics before they started speaking of elementary particles as constituting the surfaces of laptops, chairs, and tables. In such cases, individuals invoke certain aspects of their background knowledge relating to the world—for instance, the laws of gravitation or the principles of quantum mechanics—to correct, modulate, or override their perceptual beliefs.

The ontological mapmaking of the **Nyāya**, **Vaiśeṣika**, and styles of **Vedānta** is similar in certain respects to the modes outlined above of reenvisioning the world by seeking a rational equilibrium between our everyday experiences and our conceptual categories. We speak of an *appearance* of the rising of the sun in the morning sky because this characterization fits with vast stretches of our webs of belief relating to the world—these stretches would have to be significantly rewoven and recalibrated before we could employ the idiom of the *rising* of the sun. Likewise, Nyāya-Vaiśeṣika philosophers claim that the nonphysical self (*ātman*), which cannot be pointed out in the manner of a cat sitting on the mat, has to be postulated as the best explanation for certain facts about memory. I do not simply recall *that* there was the eating of breakfast at around eight o'clock—rather, there is the recollection that *I* ate breakfast at around eight o'clock. According to Nyāya-Vaiśeṣika, such recognitive syntheses need the explanatory support of a substantially "thick" self that endures across time. The worlds of Vedāntic exegesis (with the major exception of Advaita), **Sāṃkhya**, and **Yoga** agree with Nyāya-Vaiśeṣika that there is a real diversity of such selves—the self in little Nora is ontologically distinct from the self in her mother.

More generally, Advaita denies the reality not only of diverse finite selves but of all forms of difference. However, such forms shape the lives of all human beings, including inhabitants of an Advaita world. When we wake up in the morning, we cannot not perceive different kinds of objects in the room, and when we walk through a busy marketplace, we cannot not pay attention to vehicles, shopkeepers, and passersby. As I am typing out this sentence, I am working on a black laptop made by ABC and not a red laptop made by PQR, and both these laptops have distinctive configurations relating to the operating system, processor speed, and so on.

Toward revising such everyday descriptions of the world—as populated by multiple objects and processes out there—and showing them to be inadequate or implausible, Advaita philosophers have developed various argumentative strategies.

One way is to argue that the differences that we claim to perceive are not really there but are projected by us onto the environment. Thus, Maṇḍana Miśra, a contemporary of Śaṃkara, argues that we have a constant awareness of unchanging *brahman*, which is the supreme universal (*mahā-sāmānya*) perceived everywhere, and specific particulars are abstracted out of this universal. In other words, difference (*bheda*) is not given in perception; rather, it is a mental construction (*vikalpa*) and is subsequent to the apprehension of the form of being (*sad-rūpa*), which is the true nature of reality. If I were to point to objects in my visual field—a white cow in front of the elm tree, a brown dog under the wooden bench, and so on—and claim that these objects are ontologically real, Maṇḍana would claim that they are, in fact, conceptual projections onto *brahman*, the undifferentiated unity. However, if we claim that the function of perception is to reveal an object (*x*) and also to distinguish it from another object (*y*), Maṇḍana argues that there are no distinct moments in a perceptual cognition such that at one moment, perception reveals *x* through sense-contact and then *y*, with which there is no sense-contact.[3] Or consider the claim that we can demonstrate the reality of difference from the fact that human beings are engaged in various types of activities that they cannot accomplish unless there really are different objects. Maṇḍana responds that what this argument establishes is not the reality of difference but simply that these different activities receive distinct names. As an analogy, he notes that just because the one fire performs distinct roles such as burning and cooking, we do not say that we are dealing with different fires.[4] In sum, the apprehension of difference is dependent on the prior apprehension of *x* and the prior apprehension of *y*, but the apprehension of nondifference (*abheda*) does not depend on any prior apprehension of difference. Thus, Maṇḍana's standpoint is diametrically opposed to a Buddhist view, which holds that our experience consists of causally related streams of nonrepeating particulars (*svalakṣaṇa*).

A related way to reconsider difference as our mistaken projection onto the world is to employ reason to show certain contradictions in the concept of relation, whether between substance and attribute, cause and effect, and so on. This form of negative dialectics in Advaita seeks to demonstrate that one cannot grasp ultimate truth through reason and also indirectly point the way toward other methods of approaching reality. To the Nyāya-Vaiśeṣika claim that the world has specific structures independently of our cognitive grasp, an Advaita philosopher may reply that it is from within the circle of cognitive access that we speak of determinate objects and there is no noncognitive means of establishing whether or not the world is determinate.[5] When I observe the three apples, four oranges, and five mangoes on the brown table, I make certain perceptual claims about their colors and tastes, but independent of my observation, the world at large is indeterminate.

Here is one question that lies at the center of these philosophical disputes: Does the world have to be radically reconstructed through philosophical lenses before it becomes a habitable domain, or should our philosophical constructions be aligned with, though not uncritically, our everyday intuitions? Sureśvara offers an instance of the first response when he claims that those who speak of difference and identity between *brahman* and the world have to introduce many assumptions such as difference, nondifference, and the destruction of a real bondage of individuals to the world. For the Advaitin, however, only ignorance (*avidyā*), based on everyday experience, has to be assumed.[6] The claim, in effect, is that Nyāya-Vaiśeṣika works with an inflated ontology that can be deflated to proper size with Śaṃkara's razor—namely, the logically inscrutable principle of ignorance. For an instance of the second response, we may turn to Raghunātha Śiromaṇi (c. 1460–1540) who, working from Nyāya-Vaiśeṣika perspectives, eliminated the category of *viśeṣa* and reduced the substances of time and space to the nature of *īśvara* while adding eight categories, such as number and causal efficacy. After his revision of the ontological framework, some thinkers adopt and develop his methodological approach while creatively borrowing elements from older templates. Raghunātha concludes his *Padārtha-tattva-nirūpaṇa* ("Inquiry into the True Nature of Things") with these words: "The demonstration of these matters [which I have] carefully explained [above is one] contrary to the conclusions reached by all the other systems [of Indian philosophy]. These matters spoken of [above should] not [be] cast aside without reflection because [they are] contrary to accepted opinion; scholars should consider them carefully."[7]

We find another instance of the second response in the contemporary scholar B. N. K. Sharma, who argues that our inability to provide logically consistent accounts of everyday perceptual experiences is not sufficient in itself to override their validity: "Whatever may be the difficulties in the way of expounding the nature of difference and accounting for its perception, the fact of its experience cannot be denied. If logical difficulties are felt in elucidating the process by which it comes to be apprehended, it is open to us to go beyond the accepted theories on the subject and explore the possibilities of other suitable explanations."[8]

Deeply enmeshed in these disputes relating to describing the world and revising our everyday understanding of it is the question of whether cognition reveals it or constructs it. One of the reasons why the rope-snake analogy looms large in the dialectical contexts of Hindu ***darśana*** is because on one reading—namely, the Advaita—this event points to the insubstantiality not only of the snake but of the whole spatiotemporal world. The phenomenon of error generates a conceptual problem for styles of realism such as Nyāya-Vaiśeṣika, **Mīmāṃsā**, and theistic **Vedānta**, which defend the mind-independence of objects of cognition. Given the possibility of optical illusion, the nonrealist argues that we do not know that right now we are not inhabiting some kind of illusory situation. For instance, an Advaita philosopher may say to you, "Right now, you are reading this book, and it feels very real to you. However, illusions and dreams, as long as they last, too feel very real to you. From within the circle of these experiences, you do not have an epistemic criterion with which you can distinguish between veridical cognitions and erroneous cognitions. If you pinch yourself and it hurts, this does not demonstrate that you are not in a dream—you can feel dream-pain in your dream-self with a dream-pinch." In short, the experiential quality of a nonveridical perception and that of a veridical perception are indistinguishable. It is to this problem that different thinkers develop responses along more intellectual highways and byways than we have been able to explore in this book. The Advaita philosopher may go on to argue that we cannot move out from the circle of our experiences and make claims about "the world" out there. Their realist opponents sketch ontologies with varying degrees of complexity. For instance, the **Mīmāṃsā** exegetes who follow Prabhākara hold that the rope-snake perceptual error is to be explained in terms of the failure to make a distinction between remembering a snake perceived on a different occasion and the current perception of a coiled object on the road. All cognition is directed at real entities, and what is referred to as "illusion" is simply the nondiscrimination between a current perception and memory. In other words, the snake hovering in my visual field is not something that is inscrutably real-and-unreal; it is continuous with a robustly real snake that is present elsewhere.

One reason why configuring precise definitions of "perception" and "error" is such a crucial task across these intellectual worlds is because getting in touch with the fibers of reality is the pathway toward the cessation of the travails of worldly finitude. In **Nyāya**, the acquisition of knowledge is a type of activity and is compared to the cutting of a tree, which is possible because of the proper exercise of the means of an ax. Therefore, ***pramāṇa*** can be viewed both as a causal process and as an evidential source. Here knowledge refers not to general dispositions to hold beliefs but to cognitive episodes; the focus is not on accumulating a pile of propositions to believe but on correct epistemic operations that align one with the root of reality. One key debating point is whether the root includes the different features that we observe empirically—the green color of the grass, the rough texture of the table, the red color of the rose—or whether these features are mental projections onto the world. **Nyāya** philosophers generally argue that in the stage of indeterminate awareness (*nirvikalpaka*), even though the individual components of an object are not perceived as a relational whole, these components are really in the object. This viewpoint is echoed by Kumārila, who argues in the *Ślokavārttika* that there is an initial nonconceptualized cognition that is the apprehension of an object as not differentiated with specific features (*śuddha-vastu*), and this is the case also in the cognitions of infants where the bare "this" is apprehended. This awareness is followed by a conceptualized cognition where the object is apprehended with its distinctive features and similarities to other objects. The crucial point is that the subsequent cognition through which an object is grasped in terms of its universal and its qualities is also a perception.[9]

The question of whether a universal is reality-rooted or mind-fabricated is at the heart of various debates across the milieus of Hindu ***darśana*** and Buddhist spirituality. If someone from the eastern provinces of India goes to the desert in western Rajasthan and sees a group of camels for the first time, they would be able to report, "That's many of the same kind," even though they do not have the precise word for the "same kind"—namely, camel. Therefore, it is not the case, a **Nyāya** philosopher would argue, that a universal such as camel is simply a general feature spread by the mind across particular objects. More generally, the **Nyāya** system claims that the whole inheres in each of its parts, and we can perceive both the parts and the whole, while a Buddhist would respond that we infer, but we do not perceive, the whole. Underlying this debate is the question of whether there are timeless universals, attachment to which, according to Buddhism, generates worldly suffering. Therefore, the question "What is the nature of reality knowing which I may be liberated from worldly finitude?" recurs through significant stretches of Hindu intellectual spaces. Hindu philosophers generally argue that the self cannot construct itself but is the background constructor engaged in contingent constructive acts. For the Vedāntic traditions, the self is reflexively aware of itself as an enduring illuminator of objects, so that when I am aware of an object, I am also aware of myself, albeit implicitly, as the subject of this awareness.

Some of these viewpoints are shaped by the concepts and the subjectivities of the ***Upaniṣads***, according to which all finite beings are grounded in a unitive reality that is deeply continuous with the reality of the self. Crucially, the self is systematically elusive and cannot be objectified as the sense organs, the vital breaths, and so on—rather, the self is *that* because of which the human person is capable of processes like perception and volition. In the *Kaṭha Upaniṣad*, we encounter the parable of the chariot: we are asked to reflect on the self as the rider in a chariot, the body as the chariot, the intellect as the charioteer, the mind as the reins, the senses as the horses, and the sense objects as the pathways. The analogy sketches an ontological ascent: the senses, the sense objects, mind, intellect, the great self, the unmanifest, and the *puruṣa*, which is the highest goal. Such world-pictures raise the question of whether, in the ultimate analysis, the finite self and *brahman* are ontologically distinct or nondual. Vedāntic theists and nondualists have to grapple with two opposed types of problems—the first have to explain how the finite and the nonfinite can be related, and the second have to explain why worldly finitude seems so real. We have explored some of their ways of interweaving scripture, reason, and experience as they develop visions of human flourishing in the world and transhistorical modes of fulfilment.

Central to these ways of being-in-the-world is the dialectic of living-*in*-the-world by dying-*to*-the-world. Though their proponents hold different views about the ontological status of the world, they promote practices of envisioning the world not as an assemblage of disconnected bits and pieces but as a morally structured process that is unshakably rooted in *brahman*, the universal horizon without any spatiotemporal limitations. They claim that by overcoming one's egocentric absorption within the self-referential circle of the "I," an individual becomes transparent to all other living beings. In this way, filled with the gravity of the spirit, they will be able to travel lightly on the journey of life. If diverse forms of scarcity apply to the empirical world structured in space and time, the projected state of liberation is suffused with the plenitude of the spirit. The unfinished task of Hindu ***darśana*** in social spaces is the vexatious transition from the kingdom of necessity, marked with the inhumane deserts of discrimination shaped by caste and gender, to the promised land of the kingdom of ends.

In bringing this book to a close, we may ask what the status of Hindu philosophy is in contemporary Anglo-American settings. Some universities are slowly becoming more hospitable to the possibility that there is something recognizably "philosophical" in Hindu life-worlds, and this book has attempted to provide some intellectual content to such forms of institutional outreach. The dilemmas and the complexities of discussing philosophical content relating to the milieus of Hindu ***darśana*** are somewhat similar to those of exploring the systems of Hinduism, which are categorized as "religious." On the grounds that "religion" is a category that is heavily structured with the multiple lineages of the European enlightenment, we may refuse to apply it to the academic study of Hinduism. But what about concepts such as "God," "the divine reality," "the ultimate," "icon," "prayer," "scripture," "ritual," and "worship," all of which also have some sort of European or Christian inflections? A consistent application of the rule "Do not apply a concept whose historical origin can be traced to a Greek, Roman, or medieval Christian thinker" may lead to the conclusion that nothing can be written in the English language about Hinduism. And yet, some forms of meaningful dialogue have taken place on different sociohistorical terrains—in English and in Indic vernaculars such as Hindi, Bengali, Tamil, Malayalam, and Gujarati—between Hindus and Christians over the last two hundred years. Likewise, the claim that "philosophy" has a distinctively Greco-Roman heritage has often been applied with draconian rigor to set aside the conceptually rich cultures in Asian lands to the east of Port Said as woolly-headed or superstitious fantasies. However, as we have seen, across a diverse range of systems of ***darśana*** such as **Sāṃkhya**, Advaita, and others, somewhat counterintuitive claims about the unreality of the "I" or of the empirical world are not abruptly pulled out of a logical vacuum but are densely woven into networks of discursive reasoning, dialectical debate, and spiritual discipline.

Thus, writing in English about Hindu ***darśana*** is already an exercise in thinking across certain European and Indic intellectual borderlines. If Hindu ***darśana*** is simply another version or iteration of Western philosophy, it would seem that there is no need to study more of the same, but if it is radically distinct from the concerns of Western philosophy, it cannot be classified as "philosophy" at all. One way to engage with this dilemma is to go between its horns by keeping in mind that neither "Hindu ***darśana***" nor "Western philosophy" constitute a monolithic block. Across their internally poly-stranded milieus, systematic studies of individual traditions will reveal both strongly resonant and significantly discordant notes. This book can be regarded as a prolegomenon toward such comparative study.

At any rate, above and beyond such academic debate, we certainly all share in the human condition: we are all finite beings living on a planet with limited resources, and our lives are shaped alternately by joy and sorrow and by hope and despair. In the long run, we all face death, and we all have different views about whether there is some postmortem state or process. Should attempts to answer such questions of life and death be characterized as "philosophy"?

Generally speaking, for Hindu thinkers, such questions are an integral part of their worldviews. In this sense, they are system-building thinkers. You could even call them "holistic" thinkers who interweave topics relating to reality, consciousness, knowledge, and value in their conceptual explorations. It is precisely this holism that has given Hindu "philosophy" bad press in some Western intellectual circles. It is claimed that Hindu worldviews are based on just flights of fantasy. Such imaginative visions may be good for a sick soul on a lazy weekend, but they are not meant for healthy (Western) minds who are gifted to think clearly and carefully.

Notwithstanding this fairly widespread misconception, Hindu philosophers do not simply say, "Sit down in this yogic posture under the ancient banyan tree and meditate on empty space." To begin with, some philosophers are not directly interested in such "spiritual" matters—they would rather analyze the contents of a sentence (for instance, **Mīmāṃsā**), explore the structure of mind-independent reality (for instance, **Vaiśeṣika**), or stipulate a method for rational debate (for instance, **Nyāya**). Even those philosophers who, on the basis of scripture, gesture toward a transcendental state or entity, do so by methodically arguing their way through dense thickets of conceptual inquiry. They develop reasoned forms of discourse to show why their particular worldviews are more logically coherent and more experientially meaningful than the worldviews of their intellectual rivals.

Some Hindu philosophers may indeed prescribe certain types of spiritual discipline, but these too are moored in ways of thinking and ways of reasoning about the structures of the spatiotemporal world. If they declare, "The mind will take you away from reality," they will normally also give reasons for why the mind has this limitation. If they claim, "After a point, reason collapses under its own weight," they will generally also carefully discuss what this point is and why reason is infected with such instability.

So in Hindu philosophy, questions such as "What is the good life?" and "How do I find happiness?" are embedded in constellations of questions such as "Why am I here in the first place?" "What is it that I know about the world I inhabit?" and "How reliable is reason as a tool of human inquiry?"

If philosophy begins with wonder, then it ends with the removal of suffering—this is what many Hindu philosophers seem to be claiming. And in pursuit of that claim, they move toward various types of philosophical landscapes filled with numerous questions: Why is there so much seemingly pointless suffering in this world? What is the relation between the pursuit of knowledge and the practice of well-being? What types of action take us in the direction of deeper existential bondage, and what types of action lead us toward the infinite? What is the significance of beauty in a world steeped in misery? If I begin to envision myself as vitally interrelated with the rest of humanity, how should this understanding restructure how I live my life in the here and now?

For more than two millennia, Hindu philosophers have addressed such momentous questions. We all grapple with them in one way or the other, even if we have not heard of most of the philosophers mentioned in this book.

Glossary

Bhagavad-gītā—a central Hindu scriptural text.
Brahma-sūtras—a set of foundational aphorisms for Vedānta.
Cārvāka—a set of traditions that defend a naturalist standpoint according to which reality is constituted only of spatiotemporal entities.
darśana—a distinctively Hindu style of philosophical thinking.
Kashmiri Śaivism—a set of traditions that view the world as a dynamic manifestation of Śiva, who is the supreme divinity.
Mīmāṃsā—a worldview centered in an inquiry into cosmic and social order (*dharma*).
Nyāya—a worldview rooted in a reflective inquiry into the nature and the operation of reason.
pramāṇa—a knowledge source.
Śaiva Siddhānta—a worldview rooted in the worship of Śiva, who is the supreme divinity.
saṃsāra—cycles of reincarnation that are driven by action (*karma*).
Sāṃkhya—a worldview according to which things around us are the products of dynamic configurations of two fundamental principles, *puruṣa* and *prakṛti.*
Upaniṣads—foundational Hindu scriptures.
Vaiśeṣika—a worldview centered in atomism.
Vedānta—an umbrella term for multiple traditions such as the Advaita of Śaṃkara (c. 700 CE), the Viśiṣṭādvaita of Rāmānuja (1017–1137), the Dvaita of Madhva (1238–1317), and the Śuddhādvaita of Vallabha (1479–1531). Two central concepts are *ātman* (the spiritual principle) and *brahman* (the ultimate reality).
Vedas—foundational Hindu scriptures.
vyāpti—the concept of universal association that structures inference in Nyāya.
Yoga—a worldview centered in becoming yoked to the root of reality.

Notes

Introduction

1 W. Halbfass, *India and Europe: An Essay in Philosophical Understanding* (Delhi: Motilal Banarsidass, 1990), 160–71.

2 B. W. Van Norden, *Taking Back Philosophy: A Multicultural Manifesto* (New York: Columbia University Press, 2017).

3 R. Audi, *Epistemology: A Contemporary Introduction to the Theory of Knowledge* (New York: Routledge, 2011), 150–72.

4 A. A. Long and D. N. Sedley, eds., *The Hellenistic Philosophers* (Cambridge: Cambridge University Press, 1987), 1:155.

5 P. Hadot, *Philosophy as a Way of Life: Spiritual Exercises from Socrates to Foucault*, ed. A. Davidson, trans. M. Chase (Oxford: Blackwell, 1995).

6 B. Russell, *Wisdom of the West* (London: Macdonald and Co., 1975), 7.

7 J. Ganeri, *Philosophy in Classical India: The Proper Work of Reason* (New York: Routledge, 2001) 9.

8 C. Bartley, *An Introduction to Indian Philosophy: Hindu and Buddhist Ideas from Original Sources* (London: Bloomsbury Academic, 2015); R. King, *Indian Philosophy: An Introduction to Hindu and Buddhist Thought* (Edinburgh: Edinburgh University Press, 1999); R. W. Perrett, *An Introduction to Indian Philosophy* (Cambridge: Cambridge University Press, 2016).

9 R. King, *Orientalism and Religion: Postcolonial Theory, India and "The Mystic East"* (London: Routledge, 1999).

10 A. Sen, *Reason before Identity* (Oxford: Oxford University Press, 1999), 24.

11 D. Krishna, *Indian Philosophy: A Counter Perspective* (Delhi: Oxford University Press, 1991).

12 A. Watson, *The Self's Awareness of Itself: Bhaṭṭa Rāmakaṇṭha's Arguments against the Buddhist Doctrine of No-Self* (Wien: Sammlung de Nobili Institut für Südasien-, Tibet- und Buddhismuskunde der Universität Wien, 2006), 388.

13 J. N. Mohanty, *Reason and Tradition in Indian Thought: An Essay on the Nature of Indian Philosophical Thinking* (Oxford: Clarendon, 1992), 70.

14 D. C. Guha, *Navya Nyāya System of Logic* (Varanasi: Bharatiya Vidya Prakasan, 1968), xvii.

15 T. Burge, "Philosophy of Language and Mind: 1950–1990," *Philosophical Review* 101, no. 1 (1992): 51.

1: Unity and Its Concrete Multitudes

1 W. Halbfass, *On Being and What There Is: Classical Vaiśeṣika and the History of Indian Ontology* (New York: SUNY Press, 1992); S. Kumar, *Classical Vaiśeṣika in Indian Philosophy: On Knowing and What Is to Be Known* (Abingdon, UK: Routledge, 2013); K. Potter, ed., *The Encyclopedia of Indian Philosophies*, vol. 2, *Indian Metaphysics and Epistemology: The Tradition of Nyaya-Vaisesika up to Gangesa* (Princeton: Princeton University Press, 2015).

2 N. S. Dravid, tr., *Ātmatattvaviveka by Udayanācārya* (Shimla: Indian Institute of Advanced Study, 1995).

3 G. Jha, tr., *Gautama's Nyāyasūtras (with Vātsyāyana-Bhāṣya)* (Poona: Oriental Book Agency, 1939), 252–53.

4 Jha, *Gautama's Nyāyasūtras*, 34.

5 R. D. Dravid, *The Problem of Universals in Indian Philosophy* (Delhi: Motilal Banarsidass, 1972); K. Chakrabarti, "The Nyāya-Vaiśeṣika Theory of Universals," *Journal of Indian Philosophy* 3, nos. 3–4 (1975): 363–82.

6 G. Jha, tr., *Padārthadharmasaṅgraha with the Nyāyakandalī of Śrīdhara* (Varanasi: Chaukhambha Orientalia, 1982), 651.

7 C. Ram-Prasad, *Advaita Epistemology and Metaphysics: An Outline of Indian Non-realism* (London: Routledge, 2002).

8 G. Jha, tr., *Ślokavārttika* (Delhi: Sri Satguru, 1983), 385–86.

9 R. Prasad, tr., *Patanjali's Yoga Sutras* (New Delhi: Munshiram Manoharlal, 1998), 311.

10 G. Thibaut, tr., *The Vedānta-Sūtras, Part 1* (Oxford: Clarendon, 1890), 335.

11 S. Bhaduri, *Studies in Nyāya-Vaiśeṣika Metaphysics* (Poona: Bhandarkar Oriental Research Institute, 1975), 35.

12 B. N. K. Sharma, *Philosophy of Sri Madhvacarya* (Delhi: Motilal Banarsidass, 1986), 79.

13 Jha, *Ślokavārttika*, 282–87.

14 S. A. Nachane, *A Survey of Post-Śaṅkara Advaita Vedānta* (Delhi: Eastern Book Linkers, 2000).

2: Knowing the Roots of Reality

1 *King Lear*; ed. David Bevington et al. (New York: Bantam Books, 2005), 3: 2.49–60.

2 J. Ganeri, ed., *Indian Logic: A Reader* (Richmond, UK: Curzon, 2001).

3 M. Siderits, T. Tillemans, and A. Chakrabarti, eds., *Apoha: Buddhist Nominalism and Human Cognition* (New York: Columbia University Press, 2011).

4 B. K. Matilal, *Perception: An Essay on Classical Indian Theories of Knowledge* (Oxford: Clarendon, 1986).

5 Jha, *Gautama's Nyāyasūtras*, 1–3.

6 Jha, *Gautama's Nyāyasūtras*, 248–49.

7 G. Chemparathy, *An Indian Rational Theology: Introduction to Udayana's Nyāyakusumāñjali* (Vienna: Gerold, 1972).

8 B. Reichenbach, *The Law of Karma: A Philosophical Study* (London: Macmillan, 1990).
9 M. Dasti and S. Phillips, tr., *The Nyāya-sūtra: Selections with Early Commentaries* (Indianapolis: Hackett, 2017), 124.
10 N. S. A. Sastri, ed., *Advaitasiddhiḥ* (Delhi: Parimal, 1997), 334.
11 Dravid, *Ātmatattvaviveka*, 3.
12 K. Tripathi, ed., *Brahmasūtra-Vijñānāmṛtabhāṣyam* (Varanasi: Kashi Hindu Vishvavidyalaya, 1979), 26.

3: Therapies for Liberation

1 P. Gokhale, *Lokāyata/Cārvāka: A Philosophical Inquiry* (New Delhi: Oxford University Press, 2015).
2 A. M. Sastri, tr., *The Bhagavad-Gītā, with the Commentary of Śrī Śankarāchārya* (Mysore: G.T.A. Printing Works, 1901), 469.
3 G. Thibaut, tr., *The Vedānta-Sūtras, Part 3* (Oxford: Clarendon, 1904), 161–74.
4 R. Garbe, *Aniruddha's Commentary and the Original Parts of Vedântin Mahâdeva's Commentary on the Sâṃkhya Sûtras* (Calcutta: Baptist Mission Press, 1892), 178–82.
5 A. J. Nicholson, *Unifying Hinduism: Philosophy and Identity in Indian Intellectual History* (New York: Columbia University Press, 2010), 84–107.
6 Jha, *Ślokavārttika*, 356–59.
7 Jha, *Gautama's Nyāyasūtras*, 422–24.
8 Dasti and Phillips, *Nyāya-sūtra*, 122–23.
9 Jha, *Gautama's Nyāyasūtras*, 14–15.
10 Jha, *Gautama's Nyāyasūtras*, 498–99.
11 Jha, *Gautama's Nyāyasūtras*, 15.
12 Prasad, *Patanjali's Yoga Sutras*, 117.
13 M. Burley, *Classical Sāṃkhya and Yoga: An Indian Metaphysics of Experience* (London: Routledge, 2007).
14 S. S. Suryanarayana Sastri and C. Kunhan Raja, tr., *The Bhāmatī of Vācaspati* (Madras: Theosophical Publishing House, 1933), 39–40.
15 Sastri, *Bhagavad-Gītā*, 308–9.
16 Swami Jagadananda, tr., *Upadeśa-sāhasrī* (Madras: Sri Ramakrishna Math, 1989), 182–83.

4: Finding a Home in the World

1 W. D. O'Flaherty, *The Rig Veda: An Anthology* (Harmondsworth, UK: Penguin, 1981), 25.
2 P. Olivelle, tr., *Upaniṣads* (Oxford: Oxford University Press, 1996), 190.
3 Olivelle, *Upaniṣads*, 149.
4 Olivelle, *Upaniṣads*, 39.

5 Olivelle, *Upaniṣads*, 195.
6 Olivelle, *Upaniṣads*, 275.
7 S. Radhakrishnan, tr., *The Principal Upaniṣads* (London: George Allen & Unwin, 1953), 462.
8 Olivelle, *Upaniṣads*, 123.
9 Olivelle, *Upaniṣads*, 268.
10 Olivelle, *Upaniṣads*, 271.
11 Thibaut, *Vedānta-Sūtras, Part 1*, 9.
12 J. Lipner, *The Face of Truth: A Study of Meaning and Metaphysics in the Vedāntic Theology of Rāmānuja* (Basingstoke, UK: Macmillan, 1986).
13 Thibaut, *Vedānta-Sūtras, Part 3*, 422–24.
14 Olivelle, *Upaniṣads*, 41–42.
15 M. R. Sampatkumaran, tr., *The Gītābhāṣya of Rāmānuja* (Bombay: Ananthacharya Indological Research Institute, 1985).
16 Thibaut, *Vedānta-Sūtras, Part 3*, 47.
17 S. Dvivedi, ed., *Śatadūṣanī* (Ayodhya: Shyam Sadan, 1984), 4:197.
18 M. Comans, tr., *Advaitāmoda: A Study of Advaita and Viśiṣṭādvaita by Vāsudevśāstri Abhyankar* (Delhi: Satguru, 1988).
19 Thibaut, *Vedānta-Sūtras, Part 3*, 75–76.
20 Sharma, *Philosophy of Sri Madhvacarya*; D. Sarma, *An Introduction to Mādhva Vedānta* (Aldershot, UK: Ashgate, 2003).
21 K. T. Pandurangi, tr., *Viṣṇu-tattva-nirṇaya* (Bangalore: Dvaita Vedanta Studies and Research Foundation, 1991).
22 R. M. Gupta, *The Caitanya Vaiṣṇava Vedānta of Jīva Gosvāmī: When Knowledge Meets Devotion* (London: Routledge, 2007).
23 S. Dasa, tr., *Śrī Tattva Sandarbha: Vaiṣṇava Epistemology and Ontology* (Vrindavan: Jiva Institute of Vaishnava Studies, 2015), 268–82.
24 M. Marfatia, *The Philosophy of Vallabhācārya* (Delhi: Munshiram Manoharlal, 1967); R. K. Barz, *The Bhakti Sect of Vallabhācārya* (Faridabad: Thomson, 1976).
25 M. M. Agrawal, *The Philosophy of Nimbārka* (Agra: Bhargava, 1977).
26 R. Bose, tr., *Vedānta-pārijāta-saurabha of Nimbārka and Vedānta-kaustubha of Śrīnivāsa* (Calcutta: Royal Asiatic Society of Bengal, 1940), 1:209.
27 D. L. Haberman, *Acting as a Way of Salvation: A Study of Rāgānugā Bhakti Sādhana* (New York: Oxford University Press, 1988).
28 D. L. Haberman, tr., *The Bhaktirasāmṛtasindhu of Rūpa Gosvāmin* (New Delhi: Indira Gandhi National Centre for the Arts and Motilal Banarsidass, 2003), 5.
29 J. D. Redington, *Vallabhācārya on the Love Games of Kṛṣṇa* (Delhi: Motilal Banarsidass, 1983), 479.
30 S. N. Sastri, *Śuddhādvaitamārtaṇḍaḥ* (Varanasi: Varanasi Sanskrit University, 1966), 86.
31 N. Isayeva, *From Early Vedanta to Kashmir Shaivism: Gaudapada, Bhartrhari, and Abhinavagupta* (Albany: SUNY Press, 1995); G. Flood, *Body and Cosmology in Kashmir Śaivism* (San Francisco: Mellen Research University Press, 1993);

M. S. G. Dyczkowski, *The Doctrine of Vibration: An Analysis of the Doctrines and Practices of Kashmir Shaivism* (Albany: SUNY Press, 1987).

5: Multiple Modes of Morality

1 Jha, *Gautama's Nyāyasūtras*, 13.
2 P. Olivelle, tr., *Manu's Code of Law: A Critical Edition and Translation of the Manava-Dharmasastra* (Oxford: Oxford University Press, 2005), 235.
3 Olivelle, *Manu's Code of Law*, 94–95.
4 Swami Madhavananda, tr., *Vivekachudamani of Sri Sankaracharya* (Calcutta: Advaita Ashrama, 1970).
5 A. J. Alston, tr., *The Realization of the Absolute* (London: Shanti Sadan, 1971), 40.
6 Alston, *Realization of the Absolute*, 82.
7 Swami Ashokananda, tr., *Avadhūta-gītā* (Madras: Sri Ramakrishna Math, 1988), 163–64.
8 R. Mukerjee, tr., *The Song of the Self Supreme (Aṣṭāvakragītā)* (Delhi: Motilal Banarsidass, 1971), 153–54.
9 Y. Sawai, "Śaṅkara's Theory of Saṃnyāsa," *Journal of Indian Philosophy* 14, no. 4 (1986): 371–87.
10 P. Olivelle, *Saṃnyāsa Upaniṣads: Hindu Scriptures on Asceticism and Renunciation* (Oxford: Oxford University Press, 1992), 178–79.
11 W. Sargeant, tr., *The Bhagavad Gita* (Albany: SUNY Press, 2009), 218.
12 Y. Sawai, "Rāmānuja's Theory of Karman," *Journal of Indian Philosophy* 21, no. 1 (1993): 11–29.
13 Thibaut, *Vedānta-Sūtras, Part 3*, 699–700.
14 Prasad, *Patanjali's Yoga Sutras*, 26–27.
15 Prasad, *Patanjali's Yoga Sutras*, 59–60.
16 D. M. Wulff, *Drama as a Mode of Religious Realization: The Vidagdhamādhava of Rūpa Gosvāmi* (Chico, CA: Scholars Press, 1984), 20.
17 L. McCrea, "The Hierarchical Organization of Language in Mīmāṃsā Interpretive Theory," *Journal of Indian Philosophy* 28, nos. 5–6 (2000): 429–59.
18 D. G. White, *The Alchemical Body: Siddha Traditions in Medieval India* (Chicago: University of Chicago Press, 1996), 263.
19 P. E. Burchett, *A Genealogy of Devotion: Bhakti, Tantra, Yoga, and Sufism in North India* (New York: Columbia University Press, 2019), 42–44.
20 Swami Vivekananda, *The Complete Works of Swami Vivekananda* (Calcutta: Advaita Ashrama, 1982), 1:383.
21 S. Radhakrishnan, "The Ethics of the Vedanta," *International Journal of Ethics* 24, no. 2 (1914): 168–83.
22 S. Pande, *Medieval Bhakti Movement* (Meerut: Kusumanjali Prakashan, 1989), 98.
23 J. T. O'Connell, *Religious Movements and Social Structure: The Case of Chaitanya's Vaiṣṇavas in Bengal* (Shimla: Indian Institute of Advanced Study, 1993).
24 J. Openshaw, "Inner Self, Outer Individual: A Bengali 'Bāul' Perspective," *South Asia Research* 25, no. 2 (2005): 183–200.

25 R. N. Minor, ed., *Modern Indian Interpreters of the Bhagavadgita* (Albany: SUNY Press, 1986).
26 S. Radhakrishnan, *Indian Philosophy* (London: George Allen & Unwin, 1923), 2:644.
27 Olivelle, *Upaniṣads*, 38.
28 E. J. Thompson and A. M. Spencer, tr., *Bengali Religious Lyrics* (Calcutta: Association Press, 1922), 62.
29 Swami Paramananda, *Reincarnation and Immortality* (Cohasset, MA: Vedanta Centre, 1961), 54.
30 Thibaut, *Vedānta-Sūtras, Part 3*, 476–79.
31 W. R. P. Kaufman, "Karma, Rebirth, and the Problem of Evil," *Philosophy East and West* 55, no. 1 (2005): 15–32; M. Chadha and N. Trakakis, "Karma and the Problem of Evil: A Response to Kaufman," *Philosophy East and West* 57, no. 4 (2007): 533–56; A. Sharma, "Karma and Reincarnation in Advaita Vedānta," *Journal of Indian Philosophy* 18, no. 3 (1990): 219–36.

Conclusion

1 J. Taber, "The Theory of the Sentence in Pūrva Mīmāṃsā and Western Philosophy," *Journal of Indian Philosophy* 17, no. 4 (1989): 407–30.
2 K. R. Pillai, tr., *The Vākyapadīya* (Delhi: Motilal Banarsidass, 1971), 1.
3 S. K. Sastri, ed., *Brahma-siddhi* (Madras: Madras Government Oriental Manuscripts Series, 1937), 45.
4 Sastri, *Brahma-siddhi*, 50.
5 Ram-Prasad, *Advaita Epistemology and Metaphysics*, 121.
6 T. M. P. Mahadevan, *The Saṁbandha-Vārtika of Sureśvarācārya* (Madras: University of Madras, 1972), 94.
7 K. Potter, tr., *The Padārthatattvanirūpaṇam of Raghunātha Śiromaṇi* (Cambridge: Distributed for the Harvard-Yenching Institute by Harvard University Press, 1957), 89.
8 Sharma, *Philosophy of Sri Madhvacarya*, 95.
9 Jha, *Ślokavārttika*, 87–89.

Bibliography

Agrawal, M. M. *The Philosophy of Nimbārka*. Agra: Bhargava, 1977.

Alston, A. J., tr. *The Realization of the Absolute*. London: Shanti Sadan, 1971.

Audi, R. *Epistemology: A Contemporary Introduction to the Theory of Knowledge*. New York: Routledge, 2011.

Bartley, C. *An Introduction to Indian Philosophy: Hindu and Buddhist Ideas from Original Sources*. London: Bloomsbury Academic, 2015.

Barz, R. K. *The Bhakti Sect of Vallabhācārya*. Faridabad: Thomson, 1976.

Bhaduri, S. *Studies in Nyāya-Vaiśeṣika Metaphysics*. Poona: Bhandarkar Oriental Research Institute, 1975.

Bose, R., tr. *Vedānta-pārijāta-saurabha of Nimbārka and Vedānta-kaustubha of Śrīnivāsa*. 3 vols. Calcutta: Royal Asiatic Society of Bengal, 1940.

Burchett, P. E. *A Genealogy of Devotion: Bhakti, Tantra, Yoga, and Sufism in North India*. New York: Columbia University Press, 2019.

Burge, T. "Philosophy of Language and Mind: 1950–1990." *Philosophical Review* 101, no. 1 (1992): 3–51.

Burley, M. *Classical Sāṃkhya and Yoga: An Indian Metaphysics of Experience*. London: Routledge, 2007.

Chadha, M., and N. Trakakis. "Karma and the Problem of Evil: A Response to Kaufman." *Philosophy East and West* 57, no. 4 (2007): 533–56.

Chakrabarti, K. "The Nyāya-Vaiśeṣika Theory of Universals." *Journal of Indian Philosophy* 3, nos. 3–4 (1975): 363–82.

Chemparathy, G. *An Indian Rational Theology: Introduction to Udayana's Nyāyakusumāñjali*. Vienna: Gerold, 1972.

Comans, M., tr. *Advaitāmoda: A Study of Advaita and Viśiṣṭādvaita by Vāsudevśāstri Abhyankar*. Delhi: Satguru, 1988.

Dasa, S., tr. *Śrī Tattva Sandarbha: Vaiṣṇava Epistemology and Ontology*. Vrindavan: Jiva Institute of Vaishnava Studies, 2015.

Dasti, M., and S. Phillips, tr. *The Nyāya-sūtra: Selections with Early Commentaries*. Indianapolis: Hackett, 2017.

Dravid, N. S., tr. *Ātmatattvaviveka by Udayanācārya*. Shimla: Indian Institute of Advanced Study, 1995.

Dravid, R. D. *The Problem of Universals in Indian Philosophy*. Delhi: Motilal Banarsidass, 1972.

Dvivedi, S., ed. *Śatadūṣanī*. 4 vols. Ayodhya: Shyam Sadan, 1984.

Dyczkowski, M. S. G. *The Doctrine of Vibration: An Analysis of the Doctrines and Practices of Kashmir Shaivism*. Albany: SUNY Press, 1987.

Flood, G. *Body and Cosmology in Kashmir Śaivism*. San Francisco: Mellen Research University Press, 1993.

Ganeri, J., ed. *Indian Logic: A Reader*. Richmond, UK: Curzon, 2001.

——. *Philosophy in Classical India: The Proper Work of Reason*. New York: Routledge, 2001.

Garbe, R. *Aniruddha's Commentary and the Original Parts of Vedântin Mahâdeva's Commentary on the Sâṃkhya Sûtras*. Calcutta: Baptist Mission Press, 1892.

Gokhale, P. *Lokāyata/Cārvāka: A Philosophical Inquiry*. New Delhi: Oxford University Press, 2015.

Guha, D. C. *Navya Nyāya System of Logic*. Varanasi: Bharatiya Vidya Prakasan, 1968.

Gupta, R. M. *The Caitanya Vaiṣṇava Vedānta of Jīva Gosvāmī: When Knowledge Meets Devotion*. London: Routledge, 2007.

Haberman, D. L. *Acting as a Way of Salvation: A Study of Rāgānugā Bhakti Sādhana*. New York: Oxford University Press, 1988.

——, tr. *The Bhaktirasāmṛtasindhu of Rūpa Gosvāmin*. New Delhi: Indira Gandhi National Centre for the Arts and Motilal Banarsidass, 2003.

Hadot, P. *Philosophy as a Way of Life: Spiritual Exercises from Socrates to Foucault*, edited by A. Davidson, translated by M. Chase. Oxford: Blackwell, 1995.

Halbfass, W. *India and Europe: An Essay in Philosophical Understanding*. Delhi: Motilal Banarsidass, 1990.

——. *On Being and What There Is: Classical Vaiśeṣika and the History of Indian Ontology*. New York: SUNY Press, 1992.

Isayeva, N. *From Early Vedanta to Kashmir Shaivism: Gaudapada, Bhartrhari, and Abhinavagupta*. Albany: SUNY Press, 1995.

Jha, G., tr. *Gautama's Nyāyasūtras (with Vātsyāyana-Bhāṣya)*. Poona: Oriental Book Agency, 1939.

——, tr. *Padārthadharmasaṅgraha with the Nyāyakandalī of Śrīdhara*. Varanasi: Chaukhambha Orientalia, 1982.

——, tr. *Ślokavārttika*. Delhi: Sri Satguru, 1983.

Kaufman, W. R. P. "Karma, Rebirth, and the Problem of Evil." *Philosophy East and West* 55, no. 1 (2005): 15–32.

King, R. *Indian Philosophy: An Introduction to Hindu and Buddhist Thought*. Edinburgh: Edinburgh University Press, 1999.

——. *Orientalism and Religion: Postcolonial Theory, India and "The Mystic East."* London: Routledge, 1999.

Krishna, D. *Indian Philosophy: A Counter Perspective*. Delhi: Oxford University Press, 1991.

Kumar, S. *Classical Vaiśeṣika in Indian Philosophy: On Knowing and What Is to Be Known*. Abingdon, UK: Routledge, 2013.

Lipner, J. *The Face of Truth: A Study of Meaning and Metaphysics in the Vedāntic Theology of Rāmānuja*. Basingstoke, UK: Macmillan, 1986.

Long, A. A., and D. N. Sedley, eds. *The Hellenistic Philosophers*. 2 vols. Cambridge: Cambridge University Press, 1987.

Mahadevan, T. M. P. *The Saṁbandha-Vārtika of Sureśvarācārya*. Madras: University of Madras, 1972.

Marfatia, M. *The Philosophy of Vallabhācārya*. Delhi: Munshiram Manoharlal, 1967.

Matilal, B. K. *Perception: An Essay on Classical Indian Theories of Knowledge*. Oxford: Clarendon, 1986.

McCrea, L. "The Hierarchical Organization of Language in Mīmāṃsā Interpretive Theory." *Journal of Indian Philosophy* 28, nos. 5/6 (2000): 429–59.

Minor, R. N., ed. *Modern Indian Interpreters of the Bhagavadgita*. Albany: SUNY Press, 1986.

Mohanty, J. N. *Reason and Tradition in Indian Thought: An Essay on the Nature of Indian Philosophical Thinking*. Oxford: Clarendon, 1992.

Mukerjee, R., tr. *The Song of the Self Supreme (Aṣṭāvakragītā)*. Delhi: Motilal Banarsidass, 1971.

Nachane, S. A. *A Survey of Post-Śaṅkara Advaita Vedānta*. Delhi: Eastern Book Linkers, 2000.

Nicholson, A. J. *Unifying Hinduism: Philosophy and Identity in Indian Intellectual History*. New York: Columbia University Press, 2010.

O'Connell, J. T. *Religious Movements and Social Structure: The Case of Chaitanya's Vaiṣṇavas in Bengal*. Shimla: Indian Institute of Advanced Study, 1993.

O'Flaherty, W. D. *The Rig Veda: An Anthology*. Harmondsworth, UK: Penguin, 1981.

Olivelle, P., tr. *Manu's Code of Law: A Critical Edition and Translation of the Manava-Dharmasastra*. Oxford: Oxford University Press, 2005.

——. *Saṃnyāsa Upaniṣads: Hindu Scriptures on Asceticism and Renunciation*. Oxford: Oxford University Press, 1992.

——, tr. *Upaniṣads*. Oxford: Oxford University Press, 1996.

Openshaw, J. "Inner Self, Outer Individual: A Bengali 'Bāul' Perspective." *South Asia Research* 25, no. 2 (2005): 183–200.

Pande, S. *Medieval Bhakti Movement*. Meerut: Kusumanjali Prakashan, 1989.

Pandurangi, K. T., tr. *Viṣṇutattvavinirṇayaḥ*. Bangalore: Dvaita Vedanta Studies and Research Foundation, 1991.

Perrett, R. W. *An Introduction to Indian Philosophy*. Cambridge: Cambridge University Press, 2016.

Pillai, K. R., tr. *The Vākyapadīya*. Delhi: Motilal Banarsidass, 1971.

Potter, K., tr. *The Padārthatattvanirūpaṇam of Raghunātha Śiromaṇi*. Cambridge: Distributed for the Harvard-Yenching Institute by Harvard University Press, 1957.

——, ed. *The Encyclopedia of Indian Philosophies*. Vol. 2, *Indian Metaphysics and Epistemology: The Tradition of Nyaya-Vaisesika up to Gangesa*. Princeton: Princeton University Press, 2015.

Prasad, R., tr. *Patanjali's Yoga Sutras*. New Delhi: Munshiram Manoharlal, 1998.

Radhakrishnan, S. "The Ethics of the Vedanta." *International Journal of Ethics* 24, no. 2 (1914): 168–83.

——. *Indian Philosophy*. 2 vols. London: George Allen & Unwin, 1923.

——, tr. *The Principal Upaniṣads*. London: George Allen & Unwin, 1953.

Ram-Prasad, C. *Advaita Epistemology and Metaphysics: An Outline of Indian Non-realism*. London: Routledge, 2002.

Redington, J. D. *Vallabhācārya on the Love Games of Kṛṣṇa*. Delhi: Motilal Banarsidass, 1983.

Reichenbach, B. *The Law of Karma: A Philosophical Study*. London: Macmillan, 1990.

Russell, B. *Wisdom of the West*. London: Macdonald, 1975.

Sampatkumaran, M. R., tr. *The Gītābhāṣya of Rāmānuja*. Bombay: Ananthacharya Indological Research Institute, 1985.

Sargeant, W., tr. *The Bhagavad Gita*. Albany: SUNY Press, 2009.

Sarma, D. *An Introduction to Mādhva Vedānta*. Aldershot, UK: Ashgate, 2003.

Sastri, A. M., tr. *The Bhagavad-Gītā, with the Commentary of Śrī Śankarāchārya.* Mysore: G.T.A. Printing Works, 1901.

Sastri, N. S. A., ed. *Advaitasiddhiḥ.* Delhi: Parimal, 1997.

Sastri, S. K., ed. *Brahma-siddhi.* Madras: Madras Government Oriental Manuscripts Series, 1937.

Sastri, S. N. *Śuddhādvaitamārtaṇḍaḥ.* Varanasi: Varanasi Sanskrit University, 1966.

Sastri, S. S. S., and C. Kunhan Raja, tr. *The Bhāmatī of Vācaspati.* Madras: Theosophical Publishing House, 1933.

Sawai, Y. "Rāmānuja's Theory of Karman." *Journal of Indian Philosophy* 21, no. 1 (1993): 11–29.

——. "Śaṅkara's Theory of Saṃnyāsa." *Journal of Indian Philosophy* 14, no. 4 (1986): 371–87.

Sen, A. *Reason before Identity.* Oxford: Oxford University Press, 1999.

Sharma, A. "Karma and Reincarnation in Advaita Vedānta." *Journal of Indian Philosophy* 18, no. 3 (1990): 219–36.

Sharma, B. N. K. *Philosophy of Sri Madhvacarya.* Delhi: Motilal Banarsidass, 1986.

Siderits, M., T. Tillemans, and A. Chakrabarti, eds. *Apoha: Buddhist Nominalism and Human Cognition.* New York: Columbia University Press, 2011.

Swami Ashokananda, tr. *Avadhūta-gītā.* Madras: Sri Ramakrishna Math, 1988.

Swami Jagadananda, tr. *Upadeśa-sāhasrī.* Madras: Sri Ramakrishna Math, 1989.

Swami Madhavananda, tr. *Vivekachudamani of Sri Sankaracharya.* Calcutta: Advaita Ashrama, 1970.

Swami Paramananda, *Reincarnation and Immortality.* Cohasset, MA: Vedanta Centre, 1961.

Swami Vivekananda. *The Complete Works of Swami Vivekananda.* 8 vols. Calcutta: Advaita Ashrama, 1982.

Taber, J. "The Theory of the Sentence in Pūrva Mīmāṃsā and Western Philosophy." *Journal of Indian Philosophy* 17, no. 4 (1989): 407–30.

Thibaut, G., tr. *The Vedānta-Sūtras, Part 1.* Oxford: Clarendon, 1890.

——, tr. *The Vedānta-Sūtras, Part 3.* Oxford: Clarendon, 1904.

Thompson, E. J., and A. M. Spencer, tr. *Bengali Religious Lyrics.* Calcutta: Association Press, 1922.

Tripathi, K., ed. *Brahmasūtra-Vijñānāmṛtabhāṣyam*. Varanasi: Kashi Hindu Vishvavidyalaya, 1979.

Van Norden, B. W. *Taking Back Philosophy: A Multicultural Manifesto*. New York: Columbia University Press, 2017.

Watson, A. *The Self's Awareness of Itself: Bhaṭṭa Rāmakaṇṭha's Arguments against the Buddhist Doctrine of No-Self*. Wien: Sammlung de Nobili Institut für Südasien-, Tibet- und Buddhismuskunde der Universität Wien, 2006.

White, D. G. *The Alchemical Body: Siddha Traditions in Medieval India*. Chicago: University of Chicago Press, 1996.

Wulff, D. M. *Drama as a Mode of Religious Realization: The Vidagdhamādhava of Rūpa Gosvāmi*. Chico, CA: Scholars Press, 1984.

Further Reading

Adamson, P., and J. Ganeri. *Classical Indian Philosophy*. Oxford: Oxford University Press, 2020.

Dasti, M., and E. F. Bryant, eds., *Free Will, Agency, and Selfhood in Indian Philosophy*. New York: Oxford University Press, 2014.

Duquette, J. *Defending God in Sixteenth-Century India: The Śaiva oeuvre of Appaya Dīkṣita*. Oxford: Oxford University Press, 2021.

Grimes, J. *A Concise Dictionary of Indian Philosophy: Sanskrit Terms Defined in English*. Albany: SUNY Press, 1996.

Gupta, B. *An Introduction to Indian Philosophy: Perspectives on Reality, Knowledge, and Freedom*. London: Routledge, 2012.

Ram-Prasad, C. *Indian Philosophy and the Consequences of Knowledge: Themes in Ethics, Metaphysics and Soteriology*. Aldershot, UK: Ashgate, 2007.

Index

abhihitānvaya-vāda, 19, 152
Abhinavagupta, 118
Agni, 102
Akṣapāda Gautama, 15
Ambedkar, B. R., 142
anumāna, 12, 48
ānvīkṣikī, 6
anvitābhidhāna-vāda, 19, 152
arthāpatti, 66, 67
Aṣṭāvakra-gītā, 132
ātman: immutable basis, 28, 44–45, 52, 70–71; self and consciousness, 121, 122; self and liberation, 82, 84, 91–97, 102–10; self and morality, 126–28, 130–34, 140, 141, 155; substantial self, 12, 17, 26, 36, 37
Avadhūta-gītā, 132

Bāul, 143
Bhagavad-gītā, 7–9, 37–38, 95–101, 126–29, 140–41
Bhāgavata-purāṇa, 115, 144, 148
bhakti, 90, 106, 110, 114–17, 136, 142
Bhāmatī, 45
Bhartṛhari, 153
Bhāskara, 115
Bhaṭṭa Rāmakaṇṭha, 13
bhāvanā, 138
Bhāviveka, 12
bhedābheda, 114
brahman: basis of the world, 48, 61–62, 95–117, 121, 126–38; fundamental reality, 17, 21, 23, 37–39, 40–45; source of fulfilment, 145, 146, 148, 153, 156–61
Brahma-sūtras, 17, 37, 77, 101, 106, 112
Buddhism, 13, 17, 28, 38, 123, 160

Caitanya, 113, 114, 115, 116, 117, 143
Cārvāka, 67, 75, 76, 77, 83
citta, 86, 89

Dārā Shukhōh, 1
darśana, 6–9, 11–21, 63–64, 120–25, 141–45, 161–62
dhāraṇā, 87, 89, 90
dharma, 16, 125–30, 134, 137, 142–43
dhyāna, 84, 88, 89, 90, 136
dīkṣā, 71, 139
dravya, 25–28, 33, 34, 42
dṛṣṭānta, 48, 61
duḥkha, 14, 52, 81–85, 145–49

Gandhi, Mahatma, 8, 130, 141
Gaṅgeśa, 15, 17, 19
guṇa, 25–27, 34, 39, 42, 91, 95

Haribhadra, 12
hetu, 49
hetvābhāsa, 13

īśvara, 12, 62–63, 75, 80–82, 103–4, 157
Īśvarakṛṣṇa, 14, 87

Jaimini, 16, 137
jīva, 45, 93, 103, 106, 113–15, 132
Jīva Gosvāmin, 114
jīvanmukti, 130, 132, 139
jñāna, 16, 90, 106, 136

Kabīr, 142
Kaṇāda, 15
karma: category of reality, 16, 25, 27, 33, 34, 42, 64; generation of altruism, 119, 136, 143, 146–48; motor of liberation, 75, 79, 80, 90, 96, 106
Kashmiri Śaivism, 118
Kauṭilya, 6
Kumārila, 16, 17, 39, 67, 122, 159

līlā, 115, 116, 117, 137, 146–49

Madhusūdana Sarasvatī, 17, 69
Madhva, 8, 17, 38, 44, 100, 102, 104, 112, 113, 127
Mahābhārata, 90, 126, 129, 130, 144
manas, 26, 31, 79, 85, 86
Maṇḍana, 156
māyā, 45, 96, 97, 104, 110, 114, 130, 131
Mīmāṃsā, 11–17, 67–68, 122–23, 137–38, 153–58, 163
mokṣa, 2, 64, 84, 87, 95, 97, 108, 127

Nāgārjuna, 1
navya-nyāya, 15, 19, 20
Nimbārka, 115
nimitta-kāraṇa, 108
Nyāya, 11–22, 30–36, 43–49, 52–69, 82–86, 157–60

padārtha, 16, 25, 48
Paley, William, 63
Pāṇini, 6
Patañjali, 14, 80, 85
Prabhākara, 16, 68, 122, 158
Prajāpati, 102, 126
prakṛti, 14, 15, 79–81, 85–93, 96, 107–10
pramāṇa, 13, 52, 55, 62–68, 75–78, 159
prameya, 13, 15, 52, 62, 66
Praśastapāda, 16, 25, 34
prasthāna-trayī, 17
pratyakṣa, 52
puruṣa, 14, 74, 84–93, 108, 126–27, 160
puruṣārtha, 127
pūrvapakṣa, 13, 78

Radhakrishnan, Sarvepalli, 8, 130, 140, 143
Raghunātha, 157
rajas, 79
Ramakrishna, 148
Rāmānuja, 8, 77–81, 102–13, 127, 136, 146
rasa, 116, 117
Rūpa Gosvāmin, 117

śabda, 2, 7, 8, 12, 63, 66
Śaiva Siddhānta, 70, 71, 97
sākṣin, 14, 121, 122
samādhi, 88, 89, 90
sāmānya, ix, 25, 26, 33, 34, 44
samavāya, 25, 33, 34, 42, 43, 154
Śaṃkara, 8, 36–39, 104–6, 110–13, 130–36, 156–57
Sāṃkhya, 11–13, 67, 79–80, 96–97, 154–55, 162
saṃprajñāta-samādhi, 88
saṃsāra, 8, 70, 75, 80, 92, 146
śarīra, 107, 108, 109
satkārya-vāda, 105, 108
sattva, 69, 70, 79
siddhānta, 13, 154
Somānanda, 118
Śrīdhara, 25, 36
Śrīharṣa, 17
Śrīnivāsa, 115
Sureśvara, 131, 132, 157
svalakṣaṇa, 35, 51, 53, 156
Swami Vivekananda, 8, 130, 140, 143

tamas, 79
Tantra, 139
tarka, 8, 13, 15, 77, 83, 90, 129
tattva, 14, 55, 79

Udayana, 15, 26, 29, 63, 69, 83
Uddyotakara, 15, 65, 66, 82
Umāsvāti, 1
upādāna-kāraṇa, 70, 108
Upadhyay, Brahmabandhab, 1
Upaniṣads, 7, 17, 89–91, 99, 101–9, 144–45
Utpaladeva, 17, 118

Vācaspati, 13, 15, 52, 91
vāda, 13, 15
Vaiśeṣika, 11, 14–17, 21–26, 30–38, 42–46, 84
Vallabha, 8, 17, 105, 114–15, 117–18
varṇa, 126, 127, 128, 129
Vātsyāyana, 15, 29–30, 55, 58, 82–85, 129
Vedānta, 11, 22, 36, 45, 99, 158
Vedas, 7, 16, 81, 106, 136–38, 154
Vidyāraṇya, 12
Vijñāna-bhikṣu, 13, 70, 81
viśeṣa, 16, 25, 44, 157
Vivaraṇa, 45
vyāpti, ix, 19, 49–50, 60, 76, 154
Vyāsa, 15, 39, 86, 136
Vyomaśiva, 25

yajña, 101, 126, 136
Yoga, 11–15, 63, 70, 79–80, 89–91, 155

www.ingramcontent.com/pod-product-compliance
Lightning Source LLC
Chambersburg PA
CBHW050928240426
43671CB00019B/2959
* 9 7 8 1 8 0 0 5 0 2 7 0 3 *